Hog Butchers, Beggars, and Busboys

CLASS : CULTURE

SERIES EDITORS

Amy Schrager Lang, Syracuse University, and Bill V. Mullen, Purdue University

TITLES IN THE SERIES:

The Syntax of Class: Writing Inequality in Nineteenth-Century America
Amy Schrager Lang

Vanishing Moments: Class and American Culture
Eric Schocket

Let Me Live
Angelo Herndon

Workin' on the Chain Gang: Shaking Off the Dead Hand of History
Walter Mosley

Commerce in Color: Race, Consumer Culture, and American Literature, 1893–1933
James C. Davis

You Work Tomorrow: An Anthology of American Labor Poetry, 1929–41
Edited by John Marsh

Chicano Novels and the Politics of Form: Race, Class, and Reification
Marcial González

Moisture of the Earth: Mary Robinson, Civil Rights and Textile Union Activist
Edited by Fran Leeper Buss

Grassroots at the Gateway: Class Politics and Black Freedom Struggle in St. Louis, 1936–75
Clarence Lang

Natural Acts: Gender, Race, and Rusticity in Country Music
Pamela Fox

Transcribing Class and Gender: Masculinity and Femininity in Nineteenth-Century Courts and Offices
Carole Srole

An Angle of Vision: Women Writers on Their Poor and Working-Class Roots
Edited by Lorraine M. López

Michael Moore: Filmmaker, Newsmaker, Cultural Icon
Edited by Matthew H. Bernstein

Hog Butchers, Beggars, and Busboys: Poverty, Labor, and the Making of Modern American Poetry
John Marsh

American Socialist Triptych: The Literary-Political Work of Charlotte Perkins Gilman, Upton Sinclair, and W. E. B. Du Bois
Mark W. Van Wienen

Hog Butchers, Beggars, and Busboys

Poverty, Labor, and the Making of Modern American Poetry

JOHN MARSH

The University of Michigan Press
Ann Arbor

Published in the United States of America by
The University of Michigan Press
Manufactured in the United States of America
⊗ Printed on acid-free paper

2014 2013 2012 2011 4 3 2 1

A CIP catalog record for this book is available from the British Library.

Library of Congress Cataloging-in-Publication Data

Marsh, John, 1975–
Hog butchers, beggars, and busboys : poverty, labor, and the making of modern American poetry / John Marsh.
p. cm. — (Class : culture)
Includes bibliographical references and index.
ISBN 978-0-472-07157-9 (cloth : acid-free paper) — ISBN 978-0-472-05157-1 (pbk. : acid-free paper)
1. American poetry—20th century—History and criticism.
2. Working class in literature. 3. Labor in literature. 4. Modernism (Literature)—United States. I. Title.
PS310.W67M37 2011
811'.5093553—dc22 2011011892

Acknowledgments

Many people assisted in the making of this book. Dale Bauer, Matti Bunzl, Jed Esty, Gordon Hutner, and Robert Dale Parker refined its structure and argument. My writing group in Urbana, Illinois—Melissa Littlefield, Justine Murison, and Spencer Schaffner—read drafts of several chapters and saved me from some of my more intemperate arguments. Cary Nelson oversaw an earlier, extremely different version of this book, as did Trish Loughran, William J. Maxwell, and David Roediger. Walter Benn Michaels and Alan Wald wrote timely letters of support. My colleagues in the English Department at Penn State University have welcomed me beyond anything I could have reasonably expected and given me the time and encouragement to complete the book. LeAnn Fields has once again proven to be an extraordinary editor. She, Amy Lang, and Bill Mullen have done more to advance scholarship about class and culture in the United States than perhaps any other three people. Two anonymous readers of the manuscript, enlisted by the University of Michigan Press, improved it throughout and forced me to confront what I had tried to avoid—namely, a concluding chapter. Versions of chapters 2 and 6 appeared in, respectively, the *William Carlos Williams Review* and *American Literature.* I am grateful to the editors for allowing me to reprint that work here and grateful to the readers who offered advice about the original manuscripts.

Closer to home, I would like to thank my parents, Carole Marsh and Mike Marsh, and my sister, Kimberly Marsh, for supporting my adventures in higher education. The imminent arrival of Nora Fitzgerald Marsh spurred me to finish the book, and her presence has made finishing it that much more gratifying. Finally, Debra Hawhee read every page of this manuscript and shared every moment of its writing. Her enthusiasm, wisdom, and generosity continue, as William Carlos Williams might put it, to astonish me beyond words.

Contents

CHAPTER 1

To Make Poetry out of the Unpoetical: Modern American Poetry and the Labor Problem

In October 1912, Harriet Monroe brought out the inaugural issue of *Poetry,* the journal, more than any other, that would both publish and cultivate the so-called new poetry in the United States. Over the next several decades, Monroe would publish most of the poets who would go on—and many more who would not—to constitute the canon of modern American poetry.

In the same month that *Poetry*'s first issue appeared, President William Howard Taft was being vigorously lobbied by representatives of the American Federation of Labor, the National Association of Manufacturers, and the National Civic Federation (Adams, *Age of Industrial Violence* 41–44). Each of these groups sought to influence Taft's appointments to the nine-person committee that would administer the newly created Commission on Industrial Relations, which Congress had authorized in August. As the need for a commission suggests, industrial relations in the United States had grown rocky.[1] Two events in particular, though, spurred Congress to act. In addition to several other recent strikes, many of which turned violent, in January 1912, some twenty-five thousand workers—led by the Industrial Workers of the World (IWW)—struck the textile mills in Lawrence, Massachusetts. In the course of that strike, city authorities declared martial law and state militia patrolled the streets; local police turned fire hoses on picketing workers; a Lawrence undertaker, allegedly in the employ of one of the mill owners, planted dynamite as part of a plot to discredit the strike; two of the strike's leaders, Joseph Ettor and the poet Arturo Giovanitti, were inexplicably charged with murder when the local police shot and killed a striking woman; and, if all that did not draw enough attention to

Lawrence, when the IWW arranged to have the children of striking workers sent to supporters in New York, police and militia arrived at the train station and began clubbing children and parents alike (Kornbluh 158–64).

Even more alarming than Lawrence, though, between 1906 and 1911 unknown saboteurs dynamited bridges and other nonunion construction sites across the country. The attacks culminated in the bombing, on October 1, 1910, of the building housing the *Los Angeles Times,* whose publisher, Harrison Gray Otis, had earlier coordinated the vigorous antiunion campaign in that city. Twenty-one people died in the explosion and subsequent fire. In April 1911, the nation learned that two brothers, McManigal and James McNamara, disaffected officers of the International Bridge and Iron Workers Union, the once powerful union decimated by U.S. Steel's open shop campaign, had engineered the attacks (Adams 1–24).

Compelled by social reformers and public opinion to act, Congress created a Commission on Industrial Relations in order "to discover the underlying causes of dissatisfaction in the industrial situation and report its conclusions thereon" (*Final Report* 6).

The Commission on Industrial Relations, however, was not the first effort to take up the "causes of industrial unrest" (*Final Report* 21).[2] Beginning in the late 1870s, a generation of writers, reformers, economists, and U.S. commissioners of labor had described and offered solutions to what they invariably referred to as "the labor problem." As the anonymous author of *The Labor Problem in the United States* (1878) wrote, "Every day the evidence accumulates that the Labor Question is becoming the grand problem of the country and of the age. Whether or not we will admit the fact, we are standing face to face with a giant evil, with a prodigious difficulty" (unpaginated). For James A. Waterworth, the labor problem, as he titled his 1886 book, "was the question of the day" (20). By the turn of the century, the labor problem remained a grand problem and, like most grand problems, had also developed into a minor publishing industry. Literature on the problem had grown so prolific that by 1914 the journalist Walter Lippmann could complain about the "annual harvest of treatises on 'labor problems'" (73).

These labor problems—and the treatises that treated them—included more than just strikes and violence. They included, as one 1914 textbook outlined them, the "evils and abuses" (Adams and Sumner 3) of woman and child labor, immigration, sweatshops, poverty, and unemployment, to name but the most prominent. Nevertheless, the periodic violence of strikes, more than the background noise of poverty or other problems, gave the labor problem its urgency, especially when, beginning in 1909, it seemed like those strikes would become a permanent rather than periodic phenomenon. "We live in a revolutionary period," Walter Lippmann wrote in the aftermath of the Lawrence strike, "and nothing is so important as to be aware of it" (317). Similarly, in 1912, after Lawrence and the McNamara revelations, Cardinal John Farley, the archbishop of New York, told a meeting of the superintendents of the Metropolitan Life Insurance Company that employer and employee "look like two galleries of statues, facing one another, having no sympathy with one another whatever, no tie, no bond, each one independent. Very often they seem to be standing like two armies in battle array, waiting for the order to attack one another" ("What Others Are Saying" 111).

Nor did industrial unrest—and its underpinning labor problems—cease in the years after the Commission on Industrial Relations delivered its final report in 1915. If anything, workers grew even more restless, until, in the years just before and after World War I, the numbers of strikes and workers participating in them rivaled the more famously turbulent years of the 1930s.[3]

To put it bluntly, then, the period from 1912 to 1922—the decade of the birth of modern American poetry—coincided with what has been called "one of the most tumultuous periods of labor conflict in American history" (Stromquist 168). And while the Commission on Industrial Relations traveled across the country from one outbreak of industrial unrest to another—Paterson, New Jersey, Ludlow, Colorado—seeking causes for industrial unrest and solutions to labor problems, poets began to write the verse that would change utterly the field of American poetry.

On the surface, these overlapping events in the years 1911 and 1912—the early days of *Poetry* and the coming to crisis of the labor problem—seem like an accident of history, merely coincidental. And judging from most histories of modern American poetry, it would further seem that their paths—commissioners and poets, labor problems and lyric poems—would never cross, that, disappointing Lippmann, modern American poets, with the exception of some forgotten left-wing and protoproletarian poets, remained decidedly unaware of this "revolutionary period."

Yet a closer look reveals that modern American poets were keenly aware of the labor problem and, perhaps even more so, the laborers and working poor who constituted it. Before and after World War I, the poets who incorporated the poor and working class into their verse read like a who's who of canonical modernism. T. S. Eliot's first poem to appear in Harriet Monroe's *Poetry* ("Morning at the Window") claimed to be "aware" of cooks "rattling breakfast plates in basement kitchens" (1) and offered the arresting image of a working girl moving through the early morning city streets. Among Wallace Stevens's early poems is one titled "A Window in the Slums." In "Episode of Hands," Hart Crane recounts the binding of a factory worker's injured hand. William Carlos Williams's first poem in *Poetry* pretended to be the song of a Sicilian emigrant on arriving in the United States; Williams would later write of the Paterson silk strike of 1913 and, repeatedly, about the poor and working class, who were also, of course, Dr. Williams's patients. Most of Carl Sandburg's first volume of poetry, *Chicago Poems* (1916), is devoted to documenting the city's labor problems: poverty, unemployment, vampirelike factories. One poem even purports to be an interview (over dinner, no less) with a dreaded dynamiter. Some of Robert Frost's earliest unpublished poems depict his brief stints working in and living near New England textile mills; he would later write about isolated and overworked farmers' wives and hired laborers. Even Edna St. Vincent Millay's infamous early poem, "Recuerdo," ends with its merry bohemian ferrygoers giving away all their money to an old beggar. And Langston Hughes, Claude McKay, and other Harlem Renaissance poets would compose dozens of poems about waiters, busboys, elevator operators, porters, servants, cabaret dancers, and other Harlem service workers.

Despite all the recent work done in the fields of new modernism and modern American poetry, however, this history of modern poetry and the labor problem has gone untold. In the last decade, modernist studies has benefited from a host of critical approaches—forays into queerness, manifestos, sexuality, cosmopolitanism, critical race studies, "pulp" modernism, a whole host of "bad modernisms" to borrow the title of one edited collection—that have revealed much about the writers and historical contours of the period (Mao and Walkowitz). As a few critics have noted, however, except in the most abstract, theoretical, and as often as not eccentric ways, these approaches have not sufficiently accounted for how poverty and labor have shaped literary history. In short, canonical modern American poets have been judged to be many things—but rarely participants in or even chroniclers of this revolutionary period and its labor problems.[4]

Hog Butchers, Beggars, and Busboys: Poverty, Labor, and the Making of Modern American Poetry changes this; it excavates modern American poetry's labor problem and documents the integral but long neglected role that the labor problem and those who lived it—the poor and working class—would play in the formation of modern American poetry. I focus, in particular, on the years 1909 to 1927 and on poets (Williams, Eliot) who were later gathered together to form the canon of modern American poetry, as well as poets (Millay, McKay, Hughes, Sandburg) whose relation to the canon has remained more tenuous. But regardless of their fame at the time or their later canonical status, many—in fact most—modern American poets experimented with writing about the poor and working class.[5]

In the remainder of this chapter, I outline the dimensions of the labor problem as it appeared in the first decades of the twentieth century. Next I explore why self-consciously modern poets took up those behind the labor problem, workers and the poor, as frequently and seemingly urgently as they did. I argue that doing so allowed them, on the one hand, to break with the earlier, genteel tradition of poetry and, on the other, to register their alienation from a surging industrial capitalism. Regarding the latter, though, I suggest that American poetic modernism, as canonized, was constituted by a type of romantic anticapitalism that was also, at its root, deeply ambivalent toward workers' efforts to solve their problems. Finally, I examine why the field of modern American poetry has rarely credited this encounter between modern American poets and labor—and why it should.

So what was the labor problem and how might it have looked to modern Americans and modern American poets? Although the United States has always had labor problems—indentured servitude, slavery, poverty, exploitation, strikes—the discursive term *labor problem,* and the underlying, fundamental divisions between labor and capital it portended, only emerged with the railroad strike of 1877 or, as one of the authors of the first labor problem books called it, "the terrible crisis in July" (AN ANGLO AMERICAN, unpaginated).[6] That strike, at first a local dispute between workers and the Baltimore and Ohio railway line, soon spread north and west to include railway workers throughout the nation and general strikes in Chicago and Saint Louis. In the course of the two-week strike, "the first truly national strike in the country's history" (Clark and Hewitt 715), as a more recent textbook put it, over a hundred people would die and millions of dollars in property be destroyed. "Scenes of riot and bloodshed accompanied it such as we have never before witnessed in the uprising of labor against capital," the editors of *Harper's Weekly* reported at the time. "Commerce has been obstructed, industries have been paralyzed, hundreds of lives sacrificed, and millions of dollars' worth of property destroyed by lawless mobs" ("The Great Strike" 626). Subsequent decades witnessed still more uprisings of labor against capital: the national strike for an eight-hour day, the bomb at Haymarket Square in Chicago, the subsequent "legal lynching" (Freeman 127) of the Chicago anarchists, the pitched battle between labor and private militia at Andrew Carnegie's Homestead steelworks, and the Pullman strike, to name but a few. Moreover, the first decades of the twentieth century, as I suggest above, offered no reprieve from these "labor wars" (Freeman 189).

Yet the labor problem entailed more than just labor wars. One of the most thorough textbooks from the period, Gordon S. Watkins's *An Introduction to the Study of Labor Problems* (1922)—at the time, Watkins was an associate professor of economics at the University of Illinois—broke down the labor problem into several components. Watkins devoted chapters to problems of hours of labor, child labor, women in industry, industrial accidents and disease, unemployment, immigration, low wages, and, to be sure, industrial unrest—that is, the strikes and disruption that attended strikes. In terms of hours of labor, by the first decades of the twentieth century, limits to the workday for women and children had been established, but a majority of adult male workers still worked more than forty-eight hours per week, and a quarter of them worked sixty to seventy-two hours per week (103). Child labor, too, which had seemed to diminish by the second decade of the twentieth century, in fact increased as a result of the heightened demand for labor during World War I. By 1910, 1 out of every 5 children between the ages of ten and fifteen were "gainfully employed." And while most of these children (3 out of every 4) worked on farms, even farm work could, as Watkins feared, result "in loss of educational opportunities" and "interfere with the child's normal growth" (131). For similarly paternalistic and occasionally androcentric reasons, women's presence in industry inspired equal concern.[7] By 1920, about 8.5 million workers, or 1 out of every 5, were women. Nor were these working women limited to certain jobs—domestic or professional service, for example. In addition to dominating some fields (garment making) and being the primary victims of "the sweating system" (177), women were employed in every major industry (150). Indeed, as of 1914, women worked in manufacturing industries at the same rate (20 percent) as they worked in other sectors (149). Nor was it any secret why their numbers were increasing. As Mary Van Kleeck reported in a February 1921 article for *Atlantic Monthly,* "Managers employ them [women] because they need their labor, and, often, because they want it cheap" (255).

Both men and women alike, however, risked their lives merely by going to work. "Human Waste in Industry" was the somewhat odd term adopted to describe these deadly "industrial accidents and occupational diseases" (189–90), which, as Watkins notes, "in the wake of modern industry" exacted "from the wage-earning classes an enormous toll in human misery" (190). "In 1919, according to data prepared by the National Safety Council," Watkins reported, "more than 22,000 persons were killed and over 500,000 injured as a result of accidents in American industries" (191).[8] Equally deadly, at least in the long term, were occupational diseases, especially those that resulted from the inhalation of dusts and other fine particles (198), as in mines and cotton mills, which could cause an array of gruesome respiratory diseases. Although less dramatic, the problem of unemployment could be similarly disabling. During normal times, Watkins calculated, "more than 2,000,000 workers, or about 15 per cent of the industrial wage-earners of the country" were unemployed. During depression years, like 1921, the number of unemployed could rise as high as 4 and 5 million.[9]

But few labor problems sounded as many alarms—or led to as much new legislation—as what Watkins calls "unregulated immigration" (296). With the exception of the World War I years, beginning in 1901 a million or more immigrants entered the United States annually.[10] Immigration counted as a labor problem because in addition to the many other reasons (poverty, political and religious oppression, the desire to escape military service) immigrants came to the United States, their arrival here was made possible by—and, once here, they made possible—the industrial and commercial expansion of the late nineteenth and early twentieth centuries. Then, as now, the question of immigration divided the country. On the one hand, employers tended to support open immigration since, as Watkins paraphrased their motives, "it furnishes an unrestricted supply of cheap labor" (272). In contrast, Watkins notes, native wage earners were "convinced that the unregulated influx of immigrants menaces American standards of labor" (273) by increasing the labor supply, increasing unemployment, and, thus, decreasing wages. For different reasons, social scientists and eugenicists also opposed unrestricted immigration. With the passage of the Emergency Immigration Act of 1921, which limited new immigration to a single-digit percentage of the nationalities already residing in the United States, the restrictionists effectively won, even if, as many modern American poems attest, the legacy of the problem remained.

Yet all these labor problems only counted as problems because they led to "industrial unrest," the "strikes, boycotts, lockouts, and blacklists" (299) that, as Watkins described their effects, "may cause a complete shutdown of basic industries, paralyze transportation, and expose the public to immeasurable injury and inconvenience" (299). "Industrial unrest is, in fact," as Watkins put it, "the all-inclusive problem of modern industrialism" (298). If workers had passively suffered such problems as unemployment or decreasing wages, the only claim these labor problems could make on the nation would be moral and ethical ones. But workers did not suffer these problems gladly, and so the labor problem became everyone's problem. "The development of modern capitalism," Watkins observed, somewhat blandly, "has been characterized by increasing discontent on the part of the masses" (299). In the period between 1916 and 1920, for example, there were some 20,595 reports of strikes and lockouts involving nearly eleven million workers with an annual loss of roughly four trillion dollars (308). In essence, then, to solve the labor problem meant solving the problem of industrial unrest.

But first one had to understand the origins of unrest. Watkins, like other labor problem writers, somewhat fussily grouped the causes of industrial unrest into psychological, moral, political, social, and economic ones.[11] So, too, Basil Manly, who, in the final report of the Commission on Industrial Relations, noted that "the sources from which this unrest springs are when stated in detail, almost numberless" (30). Nevertheless, Manly noted, one could trace these numberless causes to "four main sources."

1. Unjust distribution of wealth and income.
2. Unemployment and denial of opportunity to earn a living.
3. Denial of justice in the creation, in the adjudication, and in the administration of the law.
4. Denial of the right and opportunity to form effective organizations. (30)

By the third source, Manly meant, as he glossed the phrase, that "our legislators, our judges, and executives . . . do not afford equal consideration to the workers and are concerned with protecting the rights of property rather than the rights of men, and at times even become the instruments of oppression of the poor and humble" (39). By the fourth source, he meant the right and opportunity to form unions, which, until the Wagner Act of 1935, were of dubious legality. But even these four sources could be boiled down still further. As Frank Walsh, the controversial chairman of the Commission on Industrial Relations, put it in his "Supplemental Statement" to the *Final Report,* capitalizing so that no one would miss the point, "WE FIND THE BASIC CAUSE OF INDUSTRIAL DISSATISFACTION TO BE LOW WAGES; OR, STATED IN ANOTHER WAY, THE FACT THAT THE WORKERS OF THE NATION, THROUGH COMPULSORY AND OPPRESSIVE METHODS, LEGAL AND ILLEGAL, ARE DENIED THE FULL PRODUCT OF THEIR TOIL" (153).

One can hear in Walsh's statement of the cause of industrial unrest—workers "denied the full product of their toil"—the outlines of his radical solution to it, industrial democracy.[12] But regardless of the solution, most writers agreed that the labor problem, at root, was essentially, as Walsh put it, "low wages."[13] In 1904, the pioneering sociologist Robert Hunter observed that he had "not the slightest doubt that there are in the United States ten million persons," between 10 and 20 percent of the population, living in abject poverty, but, he confessed, "I am largely guessing and there may be as many as fifteen or twenty million!" (11). For its part, the Commission on Industrial Relations determined in 1916 that "the majority of American wage earners did not receive an adequate wage" (61). A later study, from 1918, observed that while an income of "$2,242 was required to maintain an average family according to the minimum standard of health and comfort," only "14 percent of workers had incomes exceeding that sum" (61–62).[14] And with so few workers enjoying a viable standard of living, unrest, or so the thinking went, was inevitable—and potentially catastrophic.

As my earlier roll call of Eliot, Stevens, Williams, Crane, Sandburg, Frost, Millay, Hughes, and McKay attests, and as the remainder of this book demonstrates, when many modern American poets began writing poems, many began by writing about the poor and working class—began writing, that is, about workers' and the country's labor problem. Though rarely approaching these problems as problems—that is, as problems to be solved—modern poets nevertheless felt compelled to invoke these problems and those who lived, suffered, and occasionally sought to correct them. Some poets treated, directly or indirectly, quite specific labor problems: William Carlos Williams on the causes of strikes, Carl Sandburg on alienation and the factory system, T. S. Eliot on slums, and Edna St. Vincent Millay on immigration. Nearly all addressed the problem of poverty in the United States. Others, like Claude McKay and Langston Hughes, wrote about labor problems unrecognized at the time but recognizable now—that is, the emotional crucible of service labor.

Not surprisingly, modern poets began writing about the poor and working class for different reasons. Some of them grew up in comparative poverty or working-class families; as adults, some of them were part of the working class or—they were, after all, poets—themselves lived in poverty. But even poets who grew up and remained in relative affluence nevertheless led lives that brought them into contact with the poor and working class, whether as patients, domestics, objects of sexual desire, or simply in the streets and shops. Given the ubiquity of the labor problem, too, and its coverage in newspapers, few could have avoided its repercussions even if they tried. As poets will, then, they occasionally turned these experiences, these personal, direct, and indirect contacts with the working class and the poor, into poetry.

But modern poets had personal, direct, and indirect contact with lots of things, not all of which appear in their poetry as regularly as do workers and the poor. They must, therefore, have had more than biographical or sociological reasons to write about the poor and working class. One reason seems to have been that writing about the poor and working class offered a way for modern American poets to announce themselves *as* modern poets. As many literary historians have observed, the generation of poets who modernized poetry in the early twentieth century sought to distinguish themselves against the Victorian and genteel traditions dominating the poetry scene at the turn of the century. What has gone less acknowledged is how writing about workers and the poor became one of the principal ways poets could strike a blow against that tradition.

In the first decades of the twentieth century, these Victorian and genteel traditions remained powerful—and, from the perspective of modern poets and later critics, powerfully dull. Few poets captured the imitative, sentimental, and genteel tradition of poetry as well as Henry Van Dyke, the theologian, poet, and professor of English literature at Princeton University from 1899 to 1923. Van Dyke belonged to the group of influential poets and critics whom Frank Lentricchia called "the captains of lyric industry" (64), and a sample of their remarks provides a sense of the role poetry played—its function, its proper subjects—in turn-of-the-century culture. Their remarks also suggest how later, self-consciously modern poets would use workers and the poor to separate themselves from these genteel writers.

"The two things best worth reading about in poetry and fiction," Van Dyke observed in his *Essays in Application* (1905), "are the symbols of nature and the passions of the human heart" (265). A year earlier, in 1904, Van Dyke dedicated his book *The Friendly Year* to

a young woman
of an old fashion
who loves art
not for its own sake

but because it ennobles life
who reads poetry
not to kill time
but to fill it with beautiful thoughts
(4)

and later reflected in that work:

> The true mission of poetry is to increase joy. It must, indeed, be sensitive to and acquainted with grief. But it has wings given to it in order that it may bear us up into the ether of gladness. There is no perfect joy without love. Therefore love-poetry is best. But the highest of all love poetry is that which celebrates, with the Psalms, "that love which is and was / My father and my brother and God." (134)

In sum, as one might gather from Van Dyke's critical judgments, poetry was best when it was about nature and the passions of the human heart, especially love; poetry should ennoble life and fill it with beautiful thoughts; and while a little grief was fine, on balance poetry should increase joy and celebrate life.[15] Offering advice, somewhat bizarrely, to those who "had a rage for getting one's social doings into print," Van Dyke opined that "One of the best antidotes and cures for the craze of publicity is a love of poetry and the things that belong to poetry—the beauty of nature, the sweetness and splendor of the common human affections, and those high thoughts and unselfish aspirations which are the enduring treasures of the soul" (82).

Accordingly, and perhaps unsurprisingly, Van Dyke and other established critics had little good to say of modern poetry when it appeared in the years before and after World War I. They objected most to its formal aberrations. A March 19, 1916, *New York Times* article, for example, by the American poet and journalist Joyce Kilmer, titled "Says 'Vers Libre' Is Prose, Not Poetry," was basically devoted to the antimodernist views of Robert Underwood Johnson, who, in his capacity as poet and editor of *Century* magazine, was a captain of the captains of lyric industry. "In the last fifteen or twenty years," Johnson complained, "we have come into a reaction on the part of many young, revolutionary minds against what they are pleased to call the tyranny of form. This has made itself manifest in Cubism in art, in riotous formlessness in music, and in the heedless admiration of what is called vers libre, which I think may, with more truth, be called prose libre." Van Dyke shared Johnson's contempt for so-called vers libre. In the introduction to *A Book of Princeton Verse* (1919), which collected poems written by a group of Princeton undergraduates, Van Dyke acknowledged that during the war years "there has been a great revival of lyric poetry in England and America." The regrettable terms of that revival, however, made the poems in *A Book of Princeton Verse* all the more valuable. "It is surprising, and I must confess refreshing," Van Dyke wrote, "to find in this book so few pieces written in what is called *vers libre*—the Bolshevism of poetry—which promised liberty by the destruction of all order" (viii). "To found a new type of poetry on the basis of irregularity," Van Dyke howled, "is manifestly an absurd enterprise. It argues either a total misconception of what poetry is, or a temperamental laziness of mind, the spirit of an aesthetic loafer, who declines to learn the rules of an art before attempting to practice it" (viii). In other words, at least Princeton undergraduates—no Bolsheviks they—could write poems that rhymed and scanned. Similarly, in 1914, following Harriet Monroe's publication of Carl Sandburg's "Chicago" in *Poetry, The Dial,* not yet the champion of modernist aesthetics it would later become, blasted what it called Sandburg's "hog butcher" poetry. Setting the now famous opening lines of the poem ("Hog Butcher for the World / Tool Maker, Stacker of Wheat" [1–2]) against lines from Milton's "Lycidas" and Tennyson's "Tithonus," the anonymous reviewer complained that "we have to deal with the simple fact that certain persons obviously and honestly think that the characterization of Chicago blurted out in such ugly fashion may possibly have some relation to the divine art which Wordsworth defined, and Milton and Tennyson exemplified" ("New Lamps for Old" 232). "For our part," the reviewer asserted, "we deny the relation altogether" (232).

As *The Dial*'s "hog butcher" epithet suggestions, Van Dyke and other lyric-industry captains objected to more in modern poetry than its Bolshevist free verse or that it happened to be "blurted out in such ugly fashion." They objected to its content as well. In *Not in the Curriculum: A Book of Friendly Counsel to Students* (1903), for which Van Dyke provided an introduction, the pseudonymous "Two Recent College Graduates" who authored the book advised would-be university students that "A man of culture must be well-read. Cultivate a taste for that which is best in prose and poetry." In cultivating this taste, however, the authors advised students to avoid "literature which poisons the mind or stimulates an impure imagination. You don't have to learn all the filthy details of vice to hate it. You don't have to immerse yourself in a cesspool to appreciate its pollution. Don't be afraid to be ignorant of some things" (32–33). Robert Underwood Johnson, too, preferred that poetry, and readers of poetry, remain ignorant of some things. "I have gone carefully over the 'Spoon River

Anthology,'" Johnson told Kilmer, discussing Edgar Lee Masters's 1916 collection of first-person epitaphs, "with the purpose of discovering how much poetry there is in it. It is, in parts, stimulating, vigorous, humorous, and poignantly pathetic, but on the whole depressing in its realism. Its atmosphere . . . is throughout distinctly anti-poetic and matter-of-fact." If, as Van Dyke held, poetry should ennoble life and fill it with beautiful thoughts, poetry should in turn limit itself to the beautiful and ennobling. If it failed to do so, if it reflected the decidedly unbeautiful and degrading aspects of modernity, it became, so much the worse, "anti-poetic," the very opposite of poetry. Indeed, as in Johnson's judgment of Masters's *Spoon River Anthology,* "realism" and "matter-of-fact" are not complements. Poetry was supposed to soar beyond such vulgarities. "Of course," Frank Lentricchia writes, genteel poets "were attacked . . . for being out of touch" (xi–xii). As he rightly notes, however, "they intended to be out of touch; it was the nature and function of poetry to be out of touch" (xi–xii).

To be sure, the genteel tradition could occasionally produce less deliberately out of touch poets.[16] Nevertheless, and by contrast, modern poets sought to be distinctly in touch. "Love in country lanes, the songs of birds, moonlight—," the poet and critic Ford Madox Hueffer (later Ford) wrote in an early essay for *Poetry,* exaggerating only slightly, "these the poet, playing for safety . . . will deem the sure cards of the poetic pack. They seem the safe things to sentimentalise over, and it is taken for granted that sentimentalising is the business of poetry" (182). As for modern poets, Hueffer advised, "If you practice poetry, it is in fact better to be vulgar than affected" (187). Twenty years later, surveying the shift in literary taste, Malcolm Cowley agreed. "The general tone," Cowley, writing in 1937, summarized the genteel tradition, "was refined and bloodless." "Culture," he continued,

> was regarded as a foreign accomplishment to be learned and exhibited like golf or table manners—almost as a commodity to be bought like a new Keats manuscript for Mr. Morgan's library. In any case, it had nothing to do with the back streets where people quarreled and made love and died without benefit of Coleridge or Pater. (19–20)

Poets ultimately broke this "refined and bloodless" tone through formal experimentation, changes in diction, discontinuous composition, free verse, and new publishing venues—everything, David Perkins observed, that distinguished modern poetry from its Victorian and genteel predecessors (293–328). Yet, as complaints against Masters's realism or Sandburg's hog butcher poetry suggest, in addition to Bolshevist free verse, one of the primary ways poets could distinguish themselves from the Victorian and genteel tradition that preceded them was by taking up, as Cowley put it, "the back streets" and the people who lived there. Modern poets, in contrast to the students whom the "Two Recent College Graduates" advised, would immerse themselves in the cesspool. "And then one day I got a true look at the poor," Carl Sandburg wrote in 1916, "millions of the Poor" ("Masses" 5). For his part, Ford Madox Hueffer observed, "I would rather read a picture in verse of a Googe Street anarchist than recapture what songs the syrens sang" (185). Similarly, in a talk given in 1950, T. S. Eliot remembered that as a young poet he had learned from Europeans like Charles Baudelaire and Jules Laforgue that "the source of new poetry might be found in what had been regarded hitherto as the impossible, the sterile, the intractably unpoetic," in "the more sordid aspects of the modern metropolis," and in "the sort of experience that an adolescence had had . . . in an industrial city in America" ("What Dante Means to Me" 126). "The business of the poet," Eliot concluded, "was to make poetry out of the unexplored resources of the unpoetical"—a practice, he also noted, that as late as the first decade of the twentieth century had "never [been] developed by any poet writing in my own language" (126).

As Eliot's recollections suggest, one of the ways modern poets could "make it new," as Ezra Pound commanded, was by "widening [the] subject matter" (300), as David Perkins puts it. That is, modern poets must write into their poetry what the popular, conventional American magazine verse suppressed: the harsh, nonliterary elements (the cesspool) earlier taken up by European avant-garde poetry, as well as by contemporaneous realist and naturalist fiction. And in the first few decades of the twentieth century, one of the harshest, one of the most nonliterary, and therefore one of the most "modern" of these elements was the poor and working class—figures who indeed turn up in countless modern poems.

In this respect, as I argue in a chapter on William Carlos Williams, workers and the poor played no small role—perhaps one of the central roles—in ushering poets and readers into modernity and modern verse. As Williams figured it, adopting a cesspool metaphor of his own, poets needed to immerse themselves in the waters of the poor and working class and readers needed to immerse themselves in the poetry these newly baptized poets could now write about the poor and working class. Short of abandoning iambs and pentameters or leaving lines unrhymed, a good number of poems composed in the 1910s and 1920s suggest that writing about the poor and working class offered one of the surest ways to make a decisive break with the genteel tradition and to announce one's modernity.

Although primarily a revisionary history of literary modernism and an exploration into how certain poets made the labor problem their own, this book does offer one general thesis about modern American poetry and the labor problem that frames and unites each of the chapters. In addition to the anti-genteel motives poets had to write about the poor and working class, each of the poets I treat looked skeptically, often regretfully, on capitalism and the poverty and alienation thrown up in its wake. Nor were they alone in resenting capitalist modernity. As Seth Moglen has recently argued, most if not all American modernists remained hostile to the new economic order (9). As Moglen tells it, while many Americans "perceived that the burgeoning of advanced capitalism brought benefits," just as many, including most literary modernists, "could also feel that the emerging economic order was inflicting terrible wounds: intensifying economic exploitation, extreme social and material inequality, the betrayal of democracy, and, beneath it all, a pervasive feeling of alienation" (xiii). Out of these feelings, Moglen argues, "modernist writers invented a set of cultural practices through which they could express and manage the loss, disappointment, and injury endured by those who lived within the emerging center of global capitalism" (xiv). For Moglen, drawing on Freud's distinction between a dialectical mourning and an inert, indefinite melancholy, literary modernism divides into two camps: those, the mourners, mostly on the political and literary left, who could discern the causes—namely, capitalism—behind the suffering they witnessed; and those, the melancholics, who, as Moglen puts it, "represented the crisis of modernity as an inexorable and mysterious trauma, [who] grieved with a melancholic psychological paralysis that manifested itself as a beautiful and poignant despair" (xiv). In Moglen's view, the melancholics won out—canonically, at least—inasmuch as it was their response to modernity ("the literature of despair" [xiv]) that critics celebrated.

Regardless of their canonical fates, though, by casting melancholic modernists as capable only of despair, Moglen ignores the alternatives, albeit mostly backward-looking ones, that many modernists offered in response to "the suffering that had accompanied modern capitalism" (xiv). In fact, it is because modernists could look to the past—an imagined pre- or less capitalist past—that they could, as Michael Löwy and Robert Sayre put it, "criticize the present with so much acuity and realism" (11). If so, it seems more appropriate to count melancholic modernists, including modern poets, as the American instantiation of romantic anticapitalism: the critique of modern, industrial society driven by and taking the form of, in most cases, a nostalgia for the past. More than anything else, this strain of romantic anticapitalism on the part of modern poets seems to have influenced—if not determined—how workers and the poor made their way into modern American poetry.

As its chief chroniclers, Michael Löwy and Robert Sayre, propose, romantic anticapitalism is effectively synonymous with romanticism since what unites "the Romantic movement in most if not all its manifestations is opposition to the bourgeois world" (10). Romanticism, that is, functions "as a critique of modernity" (13). Yet what makes the bourgeois, modern world bourgeois and modern is capitalism, so it is more accurate, Löwy and Sayre argue, to describe the phenomenon romanticism as romantic anticapitalism, "essentially a reaction against the way of life in capitalist societies" (17). For Löwy and Sayre, then, romanticism extends beyond the late eighteenth and early nineteenth centuries. While the romantic worldview—that is romantic anticapitalism—developed in the second half of the eighteenth century along with capitalism, "it has not disappeared yet" (17), they argue, because the economic and social transformations that gave rise to it—that is, capitalism—have not disappeared yet either. Thus "the [romantic] worldview," they conclude, "is coextensive with capitalism itself" (17). Hence that worldview applies "to authors, trends, and periods that are usually not viewed as Romantic or that themselves reject the label" (16). Thus could moderns, including modern American poets, be romantics—or romantic anticapitalists, anyway. "The most obvious feature common to all the arts of Western nations after 1750," Löwy and Sayre somewhat sweepingly claim, "was the refusal to validate the contemporary social world" (49).

In refusing to validate a contemporary world, Löwy and Sayre argue, romantic anticapitalists often idealized a past one. For romantic anticapitalists, that is, "what is lacking in the present existed once upon a time, in a more or less distant past" (23). Thus romantic anticapitalists looked to many pasts—the Middle Ages, supposedly "primitive societies," Greek and Roman antiquity—that could provide an imaginative, potentially redemptive contrast to modernity. In addition to drawing on an imagined, precapitalist past, romantic anticapitalists could also make an idealized "past" out of the present, re-creating "paradise in present reality" by "transforming . . . one's own life" to reflect those lost, past values (23). One did this, primarily, by revalorizing the nonrational over against capitalism's market quantification and spirit of rational calculation. Hence the centuries-long romantic anticapitalist cultivation of intuition, aesthetics, craftsmanship, love, childhood, nature, the supernatural, and even poetry itself, in short, anything that capitalism had made redudant.

In the chapters that follow I make the case that modern poets in fact belong to this backward-glancing, antirational, romantic anticapitalist tradition. If so, then the possibility existed that modern poets might join, or at least sympathize with, those other occasional haters of capitalism, modern workers and the poor. Löwy and Sayre have less to say about this possibility, but as Raymond Williams tells the story, to the degree that working-class, socialist, and anarchist movements identified "the bourgeoisie as the agents and organizers of capitalism and thus the specific source of the reduction of all broader human values, including the values of art, to money and trade, there was an opportunity for artists to join or support a wide and growing movement which would overthrow and supersede bourgeois society" ("Politics" 55). In other words, the possibility existed for "a negative identification between the artists and the workers, each group being practically exploited and oppressed" (54).[17] As Williams notes, however, in most cases, that identification, even negative, did not happen. The politics of the moderns and the avant-garde turned right at least as often as it turned left, drifting into fascism or a "rejection of all politics" (59). So while a hatred of industrial capitalism on the part of modern poets could rather easily lead to hating the alienation and poverty of the spirit capitalism brought about, there seem to have been limits to the sympathy one could summon for those—workers and the poor—that the hated system had engendered and continued to dominate. For modern writers, the enemy (workers) of their enemy (capitalism) never quite turned into a friend.

But, as Williams also notes, this outcome was not predetermined, and "the politics of the avant-garde, from the beginning, could go either way" (62)—including the way of joining working-class anticapitalist efforts. As is evident in each of the chapters that follow, though, like their European counterparts, only rarely did modern American poets follow that path. With the exception of Hughes, McKay, and perhaps Sandburg, the poets who would later form the canon of modern American poetry were not socialists and did not, as Raymond Williams describes one possible form of avant-garde anticapitalist politics, "commit themselves, in their art and out of it, to the larger causes of the people or of the workers" (55).

As I have suggested and demonstrate throughout this book, though, even if modern poets did not commit themselves to the larger working-class cause they nevertheless felt compelled to include the poor and working class in their verse. The more pressing question, then, became how poets would reconcile these otherwise conflicting impulses: first, to indict capitalism; second, to include the poor and working class in their poetry; and third, to avoid having their anticapitalism or representations of the poor and working class align with "the larger causes of the people or the workers" (55). In other words, if you cannot represent the poor and working class as the oppressed of capitalism or as its heroic antagonists—either of which might drift dangerously close to writing socialist verse—yet in order to be modern they must be represented, what should workers and the poor do in your poems?

In retrospect, the poets I examine seem to have adopted one of two strategies in the face of this impasse. For some poets, because workers and the poor, especially immigrants and migrants from supposedly less civilized regions of the globe or nation, remained incompletely incorporated into the modern, capitalist bourgeois order, they could function as an implicit rebuke to it. As the chapters on Eliot and Williams suggest, what appealed to modern poets was not workers' class consciousness but the belief that their consciousness remained somehow pre- or antimodern. In this sense, modern romantic anticapitalist poets valued workers and the poor for the same reasons romantics valued "the primitive": because each could supposedly put one in touch with, as Raymond Williams put it, "the unformed and untamed realm of the prerational and the unconscious"; that is, each, the primitive and workers and the poor alike, could enable poets to access "the vitality of the naïve," as Williams called one of the "leading edge[s] of the avant-garde" (58). According to this line of thought, created and moved about by capitalism, workers and the poor nevertheless stand outside it, and their outsider status could be parlayed into anticapitalist modern poetry.

For other poets, including those originally attracted to workers' naive vitality, the suffering and alienation of the poor and working class could also become the occasion to rehearse romantic, nostalgic, and nonsocialist solutions to the crisis of industrial capitalism, including its labor problems. Thus each of the poets I examine sought to cast the labor problem—and solutions to the labor problem—in ways that look far different from, say, how the Commission on Industrial Relations or any of the labor problem textbook writers did. For those writers, the solution to the labor problem involved a redistribution of resources, which usually also involved a redistribution of power, from employers and the state to unions and a state more sympathetic to workers' interests. By contrast, what routinely surprises about the group of poets I examine here is how reluctant they are to embrace such solutions, how eager they are to reframe the labor problem—and its solutions—in romantic terms, or how often they turn would-be labor problems, especially poverty, into solutions to their problems with modernity. Rarely, however, do poets focus on anything so prosaic—poetically and politically—as reforming capitalism or raising wages. Instead, as romantic anticapitalists would, they look to the past (or to remnant values of the past) to solve their labor problem. These backward-looking solutions took many forms. For Carl Sandburg, modern capitalism would be redeemed by the soul-fulfilling possibilities of preindustrial craft work. For Langston Hughes and Claude McKay, leisure, especially music and dance, and especially music and dance that put one in touch with an imagined African past, could potentially redeem workers' exploitation and emotional alienation. For Eliot, the irrational, Bergsonian world of dreams and memory could counter the trend toward modernist hyperrationality and automatism. For other poets, poverty itself could incubate certain premodern and thus venerable qualities. For these poets, poverty became the past salvaged from the capitalist present, a more authentic mode of existence: a way of being free from meaningless labor (Millay) or free from the linguistic and experiential simulacra of modernity (Williams). Despite their outward differences, then, and despite their extraordinarily diverse political leanings, each of these modern poets hated capitalism, and each softened that hatred by turning to remnants of the past. In doing so, however, they more often than not left the actually existing labor problems—and the victims of those problems—to fester.

By now it should be clear that when I invoke modern American poetry I am speaking of a fairly narrow canon of poets, a canon that recent scholars in the field have rightly learned to distrust. While I examine both popular and high modernists, as David Perkins divided the field, my study is effectively limited to poets who published in *Poetry* magazine and who, today, populate the conventional anthologies of modern American poetry. (Each of the poets I examine, for example, appears in the *Norton Anthology of Modern Poetry.*) My study mostly ignores, then, as Cary Nelson calls them, the "modern poems we have wanted to forget," which for Nelson are mainly the poems of the American political Left, including, as he describes it, "the tradition in America" of "professional writers taking up labor issues and agitating in verse for decent wages and working conditions" and the tradition of "working people themselves producing their own rousing songs and poems" (*Revolutionary* 16). Certainly, if one looked to other publication venues—newspapers, ephemera—or other, less canonical or noncanonical poets, one could write a far different history about modern American poetry and its encounter with the labor problem. That history would involve an anticapitalism perhaps equally romantic but far more radical, one much more likely to forge a positive identification with "the larger causes of the people or of the workers" (55), as Raymond Williams put it. One might also find, as Nelson's comment suggests, poets who did not have to forge an identification with workers since they themselves were, in addition to being occasional poets, also workers. Moreover, that story, about those poets, would doubtless make for a far more politically appealing one than the one I offer here, which, as I have hinted, is mostly a story of displacements, evasions, bad faith, and occasionally stunning displays of solipsism.

So it is fair to ask why I have chosen to give this history and to focus on the poets that I do. It is not that my taste, as Frank Lentricchia describes his, "is hopelessly canonical" (ix). Rather, I have chosen to examine these poets and write this history about them in order to trace the influence and importance of labor and poverty in realms—in this case, canonical modern poetry—where they are not supposed to have had influence or importance. Along with Cary Nelson, though with slightly less confidence than him, I hope that "contempt for workers might be less easily mustered if we had sustained our awareness of their place in literary history" (55). To be sure, the place I describe workers occupying in this literary history—distorted, abandoned, their problems frequently made to fit poets' quixotic politics—is not an inspiring one. Nevertheless, as long as this story of poets' encounter with labor remains untold, our history of modern American poetry—its origins, its effects—will remain fundamentally incomplete. So, too, to some extent, will our history of modern American capitalism. Somewhat surprisingly, one can learn a great deal about workers and the poor in the early years of the twentieth century by examining what modern poets did (and did not) write about them.

Notwithstanding some valuable exceptions, however, until now this history of modern American poetry's encounter with the labor problem has gone untold, whether for the longest-running canonical poets (Eliot, Williams) or the marginal and more recent entrants (Sandburg, Millay, Hughes, McKay). One possible explanation for why this history has mostly escaped scholars' attention may be that critics who have been drawn to issues of class and radical politics in U.S. literary history have tended to focus, until recently and perhaps understandably, on the depression decade of the 1930s, whether to recover works or writers that have dropped out of the canon or to keep alive the radical politics of that decade. As I have tried to suggest, however, the decades before the Great Depression, especially the decade between 1912 and 1922, in many ways matched the 1930s in terms of labor problems, industrial unrest, and the pressure poets felt to raise these specters. Thus the questions critics have tended to ask about the 1930s—the relation between poetry and political economy, lyric and labor—seem at least as alive for these decades as for the 1930s.

Another reason this history has gone untold has to do with the formation of—and the terms of the revisions to—the canon of modern American poetry over the last seventy years. As early as the 1930s, for example, critics appear to have assumed that high modern poets remained fundamentally uninterested in questions of labor and poverty, all poetic evidence—the many slums, strikes, and prostitutes in these poems—to the contrary. For the New Critics, poets entered the canon on the condition that they wrote poetry and not "propaganda," as Cleanth Brooks divided the modern poetry world, including propaganda about the labor problem. Those who did write so-called propaganda—Langston Hughes was one of Brooks's examples—would be shown the door.[18] By contrast, for left-leaning critics of the 1930s and after, in order for the proletarian 1930s to displace the decadent 1920s, the 1930s needed to have a nearly exclusive claim on poetry and literature of the labor problem.[19] Whether from the political Left (Mike Gold, György Lukàcs) or elsewhere on the political spectrum (Brooks and the New Critics), these critics, as well as ones to follow, had a stake in demonstrating that the high moderns dodged—or wisely avoided, depending on your poetics and politics—these various labor problems. (As this book demonstrates, that was decidedly not the case.) Finally, for later critics seeking to expand the canon, the poets whom they recovered—in this volume, Edna St. Vincent Millay, Langston Hughes, and even Claude McKay—were recovered in ways that occassionally masked their encounter with labor.[20]

Whether sins of commission or omission—that is, whether deliberate exclusion or recovery of other poets on other terms—the result has been to leave the field of modern American poetry equally open to the charge made against American studies, that of neglecting questions of class, labor, and poverty. As Larry J. Griffin and Maria Tempenis have argued, "American studies . . . has never much 'done' class" and "class . . . has never really had its 'particular moment' in the field" (93). Yet that account grows flimsier by the publishing and conference season. In the last decade class *has* begun to have its particular moment in the field of American studies, as evidenced by numerous panels, conferences, books, and even book series. For the most part, however, poetry generally and canonical modern American poetry specifically have not had their moment within that class moment.

If so, then the problem may no longer be that Americanists shy away from class but, rather, that they shy away from poetry. Whole books that promise class-devoted rereadings of American literary history, for example, go by with barely a line of verse examined. Even scholarship on the 1930s, to say nothing of class-informed scholarship on earlier periods, has done a mostly woeful job of incorporating poetry into its literary histories.[21] As with everything else that scholars regret about the discipline, this critical predilection for prose can also be laid at the steps of the New Critics. Under their tutelage, Joseph Harrington argues, "poetry constituted the most autonomous form of literature, an alternative to the public, the popular, and the mass" (504)—not altogether unlike what Henry Van Dyke thought it should be, ironically enough. That reputation for autonomy, however, did not endear poetry, especially canonical modern American poetry, to a discipline newly committed to cultivating the historical contexts of works. Rather than reject or revise the supposed autonomy, however, critics, speaking very broadly, tended to grant it and turn instead to other, supposedly more historicized genres, namely, prose. In short, as Harrington summarizes the conventional critical wisdom, "we go to novels to find historical reality because novelists represent historical reality" (509), and we go to poetry, as the New Critics bid us to, to escape history. The result casts "prose narrative as the bearer of historical value . . . and poetry as the repository of aesthetic value" (509). And while that scholarly wisdom has changed since Harrington's article, and (obviously) much historicizing poetry criticism has appeared, scholars of modern American poetry still live with its legacy and its gaps—including, in this case, the absence of any history of canonical American poetry and its encounter with labor and poverty. And despite the critical conventional wisdom, far from muting or distancing itself from the labor problem, poetry may have been the genre in which these questions were most intensely played out.

But why the history has gone untold matters less than the history itself. In what follows, I argue that at its foundational moment in the early decades of the twentieth century, modern American poetry, like the rest of the culture at large, was haunted by the labor problem. That haunting took many forms, but for most modern poets it involved, through a romantic anticapitalist transformation, making the ghosts less scary and more manageable than they in fact were. Chapter 2, on William Carlos Williams, examines his deliberate remaking of one of the oldest modes of working-class poetry, the pastoral. Throughout his early work, but especially in his first mature collection of poems, *Al Que Quiere!* (1917), Williams borrows images and insights from his career as a doctor attending to the poor and working class of Rutherford, New Jersey, in order to challenge the modern pastoral fantasy of unchecked suburban prosperity. Nevertheless, as Williams argued in various essays and letters, he wanted to avoid reproducing the stigma associated with poverty and the poor. He would write poems about the poor, then, not to expose them to the light of reform, not to aid their escape from poverty, but to learn from them, admire them, and let others learn from and admire them as well. By representing the poor and working class, Williams believed, he could renew his readers' contact with the world. According to this way of thinking about poverty, which other poets would also adopt, the poor are not a problem of or for modernity but a possible solution to it. Chapter 3 focuses on T. S. Eliot and how, in his early, mostly unpublished notebook poems, he turned his midnight strolls through the working-class neighborhoods that surrounded Harvard University into some of the first recognizably modern poems. Like Williams, in these early poems Eliot seeks to distance himself from the conventional wisdom about slums and their inhabitants—namely, that they were problems in need of solutions. Instead, or, rather, in order to achieve this distance, he represents the slum and its dwellers as living repetitive, at times mechanistic lives, a representation that would be reinforced by his reading of the French philosopher Henri Bergson. In the first decade of his career as a poet, this trope of the poor and working class as mechanistic, repetitive, and without self-consciousness will inform most of Eliot's major works, including the poems he collected in *Prufrock and Other Observations* (1917), as well as *The Waste Land* (1922). In the course of these poems, Eliot will, in turn, be horrified by the narrow possibilities of such an impulsive life, embrace them, and then be horrified by them again. His recurrent horror, however, is such that in several poems he appears to reject, as other romantic anticapitalists would, rationality itself, which, in addition to underwriting capitalist modernity, is also held to be responsible for producing such automatic, repetitive, and unselfconscious existences in the first place.

The second half of the book examines poets whose relation to the canon, as I have noted, remains more marginal. Nevertheless, for the most part—there are exceptions and misgivings—these poets approached the labor problem and capitalism with similarly romantic attitudes. The fourth chapter examines the poems collected in Edna St. Vincent Millay's *A Few Figs from Thistles* (1920), which below their deliberately charming surface imply a surprisingly stark attitude toward questions of poverty and labor, one that seems to emerge out of the uneasily shared space of Greenwich Village, home to bohemian artists and writers like Millay, on the one hand, as well as the immigrant and working poor, on the other. This uneasily shared space, I argue, produced a particularly bohemian approach toward the urban poor, one that championed poverty yet sought to distinguish itself from the actually existing immigrant poor. As with Williams, for Millay poverty—especially the bohemian version of it—becomes something to be cherished and cultivated rather than abolished. The fifth chapter turns to Claude McKay and Langston Hughes, some of whose earliest poems, collected in *Harlem Shadows* (1922) and *Fine Clothes to the Jew* (1927), respectively, emerge from and comment on these poets' and other African Americans' confinement to service work: waiting and bussing tables, washing laundry, and dancing in cabarets, among other jobs. As both poets were keenly made aware, service work required a strict management of emotions and an arsenal of strategies—revenge fantasies, quitting fantasies, religion, music and dancing—to manage the management. It is the last of these strategies, the music (jazz) and dancing of the cabaret scene, that each poet offers, though not without reservations, as the tonic for the racial and emotional ailments produced by service labor. Subsequent critics have joined Hughes and McKay in making this argument, celebrating jazz as the marginalized yet empowering creation of an exploited minority, and while there is something to it, I argue that, as Hughes and McKay ultimately saw, such an attitude risks, as Theodor Adorno might put it, celebrating splendid underdogs (and their music) by celebrating the splendid system of racialist capitalism that made them so (*Minima Moralia* 28). Finally, in the last chapter, I return to an earlier moment in modern American poetry, placing Carl Sandburg in one of the most widespread and influential—if largely forgotten—reform movements of the early twentieth century, the American arts and crafts. Like other arts and crafts reformers in and around Chicago in the first two decades of the twentieth century, Sandburg imagined remaking the increasingly degraded forms of work under industrial capitalism into crafts capable of expressing rather than alienating workers' souls. For his first collection of poetry, *Chicago Poems* (1916), Sandburg would incorporate many arts and crafts ideals into his representation of workers, work, and the products of that work—whether fish, ballet, guitars, churches, the widespread death and destruction of World War I, or, most important, skyscrapers. However, as his major poem from that volume, "Skyscraper," suggests, Sandburg would eventually move away from a backward-looking arts and crafts movement in order to celebrate the new workers of industrial capitalism—no longer (if ever) craft-practicing artists but nevertheless entitled to certain rights, decencies, and respect. Sandburg, along with Hughes and McKay, thus represent poets whose romantic anticapitalism becomes slightly less romantic even as it remains fundamentally anticapitalist and pro-labor. They are, I believe, the exceptions that prove the rule. In the concluding chapter, I explore how the poets treated in this volume would continue to confront the labor problem and offer a summary judgment of their accomplishment.

In written notes for a lecture he never delivered, titled "The Tramp and the Strike Questions" (1879), Walt Whitman, arguably the first modern American poet—and arguably the first modern American poet of the labor problem—insisted that "Beneath the whole political world, what most presses and perplexes to-day, sending vastest results affecting the future, is not the abstract question of democracy, but of social and economic organization, the treatment of working people by employers, and all that goes along with it" (329).[22] "If the United States," Whitman concluded, "like the countries of the Old World, are also able to grow vast crops of poor, desperate, dissatisfied, nomadic, miserably-waged populations, such as we see looming upon us of late years—steadily, even if slowly, eating into them like a cancer of lungs or stomach—then our republican experiment, notwithstanding all its surface-successes, is at heart an unhealthy failure" (330). By the time Whitman noticed "the Poverty Question," as he put it later in the lecture, and its pathological implications for democracy, he had for the most part stopped writing poetry. In contrast, the modern American poets who would remake the genre in the 1910s and 1920s began their careers at just the moment when the labor problem had again grown pressing and perplexing. In a note dated February 1879 and appended to his notes for "The Tramp and the Strike Question," Whitman marveled, "I saw to-day a sight I had never seen before—and it amazed me, and made me serious; three quite good-looking American men . . . plodding along, their eyes cast down, spying for scraps, rags, bones, &c" (330). Modern American poets, I am arguing, were equally amazed and made serious by such sights. Moreover, whether judged domestically or internationally, such sights—of anxious work and desperate poverty—continue to haunt. The modern American poets I examine in this book have much to say about these ongoing problems, even if one does not always like what they had to say about them or if their solutions to them seem, in retrospect, appallingly insufficient.

CHAPTER 2

"Thinking / Of the Freezing Poor": The Suburban Counterpastoral in William Carlos Williams's Early Poetry

"The Voice of April" may not be the worst poem written in the twentieth century, but a list of the one hundred worst would seem somehow incomplete without it. Written by Madison Cawein, a prolific early-twentieth-century American poet known as the "Keats of Kentucky"—as Louis Untermeyer would put it in 1921, "the alliteration was tempting" (*Modern* 97)—"The Voice of April" appeared in the 1913 edition of *The Lyric Year,* a well-known anthology of the best contemporary American verse. Here are the poem's opening stanzas.

April calling, April calling, April calling me!
I hear the voice of April there in each old apple-tree;
Bee-boom and wild perfume, and wood-brook melody—
O hark, my heart, and hear, my heart, the April ecstasy!

Hark to the hills, the oldtime hills, that speak with sea and sky!
Or talk in murmurs with God's winds who on their bosoms lie:
Bird-call and waterfall and white clouds blowing by—
O hark, my heart, O hear, my heart, the April's cosmic cry!

(1–8)

That such a poem appeared in an anthology of the best contemporary American verse suggests that a great many people once very much liked "The Voice of April"—or, at least, that a few people (namely, the editors of the anthology) thought that a great many people should like it. What has happened between then and now to make the poem go from best to worst, of course, is the modernist revolution in poetry and sensibility. "The Voice of April" is bad because, formally, it "does" every one of the "few don'ts" Ezra Pound and F. S. Flint famously warned poets against in the March 1913 edition of *Poetry*—advice that has become next door to dogma. In terms of content, "The Voice of April" is bad because of its deliberately antiquated diction, its contorted syntax, and its laughable personification but also because it takes place in a pastoral no-place, seemingly unbothered by any crisis or doubt except perhaps that of winter. By 1913, to say nothing of today, these poetic affectations could seem not merely escapist but, even worse, absurd. By 1921, Louis Untermeyer was describing Cawein's poetry as "unreal, prettified, remote" (*Modern* 97). "Every now and then, with an irritating frequency," Untermeyer continued, "Cawein tried to transport his audience to a literary Fairyland; but the reader is quickly wearied by the almost interminable procession of fays, gnomes, pixies, elves, dryads, sprites, pucks, fauns—be they ever so lyrical" (97).

For all its lyrical and fairyland faults, though, modern American poetry may not have evolved without "The Voice of April" and poems like it, if only because Pound and others articulated what not to do (and thus what to do) through poems like Cawein's. Modern poets learned not to ape Cawein's chopped iambs, for example, nor his predictable rhymes, but they also learned what not to do (and, again, what to do) when working in a similar mode as Cawein—that is, the pastoral. Indeed, the pastoral did not disappear after 1913, as readers of Robert Frost or Amy Lowell or H. D. surely know, but instead it was, as with so much else, made new. And it was Pound's college friend, fellow modernist, and, as I will argue, pastoral poet, William Carlos Williams, who perhaps more than any other poet from this period helped to make it new.

As many literary historians have noted, 1913, when Madison Cawein's "The Voice of April" appeared in *The Lyric Year,* is a definitive year both for the development of modern poetry and for Williams's development as a poet. Until that year, Williams had been writing verse closer in spirit to Cawein's—with puffed-up titles like "Hymn to the Spirit of Fraternal Love" and "Ballad of Time and the Peasant"—than anything we would now associate with the poet. Nevertheless, 1913 also saw Williams asking, in one of his first definitively modern works, "The Wanderer," "How shall I be a mirror to this modernity?" (18). That is the same question I ask in this chapter—or, to phrase the question slightly differently, I ask how Williams plugged his ears to the siren's call of "The Voice of April" and became a modern poet. My answer, in brief, is that Williams mirrored his modernity at least in part by mirroring the workers and the poor he saw all around him—a mirror that few of his contemporary poets had yet bothered to hold up.

Many critics have noted the importance of workers and, even more so, the poor, to Williams's poetry, but I focus much more closely on how workers and the poor helped Williams to remake (as Pound put it) "the bad poetry now accepted as standard and classic" (932) by helping him to remake one of the most common modes of that bad poetry, the pastoral. Throughout his early work, especially the poems he collected in *Al Que Quiere!* (1917), Williams challenges the inherited conventions of the pastoral that continued to make a poem like "The Voice of April" not just possible but, alas, anthologizable. Williams does so formally—that is, his pastorals will neither rhyme, scan, nor, for that matter, let hills speak to the sea and sky, but he also does so politically. Whereas conventional pastoral poets tended to elide or romanticize rural labor and rural poverty, Williams casts a spotlight on the rural poor and working class in all their degraded, despoiled specificity.[1] He does so, I argue, not just to experiment with making a worn out mode modern but also to intervene in his hometown (Rutherford, New Jersey) and its politics, which suffered from their own "unreal, prettified, [and] remote" tendencies. While Rutherford, the adjacent town of Passaic, and nearby Paterson had more than their share of rural and urban poverty, immigrants, slums, and, especially in the case of Paterson, where silk workers went on strike in 1913, labor violence, the citizens of Rutherford did their best to pretend otherwise. Many of Williams's early poems, including his pastorals, sought to disabuse them of this fantasy.

Beyond these local politics, though, or related to them, I also argue that Williams's remaking of the pastoral belongs to his overall poetic project of renewal, of what he elsewhere called "contact." As these counterpastoral poems and Williams's long poem "The Wanderer" all reveal, what Williams expected, even required, poets and readers to come into contact with was the poor and working class. As such, my account places the labor problem—and the laboring poor—at the fulcrum point not just of Williams's remaking of the pastoral but also, and perhaps more important, of his making of himself as a modern poet.

Yet while seeking to include the poor and the working class in his poems, Williams faced a dilemma shared by other modern American poets. Put briefly, that problem was how to be modern without being Marxist. While Williams may have wanted to renew his readers' contact with the soil, with reality—which, as I argue, partly or even mostly meant he wanted to renew their contact with the poor—he nevertheless wanted to avoid propagandizing, to avoid being, as David Frail has established, a conventional political poet. The second half of this chapter examines the results of these competing desires, on the one hand, Williams's desire to make modern poetry out of the labor problem, to include the poor and working class in modes, like the pastoral, that tended to crop them out of the picture, but also, on the other hand, his need to steer clear of the dominant political philosophies of the time (whether Marxism or social Darwinism) that sought to explain why people are and remain poor at all. This ambivalence resulted in Williams's desire to portray the poor as they really are and not how others saw them or wanted to see them—that is, it resulted in what critics and Williams himself praised as the poet's "objectivity." Yet objectivity is a dubious goal, as well as a problematic assumption, especially when, as Williams does, it is offered as the sturdiest perch from which to view the labor problem or, more specifically, the problem of poverty. To insist, as Williams will, that we really see the poor and not, say, make the poor less poor, ultimately suggests that the problem with the poor is not that they lack resources but that we fail to appreciate or understand them as they are. For Williams, then, as for other modern American poets, the poor, far from being a problem of or for modernity, could become the solution to it—if only we opened our eyes.

Discussing *Al Que Quiere!* with an interviewer in 1958, Williams recalled of the book that "without knowing Greek I had read translations of *The Odes of Theocritus* and felt myself very much attracted to the pastoral mode" (*I Wanted to Write a Poem* 21). By the time Williams took it up in the early 1910s, however, the pastoral mode had grown rather shopworn. The most provocative account of its history is given by Raymond Williams, who, in *The Country and the City* (1975), outlines what he calls the "aristocratic transformation" of the pastoral (21). For Williams, the earliest works of the pastoral (or Georgic) tradition—Hesiod's *Works and Days*, Theocritus's *Idylls*, Virgil's *Eclogues*—have as their background or base such laboring activities as "the herding of goats, sheep and cattle" or, in the case of Hesiod, "plowing, tending vineyards, [and] keeping pigs and goats" (14). That is, these works remain in "contact with the working year and with the real social conditions of country life" (16). Thereafter, however, especially in the early modern period and the poetry of writers such as Andrew Marvell, Ben Jonson, and Thomas Carew, the pastoral undergoes a gradual process of abstraction from country life and workers, an abstraction, Williams argues, very much suited to the "interest of a new kind of society, that of developing agrarian capitalism" (39). No longer connected to the real social conditions of country life, the pastoral shepherds and nymphs in early modern pastoral poems "now begin to appear [as] lay figures in an aristocratic entertainment" (20). Not long after, too, the shepherds and nymphs drop out altogether, their place taken by "a renewed intensity of attention to natural beauty," which "is now the observation of the scientist or tourist," Williams adds, "rather than of the working countryman" (20). The result, Williams concludes, is "an ideological separation between the processes of rural exploitation, which have been, in effect, dissolved into a landscape" (126). "The achievement, if it can be called that," Williams observes, "of the Renaissance adaptation of . . . these classical modes is that, step by step, these living tensions are excised, until there is nothing countervailing, and selected images stand as themselves: not in a living but in an enamelled world" (18).

While this is a rather sweeping characterization of the pastoral, it does help place Williams's (i.e., William Carlos Williams's) pastorals, which, while certainly made new, also belong to that tradition of eighteenth- and early-nineteenth-century British counterpastoral poets—Stephen Duck, John Clare, George Crabbe, and Mary Collier—who emerge as the heroes and heroines of the first half of Raymond Williams's *The Country and the City.* By representing rural exploitation and the real social conditions of country life, these counterpastoral poets kicked against the pastoral poets of the period who sometimes forgot (or for whom it did not seem relevant) that fields needed threshing or that rural labor involved as much or more starving as singing. Something like this same counterpastoral mode inspired William Carlos Williams and appears as early as 1914, when in a poem entitled "Idyl," Williams borrows the title of Theocritus's collection of pastorals but sets his version in a winter snowstorm, the poet safely tucked away inside his home.

They say to me, "There is
A roaring god outside
Beating the trees!"
I go hurriedly
And find
Two unfortunates
Cowering in the wind.
I think of this
As I lie here, warm
Watching the blinding white
That was saffron

Change to blue steel
Behind shaking trees.

I raise my head and
Sight leaps twenty miles
To the bleak horizon,
"But my desires,"
I say to myself
"Are thirty years
Behind all this."

It is late.
My wife comes out
And tucks me in
Telling me
Not to hurry—
—Not to hurry!
She brings our baby
And puts him
In the bed beside me.
I move over
Into the cold sheets
To make room for him
And thinking
Of the freezing poor
I consider myself
Happy—
Then we kiss.

(1–37)

"Idyl" belongs to the "leading citizens" genre of poetry that Williams frequently wrote during the 1910s (Frail 43). In this body of thematically linked poems, Williams directly addresses the well-to-do, white-collar Republicans of his hometown of Rutherford. In "Idyl," these leading citizens, the "They" of the first line, instruct the speaker of the poem that "There is / A roaring god outside / Beating the trees!" (1–3)—yet when the speaker goes outside, he finds "Two unfortunates / Cowering in the wind" (6–7). The episode underscores Williams's lifelong secularism but also, more subtly, how our beliefs about the world determine what we see and do not see in it. Those who believe in an animistic universe—and in the early twentieth century there were many who believed just this—will, by definition, see God's (or many different gods') work everywhere, including in a winter snowstorm. Yet that same providential belief risks obscuring, or at least lessening the priority of, those who suffer in this world; that is, their suffering may be felt merely to be a part of God's plan. In contrast to this providential view of the universe, the speaker of the poem sees human suffering in the snowstorm and is haunted by this vision, so much so that it follows him back inside to his bed, where he can only think of the storm and his life in relation to that suffering.

In the stanza that follows, though, the speaker seemingly loses sight of the "Two unfortunates / Cowering in the wind" (6–7), when, instead of occupying his thoughts, they become the occasion for reflecting on his own crisis, that of finding himself in a situation—married, a new father, literally and ironically looking forward to "the bleak horizon" (16)—that his "desires" (17) did not choose but which they must always catch up to, whether they desire it or not. The "this" (8) that the speaker thinks of in the first stanza—that is, "Two unfortunates / Cowering in the wind" (6–7)—thus develops into the "this" (20) of the second stanza: the bleak horizon of a middle-class, suburban life that has developed independent of the speaker's will. The appearance of the couple's baby, however, interrupts these misgivings and reintroduces the freezing poor to the speaker's thoughts—in fact, ironically aligns the two. In order to make room for his baby, the speaker must "move over / Into the cold sheets" (30–31), which leads him to think again of "the freezing poor" (35) who must still be "Cowering in the wind" (7) and cold. By comparison to their unfortunate lives, though, his life seems quite fortunate, and while not innately happy, the speaker nevertheless "consider[s]" (35) himself happy. At any rate, the speaker has no choice (he is immobile, tucked in), and the kiss from his wife puts the matter—and the poem—to rest.

Much of the poem turns on this word *fortune,* which describes both the freezing poor—inasmuch as they are the "Two unfortunates" (6)—and the speaker's relative comfort. Etymologically, *fortune* means "chance," with, of course, an additional meaning of "money."[2] The "Two unfortunates / Cowering in the wind" (6–7) suffer from both these senses of the word: bad luck has stranded them in a winter snowstorm without enough money to secure shelter. But luck and money equally determine the speaker's life—they just happen to have determined it for the better. In the second stanza, the speaker fears that his "desires" (17), his will, have not controlled his life at all but must catch up to what has happened to him. Even so, he has a house and family to keep the cold out. Thus, in contrast to the opening "They" (1), who see God's will in everything, by its end the poem offers a vision of a world ruled—for better and for worse—by chance, by fortune. Moreover, and despite how little a part they may have played in it, people, the poem suggests, will nevertheless consider themselves "Happy" (36) (or "unhappy") at least partly in relation to others. In other words, if the middle class (as Barbara Ehrenreich put it) have a fear of falling into the netherworld of uncredentialed poverty, that fear also allows them—perhaps *compels* them—to appreciate their relative prosperity.

However intricate its structural theory of happiness, the poem does not, with the exception of its title, seem to have much to do with the pastoral mode. Instead of professing their love or challenging each other to a song contest, Williams's shepherds are freezing to death in a rural landscape that, far from being "idyllic," is being battered by a winter snowstorm. Yet Williams chose his title for a reason. If the idyll conventionally portrays a simple, peaceful scene of rural or pastoral life, then the poem must count as one, although it is not the shepherds outside freezing but the young father and baby, tucked into a warm bed in a big house by an adoring wife, who constitute the protagonists of this simple, peaceful scene. Unlike other idylls, though, which efface or romanticize the rural and working poor, Williams's version shows how that simple, peaceful scene transpires in (and to some degree psychologically depends on) poverty, the presence of the freezing poor outside. Moreover, if the usual idyll relies on the intrigues and injustices of the city to give moment to its peaceful and utopian countryside, Williams's "Idyl" starts in the country (or, rather, the suburbs) and stays there. Finally, the poem reveals that countryside to be a place of suffering and, far from the home of a benevolent Arcadia ruled by benevolent gods, the site of a cruel, indifferent nature ruled by no one at all. The poem probably deserves its pastoral title, then, but only because Williams refigures rather than reproduces the conventional qualities of that mode. He does so, first, by acknowledging that there is such a thing as rural poverty and suffering; second, by making that poverty and suffering the starting point for the mode that tended to shunt it aside; and third, by implicating middle-class prosperity for its blissful awareness of that poverty and suffering.

This concern for the relation between the poor and the middle class becomes a preoccupying theme of Williams's counterpastorals and his early poetry. It appears, perhaps most forcefully, in another Williams poem from this period. Unlike "Idyl," from 1914, this poem was published in 1917 in *Al Que*

Quiere! Like "Idyl," though, it alludes to the pastoral tradition through its title, in this case, simply enough, "Pastoral."

When I was younger
it was plain to me
I must make something of myself.
Older now
I walk the back streets
admiring the houses
of the very poor:
roof out of line with sides
the yards cluttered
with old chicken wire, ashes,
furniture gone wrong;
the fences and outhouses
built of barrel-staves
and parts of boxes, all,
if I am fortunate,
smeared a bluish green
that properly weathered
pleases me best
of all colors.

No one
will believe this
of vast import to the nation.
(1–22)

In the earlier poem, "Idyl," the "They" of the poem urge the poet to see God in a snowstorm, and he disappoints their expectations by only seeing the poor. Here, too, however, he disappoints—also by seeing the poor (3). In "Pastoral," the speaker implies that contrary to the expectations that he "must make something of [him]self," what he has made of himself is a less than admirable admirer of "the houses / of the very poor" (6–7). In other words, he has made of himself a poet, and not just any poet, but one who finds inspiration and even beauty in the living conditions of others who have also not made something of themselves—that is, the living conditions of "the very poor" (7).

To most of his contemporary readers of poetry, those eagerly awaiting their copies of *The Lyric Year* or those whose hearts harked to the April ecstasy, for example, it would seem perverse to find any of the details Williams lovingly catalogs—roofs out of line, yards cluttered, buildings carelessly made of shoddy material—as in any sense admirable or beautiful or poetic. Yet to Williams and other modern poets, the capacity to make poetry out of the unpoetic, as T. S. Eliot put it, functioned as one of the common denominators of modern poetry. As I argue in chapter 1, it was, in addition to innovations in form, this "widening of subject matter" (Perkins 300) to include poverty, prostitutes, and other speakers of what in 1913 Charles Hall Grandgent, then president of the Modern Language Association, dismissively referred to as "gutter slang" (105) that distinguished modern poetry from its Victorian and genteel predecessors.[3]

The poem thus shows Williams further remaking the pastoral, this time by not just including the poor in its pastoral scene—and showing them suffering instead of singing—or by showing how so much depends upon them, but by taking a somewhat perverse pleasure in their abject living conditions. Whereas in the conventional pastoral one is allowed to forget poverty and suffering and bask instead in the country and its charms, in Williams's pastoral one arrives in a country whose poverty is precisely its charm. "If I am fortunate," he writes in "Pastoral," the fences and outhouses will be "smeared a bluish green / that properly weathered / pleases me best / of all colors" (15–19), and again note that word *fortune.* Just as in "Idyl," the poet's "fortune"—his pleasure, his poetry—depends on the poor's lack of it. As in several poems by T. S. Eliot, taken up in the next chapter, Williams substitutes questions of aesthetics (which colors please him best) for questions of ethics (what is to be done about poverty). Yet finding poverty charming or taking pleasure in it poses certain nagging ethical problems. At worst, the poem risks replacing one sort of pastoral dilettantism ("April calling, April calling, April calling me!") with another ("Poverty calling, Poverty calling, Poverty calling me!"). More generously, the poem may implicate readers in the moral and aesthetic ambiguities of modern poetry. In other words, both readers of traditional pastorals and modern ones turn to poetry at least in part for aesthetic pleasure—even if what they find aesthetically pleasing differs from (as in Cawein) "Bee-boom and wild perfume, and wood-brook melody" (3) to (as in Williams) "the yards cluttered / with old chicken wire" (9–10). In seeking to become more "real," however, modern poetry did not seek to become less aesthetically pleasing. The problem is in what modern poetry occasionally began to find aesthetically pleasing—that is, other people's suffering.[4]

In any case, the speaker seems to regret that few of his fellow citizens will find poverty or the poetry of poverty very important. "No one," Williams concludes in the last stanza of "Pastoral," "will believe this / of vast import to the nation" (20–22), and I have to confess that I am tempted to take the nation's side on this one. Perhaps no one cares about which colors on the poverty spectrum please poets best because it is not in fact of vast import to anyone. Nevertheless, and as many critics have noted, the "this" (21) of these last lines remains ambiguous. It can refer to either the aesthetic pleasure the poet finds in rural poverty (i.e., to the poem itself) or to the poverty itself. Or, as is most likely the case, the "this" (21) is meant to refer to both, thus returning to the first stanza and further aligning poet and the very poor as overlooked failures. As John Lowney writes of the poem, mistaken only about where it takes place, "Not only is the urban slum ignored by the 'nation', but Williams's poetic treatment of such a topic presumably is ignored as well" (60).

But the "national" may be the wrong context here. As David Frail has established, the local—including Williams's hometown of Rutherford and its at times heated civic debates—remained crucial to Williams's early poetry and politics, and these local concerns may lie behind Williams's remaking of the pastoral and his provocative—even if ethically suspect—claim to find beauty in poverty. For at least he could see poverty, unlike the leading citizens of Rutherford who, by the time Williams wrote "Pastoral," had seemed to retreat into a sort of suburban pastoral fantasy, one that closed its eyes to the poverty that surrounded it. As Frail notes, the town of Rutherford was established in the hopes of it being "a haven for the right sort of white-collar professionals and entrepreneurs who [would take] one of 63 passenger trains a day home from their jobs or businesses in Manhattan to rest in what they . . . felt was a pastoral middle ground between the untamed Jersey hills and the city" (110). In other words, for the leading citizens of Rutherford, their bedroom community was to offer a pseudopastoral suburban idyll, perilously but comfortably poised between the urban chaos of New York City and the mephitic, hardscrabble backwaters of New Jersey.[5] As the local newspaper, the *Rutherford Illustrated,* bragged in 1892, "Rutherford is nearly all one vast park whose primitive charms are enhanced rather than marred by the macadamized roads and pretty cottages" (qtd. in Frail 110).

Despite considerable growth in population and infrastructure in the first years of the twentieth century, the town would desperately try to hold on to the aura of those "primitive"—but not too primitive—"charms" well into the 1910s and 1920s. Indeed, the town tried to dissuade prospective manufacturers from establishing industries in the area since, as Frail puts it, and unlike the macadamized roads and pretty cottages, "industry and a laboring population threatened to mar its primitive charms" (110). Despite the town's boosterism and best efforts, though, "there was clearly some real poverty" (19) in Rutherford, as Williams well knew since his medical practice, at least in its early years, consisted almost exclusively of these poor and working-class patients. In nearby Passaic, where Williams would open up a second practice in 1927, tens of thousands of immigrants (mostly Slavs) worked in the woolen mills and lived in a sort of perpetual working poverty. As Mike Weaver writes, these impoverished immigrant workers and their families "flowed over into East Rutherford, and other towns across the Passaic river" (89).[6] Nevertheless, Rutherford downplayed that poverty in order to maintain, as Frail puts it, "its self-image as a pastoral community governed by small-community values and middle-class respectability and refinement" (110).

Given this head-in-the-sand worldview, Williams did not—or not just—wish to remake the pastoral in order to mine the heretofore untapped sources of beauty to be found in poverty but, rather, to make his pastorals of the poor compete with—in some way triumph over—the Rutherford pastoral fantasy of unbroken suburban prosperity. Indeed, Williams claimed to only want readers who would share his interest in the poor—or so he announces in "Sub Terra," the lead poem of *Al Que Quiere!* and the poem that precedes "Pastoral" in that collection. Williams begins the poem by asking where he shall find "you / my grotesque fellows, / that I seek / everywhere / to make up my band?" (1–4). He regrets that, as in "Pastoral," "None, not one" has "the earthy tastes I require" (5–6). While awaiting the arrival of his band, Williams states what he expects of them.

You to come with me
poking into negro houses
with their gloom and their smell!
In among children
leaping around a dead dog!
Mimicking
onto the lawns of the rich!
You!

To go with me a-tip-toe,
head down under heaven,
nostrils lipping the wind!
(34–44)

Like the poet he was reading at the time, Walt Whitman, Williams claims free passage into worlds inaccessible—and frankly undesirable—to the usual readers of poetry. Williams seems to regret, however, that so few of those readers will be willing to follow the poet into "negro houses"—or respect his desire to go at all. As John Lowney observes of "Sub Terra," "the poem mourns the scarcity of readers receptive to [his] aesthetic" (*The American Avant-Garde Tradition* 54).

While Williams doubtless remained aware of how few readers would want to go sniffing out gloom and smells, how little import these would have for the nation, and how few people, myself included, would find any of this beautiful, to say that he "mourns" this situation perhaps puts too gloomy an interpretation on it. In poems like "Apology"—also from *Al Que Quiere!*—Williams insists with some pride that the poor, and not the leading citizens of the town, remain his fundamental inspiration. "Why do I write today?" (1), Williams asks, and goes on to answer his own question.

The beauty of
the terrible faces
of our nonentities
stirs me to it:

Colored women
day workers—
old and experienced—
returning home at dusk
in cast off clothing
faces like
old Florentine oak.

Also
the set pieces
of your faces stir me—
leading citizens—

but not
in the same way.
(2–18)

The "nonentities" of the first stanza belong to the same category of the "this" that is of no import to the nation in "Pastoral" but of vital import to Williams the poet. He finds beauty in their "terrible faces" just as in "Pastoral" he finds beauty in their terrible yards and terrible sheds. In contrast, the poet claims to be stirred by the "set pieces" of the faces of the leading citizens, "but not / in the same way"—which raises the question, of course, "In what way?" One answer is that the poor and the leading citizens in "Apology" and elsewhere in Williams's early poetry may not be mutually exclusive stirrings but very much connected. Leaving aside whether the terrible faces of poverty can in fact be beautiful, the poet may be stirred to represent those faces in order to rearrange the "set pieces" (14) of the leading citizens' faces—just as the freezing poor led the speaker of Williams's "Pastoral" to rearrange his own middle-class, midlife crisis and the terrible faces of this poem "stir" the poet to write. Williams is not only interested in the poor in and of themselves, then, but equally in their capacity to affect the well-to-do readers of his poetry and residents of his town. To put it another way, if the town of Rutherford looked away from poverty, if it behaved like some anxious mayor who hides the poor when visiting dignitaries come to town, then Williams's pastorals would pull them out of the shadows and into the stirring light. *Ecce homo pauper.*

Take "K. McB.," for example, also from *Al Que Quiere!* The "K. McB." of the title is Kathleen McBride, a young girl from the state orphanage whom the Williams family employed as a nursemaid for their two young boys. In the poem, the speaker addresses Kathleen directly.

You exquisite chunk of mud
Kathleen—just like
any other chunk of mud!

—especially in April!
Curl up round their shoes
when they try to step on you,
spoil the polish!
I shall laugh till I am sick

at their amazement.
Do they expect the ground to be
always solid?
Give them the slip then;
let them sit in you;
soil their pants;
teach them a dignity
that is dignity, the dignity
of mud!

(1–19)

Kathleen McBride is "like / any other chunk of mud" (2–3)—that is, common and filthy—but also "exquisite" (1), carefully done and elaborately made, beautiful and lovely, just as in "Pastoral" and "Apology" the houses and faces of the very poor seem common and filthy but nevertheless exquisite to the poet. Like the "Two unfortunates / Cowering in the wind" (6–7) in "Idyl" and the "Colored women / day workers" (5–6) from "Apology," too, Kathleen exists to unsettle middle-class lives, perhaps, in this case, Williams's two boys, but also, more generally, each of Williams's readers. The speaker orders Kathleen McBride to "Curl up round their shoes," to "spoil the polish," and the speaker relishes the possibility, especially since "they" have lost contact with reality. "They expect the ground to be always solid" (10–11), and K. McB. is to bring them back into contact with it, reality, by bringing them back into contact with the muddy ground itself—or, what amounts to the same thing, the muddy ground *herself.* (K. McB. is, remember, "like / any other chunk of mud.") "Give them the slip then" (12), the speaker commands, and expects that her doing so will "soil their pants" (14) and "teach them . . . the dignity / of mud" (15–17), which will also teach them something about the dignity of the poor, as well as their own unearned senses of dignity. Williams, admiring the dignity of mud, which is also the dignity of the poor and working class, wishes to immerse others in a similar admiration.

If Williams recommended a mud bath in the poor and working class to others, it is perhaps because it had done him so much good, had, in fact, made him a modern poet. In "The Wanderer"—a long, ambitious poem written in 1913 but lightly revised and inserted as the concluding poem of *Al Que Quiere!*—Williams documented his own immersion in the poor and working class. The poem is, in essence, Williams's *Prelude,* a poetic bildungsroman. In it, Williams reproduces the consciousness of a premodern, pastoral-devoted poet who—through the machinations of a shape-shifting muse figure—is made to confront workers and the poor for the first time. While shocking, the experience is also liberating.

Prior to this confrontation between poet and workers, though, the muse figure, in the form of a prostitute, challenges the poet to look at the crowds on Broadway, where he has the following vision, which is not of the beauty of the world, which he expects the muse to show him, but of the quiet desperation of the city's inhabitants.

And instantly down the mists of my eyes
There came crowds walking—men as visions
With expressionless, animate faces;
Empty men with shell-thin bodies
Jostling close above the gutter,
Hasting—nowhere!

(67–72)

Not prepared for these visions of urban modernity, the poet wishes to escape the "terror" of the city and its hollow men and gain, instead, as he begs of the muse, "A new grip upon those garments that brushed me / In days gone by on beach, lawn, and in forest!" (106–7). In other words, these visions of the "death living" (109) on Broadway leave the speaker hungry for poetry inspired by and realized in beach, lawn, and forest—that is, the pastoral and genteel mode proper. He is, as it were, not quite ready for Broadway.

The joke is on him, though, for the next place the muse sends the speaker (in the section titled "The Strike") is even worse than Broadway. She sends him to "the deserted streets of Paterson," New Jersey (120), where, in 1913, striking workers had brought the town and its silk mills to a halt. Although he did not visit Paterson during the strike, Williams followed its progress from nearby Rutherford, and, as "The Wanderer" suggests, it seems to have greatly affected him. The poem culminates in the following description, given by the poet to his muse, of workers during the strike.

"Heavy drink were the low, sloping foreheads
The flat skulls with the unkempt black or blond hair,
The ugly legs of the young girls, pistons

Too powerful for delicacy!
The women's wrists, the men's arms red
Used to heat and cold, to toss quartered beeves
And barrels, and milk-cans, and crates of fruit!

"Faces all knotted up like burls on oaks,
Grasping, fox-snouted, thick-lipped,
Sagging breasts and protruding stomachs,
Rasping voices, filthy habits with the hands.

"Nowhere you! Everywhere the electric!

"Ugly, venomous, gigantic!
Tossing me as a great father his helpless
Infant till it shriek with ecstasy
And its eyes roll and its tongue hangs out!—

(142–60)

Williams's image of workers' "faces all knotted up like burls on oaks" recalls the one he uses in "Apology" to describe the "Colored women / day workers . . . returning home at dusk" (6–9) with "faces like / old Florentine oak" (11–12), except in that poem the day workers illustrate "The beauty of / the terrible faces / of our nonentities," a beauty that Williams claims stirs him to write (2–4). In "The Wanderer," those faces have also stirred him to write but not because of their beauty and not out of any great sense of sympathy with their condition. Unlike Kathleen McBride, the subject of Williams's largely worshipful "K. McB.," there would seem to be considerably more mud than dignity in his poet's representation of these striking Paterson silk workers. Workers are drunks, Neanderthals, disheveled, vile, machinelike, ungainly, bestial, and worse. The passage could have been written by a particularly class-conscious eugenicist. And all the effort in the world will not make this representation of workers more palatable than it is, except to say that the point is that it be unpalatable. In other words, the passage represents what the striking workers of Paterson would look like to an ambitious though conventional poet circa 1913. Such a vision, the poem also implies, is the necessary, albeit revolting, first step toward a more modern sensibility, including a more modern poetics.

That reading is in keeping with the one Williams offered about this section in a 1947 letter he sent to the poet Babette Deutsch, who, to gather from the context of the letter, must have asked Williams about "the labor violence which has had Paterson as its scene during the last thirty or, perhaps, hundred years" (*Selected Letters* 258). He confesses that he had "found little [he] wanted to say about it," excepting "The Strike" section of "The Wanderer" (258). He writes:

> You have found "The Strike." Good. You will find more in the prose of *Life Along the Passaic,* especially the first account contained therein. However, in *Paterson* the social unrest that occasions all strikes is strong—underscored, especially in the 3d part, but I must confess that the aesthetic shock occasioned by the rise of the masses upon the artist receives top notice. (258–59)

Although by the end of the passge Williams is discussing *Paterson,* his later epic poem, his comments about that poem and its treatment of labor unrest apply as well to "The Strike" section of "The Wanderer." He even adopts the same metaphor. In his letter to Deutsch, he writes of the "aesthetic shock" that the artist receives on witnessing the rise of the masses, and in the earlier poem the poet complains that instead of the muse, he finds only "Everywhere the electric!" (156). Williams's letter to Deutsch offers a clue, then, and what it suggests about this ugly little portrait of striking workers is that *this* is how workers would appear to the premodern artist or poet. The purpose of the "Strike" section, and the poem as a whole, is to expose this pre-modern vision of poetry to "the aesthetic shock occasioned by the rise of the masses." Rather like tossing a vampire into sunlight, it does so by confronting the representative poet of that genteel tradition with that which it cannot tolerate—the striking workers of Paterson.

Yet the experience is also transforming. In the next-to-last stanza of the "Strike" section just quoted, the vision of these striking and fighting workers repulses and infantilizes the poet. The scene is "Ugly, venomous, gigantic!" (157). It overwhelms the poet, "Tossing me as a great father his helpless / Infant till it shriek with ecstasy / And its eyes roll and its tongue hangs out!—" (158–60), and the only thing unexpected about these lines may be the word *ecstasy* (159). Because ecstasy tends to connote something desirable (an "ecstasy of delight"), it seems out of place in a vision "ugly, venomous, gigantic!" Yet *ecstasy* can mean being overwhelmed by any emotion, whether joy, grief, passion, or, in this case, shock. The word comes from the Greek, *ekstasis,* which means "to be put out of one's place"—or "being put out of one's place and into another place," say, a trance. Accordingly, though at first unable and unwilling to see them, the poor and working class nevertheless usher the poet out of the pastoral, genteel mode and into modernity proper. They do so through a sort of baptism that is like the more famous baptism in "The Passaic, that filthy river" (260) at the conclusion of the poem. Instead of being dunked in the river, though, this baptism involves a dunking in the poor and working class and leaves the baptized ecstatically dripping and shivering in the modern. The baptism thus offers a variation on the immersion metaphor in Williams's counterpastoral poems. In "K. McB.," Williams wished that Kathleen McBride would give readers "the slip" (12), that she would "let them sit in you" (13), that readers would be immersed in "the dignity / of mud!" (16–17) that is also the dignity of the poor and working class. In "The Wanderer," Williams recreates his own immersion, his own baptism, in the filth of starving and striking workers. In "K. McB.," he hopes that such an immersion in the poor and working class will disrupt expectations that the ground will always be solid. In other words, that K. McB. will throw her charges off—just as the poet of "The Wanderer" is disrupted, thrown off, overwhelmed, and put into a state of ecstasy by his vision of the striking Paterson silk workers.

The pattern is clear: someone plunged—or was made to plunge—into the waters of the poor and working class and came out a new person, including a new, sufficiently modern poet, reader of modern poetry, or citizen of modern suburbia. As in "K. McB.," "The Wanderer" implies that the route to modernity—and a mature modern poetry—runs through the poor and working class.

As the counterpastoral poems and "The Wanderer" all suggest, Williams attempted to remake the poetic by bringing the rural poor and urban working class into its frame, and he did so with an eye toward how those figures would affect the moral and aesthetic complacencies of not quite modern enough readers. In this section, I ask why, exactly, Williams seemed so concerned that he and his readers expose themselves to the poor and working class. The answer reveals how crucial the poor and working class would be to Williams's efforts to make himself a modern poet but also, and perhaps more important, how crucial the poor and working class would be to the reformation of modern life generally.

In "A Point for American Criticism," an essay on James Joyce from 1929, Williams wrote:

> Joyce maims words. Why? Because meanings have been dulled, then lost, then perverted by their connotations (which have grown over them) until their effect on the mind is no longer what it was when they were fresh, but grows rotten as *poi*—though we may get to like *poi*. (89–90)

As a metaphor for words turned rotten, poi is a good choice. It is a Hawaiian food made from the root of a large, tropical plant (called a taro plant), which is then mixed with water, cooked, pounded into a paste, and slightly fermented. On the first day it is made, poi is sweet, but each day thereafter it turns increasingly sour. An etymological coincidence reveals Williams's meaning: *poi-e-tes* is the Greek word for poet, and just as poi grows rotten, so, too, do poi-e-tes (poets—and their poems) grow rotten. Therefore, what Joyce and his linguistic experiments enable, Williams suggests, is, as he wrote eight years earlier in another essay on Joyce, "the forever sought freedom of truth from usage," the old and rotten made sweet and new again ("Comment" 28).

As so often happens in essays of this sort, Williams's description of Joyce's technique applies as much or more to his own ambitions as a poet as to Joyce's as a novelist. For Williams, in order to make it—poetry—new, one had to make words new as well. The modern poet had a responsibility to renew readers' perception of the world, to make them see reality beneath the accumulated layers of thought and language. The poet must put his readers back in *contact*—as it happens, the name of the little magazine Williams started in 1920 with Robert McAlmon—with the world. "If Americans are to be blessed with important work," Williams wrote in 1920 in his "Comment on Contact," "it will be through intelligent, informed contact with the locality which alone can infuse it with reality" (68). A poet created that important work by immersing himself in the local—in the case of Williams's counterpastoral poems, the Rutherford poor—but also by freeing words from usage, as Williams claimed Joyce did, and as he sought to do as well.

In *Real Thing: Imitation and Authenticity in American Culture,* Miles Orvell explicates this artistic aim in Williams specifically and the modernist project more generally.

> Realism, it was believed, had lost contact with reality, and modernists like Williams were seeking, through the work of art, somehow to restore that contact. On the face of it, modernism seemed to shift the focus of the arts away from the thing signified, as we would say nowadays, to the signifier itself, the medium of the artwork, whatever that might be—words, sound, paint, wood, movement. . . . This was a revolutionary effort, but it was also restorative, and Williams reminds us that the goal was not to escape reality, but somehow, through the work of art, to restore it. (240–41)

The artist could answer this call to restore reality, Orvell concludes, "by inventing works that asserted the artist's moral and aesthetic power of clarification" and by inventing "works that remained in contact with the soil, with local materials" (241). "Here," Orvell continues, echoing Williams on Joyce, "is the essence of the American modernist's vocation: to rebuild the ruined words" (242).

Few would argue with the spirit of Orvell's conclusions, but in seeking to distinguish realists from modernists like Williams, Orvell and other critics have perhaps overestimated the all-encompassing importance of form and "words" to modernist poets and writers. As such, they may have underestimated the importance of the realist content that would inform these revolutionary works and words of art—at least in the case of Williams's early poetry and, I would argue, for many other modernists as well. For example, Orvell writes:

> Frank Norris and the other realist writers around the turn of the century had said what sounds like the same thing: we want life not literature. But what they in fact meant was blood, sex, money, grime, garbage, immigrants, and killing snowstorms—a recognition of areas of experience previously excluded from polite literature. . . . What Williams meant by "reality itself" was, however, quite different; it was a quality of authenticity that was held to be missing from a literary "realism" that had itself grown conventional. (240)

By placing so much emphasis on words, on signifiers, and by taking the new literary "areas of experience" for granted, Orvell ends up diminishing the importance of what he calls "blood, sex, money, grime, garbage, immigrants, and killing snowstorms" to the invention of modern American poetry. I have my eye out for them, of course, but even so the Williams poems thus far examined have been about money, grime, garbage, immigrants, and killing snowstorms, and soon enough there will be ones about blood and sex.

Still, Orvell is right about what modernists sought by remaking poetry and freeing words from usage: they sought not just to revolutionize the word, but the world through the word. As Bob Johnson writes of Williams's literary politics prior to the Great Depression, "One of the most important strategies of the modernist experiment in America was to introduce into art harsh nonliterary elements, to defamiliarize language so that it might once again appear to us new, exciting, and revelatory, in other words, so that it might reflect and restore a more vital contact with the world, making it possible for people to see and experience that world with greater clarity and poignancy" (7–8). As Johnson suggests, new poetic forms could in fact "restore a more vital contact with the world," but it is surprising how often those new forms relied on what Johnson calls "harsh nonliterary elements"—Orvell's blood, sex, money, grime, garbage, immigrants, and killing snowstorms—in order to shock their readers into a renewed perception of and contact with reality. In other words, the voice of April, regardless of how new its words or forms were made, just couldn't deliver enough voltage. In seeking to revolutionize the world, I am suggesting, modernist poetry had to discover a new content as well as a new form—and, in Williams's case, that new content as often as not meant the poor and working class.

As Miles Orvell argued of Williams, the modernist project sought to create "works that remained in contact with the soil, with local materials" (241). Williams's "K. McB." and "The Wanderer" make that assertion literal, or, rather, give the soil, which literary works were to remain in contact with, a human and, importantly, a class analog. Here, as in many other Williams poems from the 1910s, what readers are supposed to come in contact with is the poor and working class.[7] In order for a poet to put his readers into contact with the poor and working class, though, *he,* the poet, had to remain in contact with them, and here Williams's own profession as doctor enters the picture. In a letter Williams published in 1940 in the poetry journal *Furioso,* he argued:

> Some experience to the sharp edge of the mechanics of living—such as blindness, political exile, a commercial theatre to support and be supported by, a profession out of necessity, dire poverty, defiance of law, insanity—is necessary to the poet. It doesn't matter what the form is, these are all of a class, to give the poet his sense of precision in the appreciation of values, what is commonly spoken of as "reality." ("A Letter" 22)

In addition to all the other experiences tinged with the "sharp edge of the mechanics of living," Williams lists "a profession out of necessity" followed by "dire poverty," and, again, one can only assume that in addition to other poets—Milton the blind poet, Yeats the commercial theater director—he is thinking of himself. Williams practiced medicine in Rutherford for forty-one years, and many of his patients, as noted earlier, came from the urban and rural poor—meaning that Williams's profession out of necessity frequently brought him into direct contact with dire poverty and what was for him, in other words, reality.

As in "Apology," he would later identify these poor as one, perhaps the major, source for his work as a poet. Williams later wrote in his *Autobiography* (1951):

> [M]y "medicine" was the thing which gained me entrance to these secret gardens of the self. It lay there, another world, in the self. I was permitted by my medical badge to follow the poor, defeated body into those gulfs and grottos. And the astonishing thing is that at such times and in such places—foul as they be with the stinking ischio, rectal abscesses of our comings and goings—just there, the thing, in all its greatest beauty, may for a moment be freed to fly for a moment guiltily about the room. In illness, in the permission I as a physician have had to be present at deaths and births, at the tormented battles between daughter and diabolic mother, shattered by a gone brain—just there—for a split second—from one side to the other, it has fluttered before me for a moment, a phrase which I quickly write down on anything at hand, any piece of paper I can grab. (288–89)

It is prose rather than poetry, but nevertheless Williams seems to have chosen his metaphors carefully. Not the "gardens of the self," though that is an interesting phrase, but the "gulfs and grottos" into which Williams's medical badge permits him to go. "Gulfs" suggest a necessary downward movement, while "grottos" suggest movement into a hidden, darkened cave. These are generic, unclassed places, to be sure, but they also suggest those out-of-the-way places into which he demanded his readers follow him in "Sub Terra"—where, with the poet, they can go "poking into negro houses / with their gloom and their smell" (35–36). Here, too, then, Williams suggests that poetry emerges (and hides) in places—gulfs and grottos full of gloom—below and inaccessible to the paths of respectable life. Moreover, as in "Sub Terra," these gulfs and grottos "smell," are "foul as they be," and are made foul by the "stinking ischio, rectal abscesses of our comings and goings." In other words, they are made foul by a number of things, none of them especially pleasant but primarily defecation. (*Ischio* is a term for the bone on which the body rests while sitting; *abscess* means "filled with pus" but also, in the original Latin sense of the word, "to go from," just as "our comings and goings" is both the act of entering and the act of leaving these places, as Williams the visiting doctor does, but also waste leaving the body.) From these foul, befouled places, "the thing, in its greatest beauty" is born and, like a bird or butterfly, flies about the room until Williams the poet seizes it on "any piece of paper I can grab."

Not surprisingly, then, Williams will attempt to bring poetry—and the readers of poetry—into contact with these same sharp edges and filthy holes of poverty as well. Digging in these befouled places, or among befouled persons like the "exquisite chunk of mud," K. McB., Williams finds something rare and beautiful, alive and true. Williams had used this metaphor before, in "Epigramme," a poem published in the little magazine *Others* in 1916. It runs in whole:

> *Hast ever seen man*
> *Dig gold in a manure heap?*
> *Then open two eyes*
> *For digging among these,*
> *Our fellow townsmen,*
> *I turn up this nugget.*
>
> (1–6)

Like a fearless explorer to another, poorer, more primitive, more filthy country, Williams returns to his civilized country with precious nuggets of golden truths. Moreover, just as slipping in the mud that is K. McB. will renew their contact with reality, these befouled but golden nuggets will open the eyes of Williams's readers.

As I will argue, the content of that "reality" remains vague, but Williams, to his credit, seeks to bridge the increasing chasms between classes that developed at the advent of the age of suburbia. That was no easy task given people's real fears about the poor and working class.[8] Whereas most critics—Kenneth T. Jackson perhaps most famously—have focused on how the suburbanization of the United States isolated the relocating middle class from the foul, disease-breeding urban poor, Williams reminds us that the suburbs isolated their inhabitants from the rural poor as well, whom one saw, if at all, through the window of an automobile or commuter train. Williams, however, because of the access to the poor he realized his medical badge allowed him, claimed to live "among these people." In contrast to those who maligned or stereotyped them, Williams claimed, "I knew them" and, as he would write in 1949, "saw the essential qualities (not stereotype), the courage, the humor (an accident), the deformity, the basic tragedy of their lives—and the *importance* of it." "It was my duty," he continued, "to raise the level of consciousness, not to say discussion, of them to a higher level, a higher plane. Really to tell" ("A Beginning" 300).

~

For all his compulsion to tell, however, and for all the essential part they play in ushering poets and readers into the modern, it is surprising just how little one would learn about the poor and working class from Williams's poetry. In

"K. McB.," for example, we know next to nothing about K. McB. except that she has "the dignity / of mud" (16–17) and should teach it to others. In "Idyl," we learn much about the midlife crisis of the speaker but only of the freezing poor that they are "Cowering in the wind" (7). In "Pastoral," we learn about "the houses / of the very poor" (6–7) but nothing about the poor themselves. We learn perhaps the most from "Apology," with its brief sketch of "Colored women / day workers" (6–7) who are "old and experienced" (8), who are "returning home at dusk / in cast off clothing" (9–10), and who have "faces like / old Florentine oak" (11–12)—but that is nothing (except for the inventive but relatively unrevealing comparison of their faces to oak with a colorful metal finish) we probably could not have guessed for ourselves. In "Sub Terra," we discover that Negro houses are gloomy and smell bad and maybe that their children leap around dead dogs. And in "The Wanderer," of course, we learn less than nothing about the striking workers. Or, rather, we learn what they look like to someone who knows nothing about them; we don't even learn why they have gone on strike!

These flat, one-dimensional sketches of the poor and working class possibly owe to Williams's aesthetic and political aims in representing them. After all, if one turns to the poor with an eye toward how they will renew or rearrange the upper or middle classes' contact with reality, one's attention is ultimately focused away from the poor and working classes and on the better off. Williams as doctor-poet may have gained access to the houses, ailments, and poetry of the poor, but those houses and ailments remained important largely in relation to where Williams had come from, where he returned to, and where he imagined his readers lived. In other words, Williams, when he selects details at all, seems to select just those details—dilapidation, filth—most likely to outrage or shock middle-class tastes but that also reveal little, beneath all that dirt, about the laboring poor themselves.[9]

Even a poem like "Sick African," which appeared in *The Masses* in 1917 and offered a revealing sketch of the working poor, one made possible by Williams's medical badge, nevertheless withholds much, mostly everything, about its subjects.

Wm. Yates, colored,
Lies in bed reading
The Bible—
And recovering from
A dose of epididymitis

Contracted while Grace
Was pregnant with
The twelve day old
Baby:
There sits Grace, laughing,
Too weak to stand.
(1–11)

As I discussed earlier, Williams felt that "some experience to the sharp edge of the mechanics of living," in his case, "a profession out of necessity," "is necessary to the poet," and "Sick African" would seem to confirm this formula. In terms of content, the poem was likely inspired by one of Dr. Williams's house calls, but formally the poem is also made by Williams's profession out of necessity. Reproducing abbreviations and racial classifications, it reads like doctors' notes. The poem, like medical discourse more generally, also aims to remain utterly objective, to report just the facts and leave the observer, whether poet or doctor, as far outside the frame as possible.

Indeed, Williams reveals so little about his subjects that critics have struggled to discern exactly what he means by representing this African American family. Barry Ahearn, for example, argues that because William Yates suffers from epididymitis, an inflammation and swelling of the testicles, the poem invites

> the reader to tag Yates as a member of the black underclass, someone unable to restrain or control his sexual desire as successfully as whites can. Behind the poem's humor . . . lies the perennial and widespread anxiety in the white community about the black man as threat. (*Birth of a Nation* had been released two years before.) Though we do not know the motive for Grace's laughter, her mirth suggests still another stereotyped view of black behavior—though beset by numerous troubles, they always find some humor in their plight. (68)

Taking something like the exact opposite position, David Frail argues that

> unless the poem is a racist joke playing on the stereotype of the potent and rampant black male, which I very much doubt, it is about power relations within a marriage, and mostly the folly of maintaining conventional moral proprieties when something funny happens to one's body. . . . [William Yates] retreats into Bible reading, perhaps taking his affliction as a sign from the Lord about having

> more children. Grace, whose affliction is not a disease but a part of life, sees the joke in his being confined for a relatively minor ailment; after going through labor, she must find his solemn response to his illness a bit silly. (105)

Critics will certainly disagree about poems and their meaning. Nevertheless, it seems remarkable that two of the sharpest Williams critics of the last twenty years could so thoroughly disagree about a single poem. Yet, as I will suggest, from another perspective it is not surprising at all. Both Ahearn and Frail grab on to the question of whether Williams does or does not trade on stereotypes. That is the right question to ask but not in the way that Ahearn asks it and not quite in the way that Frail does either.[10] Instead, Williams would hold that "Sick African" is an exemplary poem—and worthy of submission to the left-wing, broadly socialist journal *The Masses*—because by paying attention to the details, to reality, to the quality of the soil and those who live their lives close to it, by remaining, in other words, objective, the poem unsettles stereotypes about the poor.

Williams believed that his portraits of the poor offered—and must offer—a better, more faithful picture than those offered by "the institutions of church and state" or by their "betters," both of whom let their ideological assumptions about the poor interfere with their perception and representation of them. These "betters" only saw, heard, and said what maligned and stereotyped the poor and thus confirmed their and others' prejudices about them. Inevitably, of course, readers and critics will draw conclusions about William Yates and his wife, as often as not based on prejudices or their desire to read against prejudices, but Williams sought to delay that inevitability, to make readers see this family (and other specimens from the class they represented) independent of preconceived notions about them, to put readers back into contact with the reality of the rural poor. Williams would set readers straight: not by telling them what to think but by relieving them of what they unconsciously and without ground already thought.[11]

For Williams, any number of things threatened to interfere with our contact with reality, our contact with the poor. These included beliefs about God; superannuated poetic forms; words constrained by usage and convention; the conventions of the pastoral—whether alive in poetry or in the official discourse of a well-to-do, on-the-make suburb; middle-class proprieties, which would make one reluctant to go poking into Negro houses or read the poems of those who poked on their behalf; sheer physical distance between the classes; and, finally, inherited and unchallenged prejudices and stereotypes about the poor and thus the world. This last category, however, included more than just the usual prejudices about the poor generated by the church, the state, and their "betters"; it also included, Williams felt, perhaps more surprisingly, the prejudices and stereotypes generated by the political Left—including Socialists, Communists, and Marxists more generally—who sought to abolish poverty and the poor. As Williams wrote in a chapter on Benjamin Franklin in *In the American Grain* (1925), his unorthodox attempt at writing an essayistic history of the United States:

> "Don't let us have any poor," is our slogan. And we do not notice that the chief reason for this is that it offends us to believe that there are the essentially poor who are far richer than we are who give. The poor are ostracized. Cults are built to abolish them, as if they were cockroaches, and not human beings, who may not want what we have in such abundance. THAT would be an offense an American could not stomach. So down with them. Let everybody be rich and SO EQUAL. What a farce! But what a tragedy! It rests upon false values and fear to discover them. (176–77)

In this rather strange passage, Williams suggests that the poor may choose to be poor, that they "may not want what we have in abundance" and may even be better off, all things considered, than those who are not poor. Those who wish to abolish the poor must, by definition, fail to understand them, must belong to "cults"—otherwise they would not try to abolish such a satisfied people. Williams's ire might be understandable if these cults literally wished to abolish the poor, say through genocide. But his next sentence makes it clear that he means not those who would exterminate the poor but those who would abolish poverty, who would make the poor not poor—that is, make them "rich" and "SO EQUAL." Williams may have Marxists in mind as well, for his diction—"What a farce! But what a tragedy!"—alludes rather plainly to the opening sentences of Marx's *The Eighteenth Brumaire*. In any case, for Williams, unexamined political beliefs about the poor—even on the part of those who wanted to help them—could grossly distort apprehension of them and therefore of reality.

And thus follows the central dilemma of Williams's poetry of the poor and working class. Given his poetics, with its emphasis on "the local" and the need for "contact with reality," Williams needed to include the working class and poor in his poetry. But he also needed to avoid making judgments about workers or the poor. To do so would be to assume that the poor do not want to be poor or that poverty is a regrettable condition, both of which would "rest upon false values" and proceed "from a fear to discover them." It was not just their "betters" who were guilty of distorting the poor or stereotyping them, then, but even those, including poets or Marxists, who might wish to save them from poverty.

All this is to say that Williams did his best to keep what he called "politics" from his poetry, even and especially his poetry of the very poor.[12] As he defensively wrote in a letter to his publisher Ed Brown in May 1917—just after he had decided on the title for *Al Que Quiere!*—"he was no ideologue trying to create a closer bond of brotherhood through poetry" (qtd. in Mariani 790). Later he would write, "You can't use great art as propaganda—or any art. It will resist it" (qtd. in Dijkstra 23). Or, as he wrote in the letter to Babette Deutsch in 1949 wherein he explains the motive behind *Paterson* and, indirectly, "The Wanderer," "I am not a Marxian" (259). What he was, or what he sought to be, was, as Barry Ahearn summarizes it, "a kind of recording mechanism: the scrupulously unemotional scientist" (78). Politics, of either the Left or Right, could only interfere with or distort that documentary, objective, even clinical approach. It suddenly becomes possible, then, to see how two of Williams's better critics could disagree so completely about "Sick African." Although he could never do so entirely, Williams does his best not to force any conclusion about William Yates and his wife. The poem simply does not give readers enough information to determine Williams's attitude one way or the other. True, that he chose to write about them and not "their betters" constitutes a political choice, but beyond that Williams wishes to remain as objective as possible.[13] The goal of such a poem is not to politicize readers but to depoliticize them, to show the poor as they really are.

Throughout his career, Williams was quite explicit about what he felt should be the nearly mutually exclusive relation between art and politics. In his "Comment on Contact," from 1921, for example, Williams wrote that the magazine existed for artists who, among other qualities, "do not weaken their work with humanitarianism" (64). His unpublished essay "Notes on Art," from 1928, begins with the unqualified statement, "Art being a mode by which anything may be said, is amoral in its conceptions" (73). Similarly, in the 1936 essay "The Neglected Artist," also unpublished, Williams had an artist, who is rather unambiguously standing in for the poet, proclaim of another artist that he "is a fool."

> He is a fool because he thinks he is doing one thing and is really doing something else. That is a fool. And it is a pity, too, because he is full of genius. But he

> has forgotten what a painter is for. That is, to paint. He has let himself be led astray into politics and that has ruined him. In the time of Michelangelo they used to bend two trees together and tie a man's limbs to them. Then they would let go so that the trees tore him apart. But the artist did not turn aside for such cruelty. He had only to paint, to approach the world indirectly through his art. (83)

It is not that Williams believed that art or poetry had no political effects. Rather, for Williams, the artist or poet approaches the world, and the world of politics, as in the passage just quoted, "indirectly." In fact, Williams did believe that poetry could redeem humanity.[14] "The artist must save us," Williams wrote in a 1938 essay on the photographer Walker Evans. "He is the only one who can!" ("Walker Evans" 137). But the artist would save us not through his politics but through his vision—his ability to see things for what they are when others see them without really looking. As Williams claimed Joyce did, Williams would free "truth from usage," would, in the case of the poor, rob us of our "fear" so that we might "discover them." "For Williams, clearly," Bram Dijkstra sums it up, "sight and insight were one and the same thing" (17).

But sight and insight, as Dijkstra makes clear, may not be the same thing. Nor does either necessarily lead, directly or indirectly, to the artist or poet saving anyone. The esteem Williams and his critics have for poets' "sight"—their ability to arrange unfiltered "contact with reality," their capacity to be recording mechanisms and not propagandists, their role in helping readers "discover" what they fear—thus rests on a number of false, even misleading premises, especially when they are offered as *the* aesthetic approach to something as morally weighty as the reality of poverty. The first objection, of course, is the late-night dorm room one that there is no such thing as an objective representation or recording of anything—ideology, of course, always intervenes. It intervenes at the level of what an artist chooses to capture in a poem or photograph (a poor person, say) or what he or she chooses to neglect (a leaf). In his reflections on just this element in Williams's views of art and poetry, Bram Dijkstra observed, "Williams failed to recognize that no one's sight . . . is 'unimpaired.' Ideological manipulation has structured our perceptions long before we come to intellectual consciousness. Therefore any belief in the inherent purity of our visual perception is itself an ideologically determined delusion" (18). Moreover, viewers look at what is placed before them with certain built-in even inalterable predispositions. When Barry Ahearn looks at William Yates in "Sick African," he sees racism; when David Frail does, he sees satire; and when a racist looks at the poem, he may see a confirmation of all his beliefs about African American sexuality. Those differences imply more than that readers will disagree, or that interpretations will vary, but rather that objects neither have nor communicate their sole, unambiguous, apolitical meaning. In other words, there is no guarantee that the "reality" these portraits and poems uncover will be stable or obvious enough for all readers to have the same, unmediated contact with it.

The problem is not with the presence or absence of politics in Williams's poetry of the poor, then, but, rather, what those politics do and do not require. Far more serious than whether objectivity is politically possible or not is what this challenge to see the poor—encumbered by prejudice or not—leaves out. "See them!" the muse bids the poet in "The Wanderer," and "seeing them"—Paterson silk strikers—is the point of "The Strike" section of that poem and of much of Williams's other poetry from this period as well. Accordingly, the counterpastoral poems from *Al Que Quiere!* drag the poor from out of their gulfs and grottos to display them for readers who might not otherwise see them, or who see them but do not see them or discover their truth because they look with stereotyping or prejudiced eyes. But the challenge posed by poverty is not only or not even at all to see those who are poor but, rather, to make them less or even not poor. Perhaps one requires the other, but even so Williams rarely challenges his reader to do anything besides see the poor. In his poetry, Williams often seems resigned to the world as it is—asking readers only to change their valuation of elements within it.

Take one last poem, also entitled "Pastoral" and also from 1917's *Al Que Quiere!* The poem opens with a rather conventional attack on the church.

The little sparrows
hop ingeniously
about the pavement
quarreling
with sharp voices
over those things
that interest them.
But we who are wiser
shut ourselves in
on either hand
and no one knows
whether we think good
or evil.

(1–13)

Many critics have justifiably wanted to read the quarreling little sparrows as churchgoers and the "we who are wiser" (8) as those—Williams among them—who keep their distance from such goings on. In the second and third stanzas, though, Williams provides yet another perspective, one that tweaks the noses of believers and apostates alike.

> *Meanwhile,*
> *the old man who goes about*
> *gathering dog-lime*
> *walks in the gutter*
> *without looking up*
> *and his tread*
> *is more majestic than*
> *that of the Episcopal minister*
> *approaching the pulpit*
> *of a Sunday.*
> *These things*
> *astonish me beyond words.*
> (14–25)

The key word here—after *astonish* (25), of which more in a moment—is *majestic* (20), which Williams uses to refigure the relative value assigned to these two different members of a community, the Episcopal minister and the old man gathering dog-lime. Contrary to conventional wisdom, the old man gathering dog-lime is more "majestic" (great, big) than the usually exalted Episcopal minister. As other poems attest, this comparison of the exalted with the earthy (or finding the exalted in the earthy) is one of the dominant tropes of *Al Que Quiere!* and Williams's poems of the poor and working class. Dog-lime is a (literally) refined term for dog shit; the old man is gathering it to sell to farmers for fertilizer. Just as in "K. McB.," or, especially, "Epigramme," gold—or dignity or majesty or poetry—is to be found in the low, in the filthy, in mud and manure heaps, not in the high, in Episcopal ministers, or in other leading citizens.

More important than this trope of gold in dross, though, is the one present in the last stanza of the poem. "These things," Williams writes, "astonish me beyond words" (24–25). *Astonish* means "to fill with sudden wonder or great surprise," like hearing a roar of thunder that is closer than you thought. Although "Pastoral" differs from "The Wanderer" in how people should value the filthiness of the working class, the attitude they are supposed to take toward that class remains remarkably similar. At the conclusion of "The Strike" section of

"The Wanderer," the poet stands in a state of "ecstasy," overwhelmed by the scene before him; so, too, in "Pastoral" does he stand "astonish[ed]," overwhelmed, in a state of awe. Just as in "The Wanderer" the poet is infantilized, in "Pastoral," too, the speaker is astonished "beyond words" (25). As a result, the poet has nothing to say about the dog-lime gatherer—beyond what he has already said about the majesty of his tread. Like the poet, we, too, are to be overwhelmed.

But, again, the point about poverty is not that people should see it, know it, understand it, or be overwhelmed by it but that they should lessen or eliminate it. Living in a world where poverty was rampant, Williams, however, may have arrived at a different attitude toward poverty. Like Christ, he may have felt—and given its ubiquity, may have had good reason to feel—that the poor would always be with us. If so, then the challenge was not to eliminate poverty but to apprehend it, not to dehumanize those who live in it but to reveal their humanity, even majesty, to those who do not. That is, Williams's poetry seems satisfied that people know poverty, that they confront it and be changed—be astonished, be made ecstatic—by it, but not that they themselves change it. Consider again what I take to be the paradigmatic poem of Williams's poetry about the poor and working class, "K. McB." In that poem, what Williams admires about Kathleen McBride, and what he wants readers to admire about her, is her "dignity" (18). Presumably, "dignity" here means "the quality of being worthy of esteem or honor"—with an additional context of "proper pride and self-respect." It follows, then, that K. McB. merits esteem and honor because, despite her poverty, she has pride and self-respect—her dignity comes from her capacity to survive poverty. The poem follows the logic of "Pastoral" and "Epigramme": reader, you may think this person is mud or shit, but there is gold here, humanity and majesty. Accordingly, the poem bids readers not to feel sympathy for the poor or seek to change their condition but to admire their dignity, their capacity to survive poverty.

But poems like these merely object to the conventional, denigrating way of thinking about the poor; they level no such objection to the condition of poverty itself.[15] True, readers might, by coming to a new appreciation of the esteem and honor of the poor, conclude that the poor do not deserve their poverty, that they are better than it, and thus that they should not be subjected to it. But that is a roundabout way to any statement about poverty—and perhaps an overly generous interpretation of Williams's intentions in his poetry of the poor since he rarely, in poems, prose, or letters, concerns himself much with ending poverty and not just knowing it. Rather, his concern over and over again is with an appreciation for those subject to it.[16] But if the poor were not subject to poverty, there would be no grounds to admire them. Without poverty, that is, without their lack, the poor are nothing. Their nothing is what makes them something worth looking at. Through them, one could find one's way back to reality, forward to the modern.

As that last sentence implies, for Williams the poor offered more than just a path to modernism. They also represented a way out of the more regrettable aspects of modernity. For Williams, as he discusses in his essay on Joyce, "meanings have been dulled, then lost, then perverted by their connotations . . . until their effect on the mind is no longer what it was when they were fresh" (89–90). "Truth" had been enslaved by usage, and only artists could liberate it, could make the world—by making our perception of it—new again. That was why, Williams felt, Joyce must maim words. New words, new forms, and a whole new language could clear the deck of connotation and bring readers back into contact with reality. For Williams, however, that power to renew the world also rested in workers and the poor. Like maimed words, the maimed but beautiful bodies of the poor could renew readers' contact with the world. If poems like Cawein's "The Voice of April" alienated people from reality—exposed them to nothing more than bad rhymes, overused sentiments, and a mystification of the rural and rural labor—then Williams's counterpastorals would put them back into contact with reality, back into contact with the soil, which, as in "K. McB." or "The Wanderer," mostly meant putting them back in contact with the poor and working class. The poor might not be redeemed, but they did not need to be redeemed. Rather, those who avoided the poor did, and would be, if modern poems could only make them look closely enough, if only readers, as Williams put it in "Apology," would go poking into the gloom and smells they otherwise avoided.

Unwittingly, then, Williams's counterpastorals end up reproducing some of the very conventions he set out to critique. True, they acknowledge rather than obscure poverty. Yet Williams's poems also recycle some of the essential characteristics of the pastoral, including, as William Empson put it, the idea that "The fool sees true" (14). For Williams, not only do fools, or, rather, the poor, see true, they speak true, they *are* true, and they will help others to true themselves as well. More seriously, it may seem that by acknowledging the poverty of the rural poor, Williams's pastorals avoid implying, as Empson described the implications of the pastoral, "a beautiful relation between rich and poor" (11). Yet, as I have argued, while Williams may acknowledge poverty, he does not regret it. Rather, he regrets readers' distance from it. In other words, Williams may not hold the belief that a beautiful relation between rich and poor currently exists but, rather, the equally benighted belief that a beautiful relation could exist if only the rich—or the well-off—would pay proper attention to the poor.

In addition to, or rather by dint of, recycling these pastoral conventions, Williams typifies the romantic anticapitalist attitude toward labor problems. Romantic anticapitalism, as I have defined it, is the critique of modern, industrial society driven by nostalgia for the past. Although Williams has more to say about the present than the past, the present, modernity, undoubtedly comes in for critique. For Williams, to live in modernity means to be cut off from nature, to speak an exhausted language, to be estranged from reality itself. Moreover, the cure for this alienated life of the present lay in that which modernity had left behind, those elements of the past which had survived into the present yet remained uncorrupted by it, namely, the naive vitality and rejuvenating filth of the working poor: colored women day workers, Kathleens, Paterson strikers, and dog-lime gatherers. The poor could save everyone except themselves.

CHAPTER 3

Aware and Awareless: T. S. Eliot's Labor Problems

In April 1916, the journal *Poetry* published its third series of poems by a young "T. R. Eliot." (Still relatively unknown, Eliot would soon be too famous for editors to make the same mistake.) The series of poems, which included "Conversation Galante," "La Figlia che Piange," "Mr. Appolinax," and "Morning at the Window," appeared under the catchall heading "Observations." One of these observations, however, was not like the others. While the first three poems examined, respectively, a halting conversation between a man and a woman, a lovers' parting, and, allegedly, the philosopher Bertrand Russell at a Harvard tea party, the final poem, "Morning at the Window," observed a far different scene comprising a far different class of people.

They are rattling breakfast plates in basement kitchens
And along the trampled edges of the street
I am aware of the damp souls of housemaids
Sprouting despondently at area gates.

The brown waves of fog toss up to me
Twisted faces from the bottom of the street,
And tear from a passer-by with muddy skirts
An aimless smile that hovers in the air
And vanishes along the level of the roofs.

(1–9)

Grover Smith calls the poem "unimportant," "inferior," "barely plausible," and "inept" (30–31), and perhaps it deserves these judgments, but the poem also documents how workers intruded, early and often, on the consciousness of modern American poets. The poem is divided between an observed "They," workers who rattle breakfast plates or come and go, and an observing "I," who collects the fleeting sounds and images of a workaday morning. While the "rattling" (1) of the breakfast plates in the opening line suggests that the speaker at first resents this insolent claim on his attention, he soon becomes intrigued with the possibilities of observing workers at their jobs or on their way to their jobs. "I am aware," the speaker observes, "of the damp souls of housemaids" (3), and "aware" here seems to mean both on one's guard but also conscious, informed, perhaps even sympathetic. When most poems and poets simply took workers, especially domestic workers, for granted, the speaker of "Morning at the Window" registers the emotions, even the plight of housemaids: their souls are damp, perhaps made so by their work, and they sprout "despondently" (4) at area gates.[1]

The speaker's choice of the word *sprouting* (4) to describe the arrival of housemaids, however, suggests the limits of his empathy. As the following stanza makes clear, workers do not appear at work out of nowhere or sprout at area gates but must travel there. Yet to the speaker of the poem, who remains locked within his own awareness, housemaids simply materialize. In other words, his consciousness of the working class is a recording, leisured, even solipsistic one. As servants should, they come to him. That pattern continues in the second stanza when a class intermediary—the "brown waves of fog"—is required to make these workers "from the bottom of the street" available to his awareness. The metaphor of shipwrecked cargo washing ashore implies that the speaker remains the passive recipient of these sunken treasures, these cryptic messages in a bottle—the twisted faces, the muddy skirt, the aimless smile—that mysteriously find their way to him. But *recipient* does not wholly capture the speaker's position since these images and sensations ultimately escape him. As the concluding lines of the poem show, these sensations of workers arriving and traveling disappear, "vanish along the levels of the roof" (9).

"Morning at the Window" offers one among many instances of modern American poets becoming "aware" of the working class.[2] To be sure, part of what Eliot's persona becomes aware of is how difficult it is to maintain an awareness of workers, who are ubiquitous but also, unlike Prufrock wriggling on the wall, hard to pin down. Poets, however, including T. R. Eliot, would not remain nearly so passive or powerless in their consciousness of this class. And although few critics have noticed it or have spoken instead of Eliot's fascination with the city, in fact Eliot's career as a poet fairly begins with his discovery of the urban poor and more or less develops as his thinking about them develops. In this chapter, I investigate what uses Eliot made of workers and the poor once he had, as in "Morning at the Window," achieved an awareness of them. I argue that, again as in "Morning at the Window," an awareness of these figures would play a formative role in Eliot's poetic imagination, from the early, unpublished cityscape poems Eliot collected in his notebook through the satirical and philosophical poems of *Prufrock and Other Observations* (1917) and finally to *The Waste Land* (1922). To be sure, each of these moments in Eliot's working-class poetry involves a slightly different awareness of and representation of workers and the poor. Nevertheless, whether strolling through city slums, conducting philosophical experiments in verse, or satirizing bourgeois propriety, Eliot early on decides—or concludes—that, unlike other classes, the poor and working class resemble, perhaps even are, automata, closer in consciousness (or lack thereof) to animals than to reflective human beings. This conception of mechanistic workers, of the poor behaving reflexively, without consciousness or self-consciousness, remains in place throughout the early poetry. Indeed, the early poetry could not exist without it, so much does Eliot depend on the trope. What changes, however, across these early poems is Eliot's attitude toward this phenomenon that he half observes and half creates. More often than not it will repulse him, except, that is, when it seems to attract him.

In any case, that the poor and working class remain tethered to this trope of automata makes for a peculiar link between Eliot and the labor problem. On the one hand, like other modern poets in this book, Eliot treats a number of conventionally recognized labor problems: poverty, slums, prostitution, unruly servants. In a number of these poems, too, Eliot draws on a few of the conventional, occasionally stereotypical ways in which his culture imagined and represented the lower classes. On the other hand, and especially in the very first poems he wrote about the urban poor, Eliot strains to shed the "problem" part of the labor problem discourse. In other words, for Eliot labor will be a problem not, as it was for others in the modern period, because workers suffered needlessly, might rebel violently, or otherwise threatened the status quo. Rather, the poor and working class are a problem because they stand in for and act out the other sexual, civilizational, and philosophical problems with which Eliot in his early poetry is nearly obsessed. Another way to put it may be to say that Eliot has his own rather atypical labor problem, one in which workers and the poor are not so much problems in need of solutions as they are symbols made to personify his problems with modernity.

Like the other poets in this book, then, Eliot deploys these figures to question the civilization that modern, industrial capitalism has made. That is perhaps the most prominent use Eliot makes of his newly won awareness of the poor and working class. In some of these poems, workers have the capacity to disrupt modernity yet, in many more, they embody its most mechanistic, alienated, and alienating aspects. In these poems, workers are less the heroic redeemers of capitalism—or even its piteous victims—than the most intense expression of its pathologies. Eliot's solution to this labor problem, which he seems to have found in reading the popular French philosopher Henri Bergson, and which he shares with other romantic anticapitalists, is to indict rationalism altogether.

Although "Morning at the Window" was the first published poem to announce Eliot's awareness of the working class, his consciousness of that class—and its poetic possibilities—predates that poem by quite a few years. Beginning in early 1910, Eliot devoted a notebook to recording what he ambitiously called "the Complete Poems of / T.S. Eliot," afterward changing the title to "Inventions of the March Hare." In 1917, Eliot would draw on these poems to compile *Prufrock and Other Observations,* his first volume of verse, although many of the poems remained unpublished until Christopher Ricks's edition of the notebook in 1996. Intriguingly, especially for a critic interested in the relation between modern poetry and the labor problem, among the first poems Eliot collected in that notebook—and, based on Eliot's dating, the first poems he composed and chose to preserve—are a series of so-called "Caprices" set in North Cambridge, which he wrote in November 1909 and December 1910. As "Morning at the Window" allegorizes, his efforts as a serious poet appear to coincide with his discovery of the urban poor.

For present-day readers, the title of the series—"Caprices in North Cambridge"—may be misleading. Cambridge, Massachusetts, circa 1909 differed slightly from the Cambridge of today. Then, as now, Harvard University dominated the part of the city adjacent to the Charles River, but the remainder of Cambridge constituted a whole other world. As Samuel Atkins Eliot observed in his *A History of Cambridge, Massachusetts* (1913), Cambridge had grown because "many of the leading merchants and professional men of Boston make their homes" there, and also, of course, because of "the presence of the University" (120). Yet the city's "growth had also," Eliot notes, "been expedited by the establishment of numerous factories" and "great manufacturing plants" (120). This Cambridge, as the authors of *Massachusetts: A Guide to Its People and Places* (1937) later put it, unconsciously echoing lines from T. S. Eliot's *The Waste Land,* was the "Unknown City." "This Unknown City," the 1937 guidebook declared, "is the second in Massachusetts in the value of goods manufactured; it is third in all New England, outranked only by Boston and Providence" (184). As a result of this industrial expansion, workers, many of them immigrants, settled in Cambridge, especially the North Cambridge of Eliot's poems, close to the factories where they worked.[3] Inevitably, overcrowding and slums attended their arrival. Indeed, Samuel Atkins Eliot's otherwise relentlessly upbeat *History of Cambridge, Massachusetts,* ends on the disquieting note that "there is one peril which Cambridge is likely to encounter" because of its "increasing density of population," namely, "tenements housing," which, if left unchecked, would lead, as it had in other cities and had begun to in Cambridge, to the "evils" of "unhealthy premises, dark rooms, overcrowding, excessive rents, and other deplorable manifestations of the social life of modern cities" (150). The citizens of Cambridge, Eliot asserts, "must prevent the growth of slums," and the "housing evils that exist today are a reflection"—and not a positive one—"upon the intelligence and right-mindedness of the community" (152).

While Samuel Atkins Eliot may have sought to prevent the further growth of slums, his namesake, Thomas Stearns Eliot, seems to have taken a decidedly different attitude toward them. While an undergraduate at Harvard University from 1906 to 1909, Eliot wandered the immigrant and working-class neighborhoods that ringed Cambridge proper. His most thorough biographer, Lyndall Gordon, locates in these walks through North Cambridge the beginnings of Eliot's work as a poet, including *The Waste Land* but also, more obviously, the "Caprices" that bear the neighborhood's name. "Failing to find life amongst his own class," Gordon observes, "Eliot sought out the slum areas."

> In Roxbury, then, and North Cambridge, Eliot deliberately courted squalor, but found that as life-destroying as the well-to-do Boston squares. He was physically repelled by smells and depressed by slums. In St. Louis the darker and grimmer aspects of the city had passed him by; in Boston, for the first time, he conceived a horror of the commercial city, its cluster and the sordid patience of its dwellers. . . . He was both horrified and, in a way, engaged. It seemed a far

> world from his studies, the neat definitions and laws he was piling up at college, but it touched him as Harvard did not. It was his first image of a waste land, a scene he was to make his own. (18–19)

That last phrase, "a scene he was to make his own," is particularly apt since, as "First Caprice in North Cambridge" and other poems in the sequence demonstrate, Eliot would take what had become a fairly stock phenomenon, the urban slum, and transform it—or one's attitude toward it—into something that Samuel Atkins Eliot was not likely to have recognized.

Eliot's incongruous perspective on the slum is implied by his title, "First Caprice in North Cambridge." As in his other slum poems of the period, Eliot adopts a musical conceit. What would have immediately struck contemporary readers, if Eliot had shown the poem to anyone, was how the title juxtaposed high and low, light and dark, art and squalor. (A contemporary poem, for example, might be titled "Waltz in the Bronx" or "First Bagatelle in East Saint Louis.") The other meanings of *caprice,* though—a "prank, whim, a sudden, impulsive change in the way one thinks or acts"—also suggests what Eliot may have been up to in his slum poetry. While the images that comprise his "First Caprice in North Cambridge" may seem familiar, the attitude he ultimately adopts toward them, at least for its time, is not.

> *A street-piano, garrulous and frail;*
> *The yellow evening flung against the panes*
> *Of dirty windows; and the distant strains*
> *Of children's voices, ended in a wail.*
>
> *Bottles and broken glass,*
> *Trampled mud and grass;*
> *A heap of broken barrows;*
> *And a crowd of tattered sparrows*
> *Delve in the gutter with sordid patience.*
> *Oh, these minor considerations! . . .*
>
> (1–10)

"The yellow evening flung against the panes / Of dirty windows" will later surface in Eliot's "The Love Song of J. Alfred Prufrock," but "First Caprice in North Cambridge" does much more than contribute an image to the more famous poem. Perhaps most remarkably, in taking stock of a neighborhood supposedly suffering from tenements and overcrowding, the poem remains astonishingly underpopulated. One hears a "street-piano, garrulous and frail" but does not see the player. One hears "children's voices" but only at a distance. Similarly, one sees "Bottles and broken glass," in addition to "Trampled mud and grass" and "A heap of broken barrows," but there are few, none in fact, drinkers of bottles, tramplers of grass, or pushers of barrows. In short, noises and debris are abundant but not the humans who make noises or debris, until, perhaps, the final lines of the poem, when a "crowd" of sparrows that "Delve in the gutter with sordid patience" seem, to judge by their behavior, to stand in for the missing "crowd" of North Cambridge's overcrowded streets.

In the image of tattered sparrows "Delv[ing] in the gutter with sordid patience," Eliot offers two tropes that will reappear—and less obliquely—in nearly all of his early poems about the poor and working class. First, Eliot likens workers and the poor to things or animals (and, conversely, as here, things and animals to workers and the poor), and second, he associates the poor and working class with repetition, even automatism. The former trope appears in Eliot's implied metaphor between sparrows and slum dwellers: both appear tattered, whether their clothing or plumage, and both "Delve in the gutter with sordid patience" (9). Although the poor are not prone, except metaphorically, to dig in the gutter for their living, what more likely unites crowds of sparrows with crowds of slum dwellers in the speaker's mind is the "sordid patience" of each. By this phrase, Eliot seems to suggest that sparrow and slum dweller alike—except perhaps for the wailing of children—endure their invariable suffering without complaint. This ability to endure suffering, then, makes the poor "sordid," both filthy (as in the earlier "tattered" [8]) and, more figuratively, just depressingly wretched. Hence the second trope of repetition, mindlessness. As in other poems in the series, which I turn to shortly, the poor passively accept their poverty, just as, in the opening image of the poem, someone—it does not matter who—mechanically turns the crank on a street piano. As I show in a moment, too, and as is clearer in other poems in the series, by representing the poor as tolerating their poverty, Eliot draws on some of the most advanced thinking (for the time) about the causes and effects of poverty.

In any case, only in the final line of the poem does Eliot reveal anything more than hints and indirections about what attitude one should—or his speaker does—adopt toward this scene of sordid patience and the patience of the sordid, and even this attitude remains ambiguous. To be sure, the final line—"Oh, these minor considerations! . . ." (9)—can seem disarmingly indifferent to the sordid lives the poem obliquely documents. As Eric Schocket puts it, "[T]he poem seems finally like a study in bourgeois arrogance" (156), especially if one reads the "minor" in "minor considerations" as small, inconsequential. Yet in a poem that lives on musical metaphors, by "minor" Eliot may also mean sad, melancholy, and plaintive, the mood a composition in a minor key supposedly arouses. ("Strains" [3], earlier in the poem, both musical and physical, can take on a similar ambiguity.) In this case, "minor" considerations may not confirm the arrogant "Caprice" of the title but, rather, counteract it. That is, what starts out as a whimsical trip through the slums of North Cambridge is disrupted by the actual images encountered there, which command one's attention and, perhaps, even pity. Read this way, "considerations" may mean thoughtful or sympathetic regard for others, and the poem documents how the speaker is reluctantly brought to an awareness of, a consideration for, these minor-key, melancholy scenes. In short, while the poem may seem like a study in bourgeois arrogance, it can also be read much more generously as one in which bourgeois arrogance is confronted and perhaps altered by these "minor considerations."

This more charitable reading of the poem almost certainly gives Eliot more credit for sympathy and fellow feeling than he actually intends or, most likely, feels, for the tone of the poem does, finally, seem dismissive. After all, the final line begins with the sardonically poetic "Oh," ends with an exclamation point perhaps more ironic than sincere, and trails off in ellipses, suggesting that the speaker rather easily moves on from these "minor considerations." My point in raising the possibility of a reluctantly sympathetic poem, however, is to suggest that Eliot invokes even as he rejects a certain mode of apprehending poverty and slums. On the one hand, there is the mode of Samuel Atkins Eliot and other reformers, including, as I show in a moment, not a few members of Eliot's immediate family, who look on such scenes as problems in need of charitable redress or the efforts of a more sympathetic, right-minded community. These are considerations in a minor, melancholic key. On the other hand, there is Eliot's apparent mode, the minor considerations, which appreciates the aesthetics of poverty and views its sordidness less as a problem in need of reform and more as an accomplished fact, reflective, perhaps, of the speaker's own ennui. What makes Eliot's poem capricious, then, is how far it departs from the way one usually thought about urban poverty. As William Carlos Williams occasionally does, Eliot registers the aesthetic (visual and aural) power of the urban slum as a way to pass over, provocatively, its ethical or political implications.

That dismissive attitude surfaces even more clearly in "Second Caprice in North Cambridge," composed around the same time as the first. The poem shares much with "First Caprice in North Cambridge," notably that poem's tendency to depopulate the urban slum, to describe things as people, and, crucially, to oppose the aesthetic and the ethical.

This charm of vacant lots
The helpless fields that lie
Sinister, sterile and blind
Entreat the eye and rack the mind,
Demand your pity.
With ashes and tins in piles,
Shattered bricks and tiles
And the debris of a city.

Far from our definitions
And our aesthetic laws
Let us pause
With these fields that hold and rack the brain
(What: again?)
With an unexpected charm
And an unexplained repose
On an evening in December
Under a sunset yellow and rose.

(1–17)

In the first stanza, the vacant lots cast a "charm," meaning, of course, that they are attractive or delightful but also, as in the ambiguous "considerations" of "First Caprice," that they force a claim on one's attention, they "Entreat the eye and rack the mind" (4). As in "First Caprice," too, things stand in for people. In this case, a field is "helpless" (2), and it lies, somewhat incongruously, "sinister, sterile and blind" (3). Just as the sparrows exhibit a "sordid patience" because they delve, routinely and without complaint, into the gutter, here, too, the field—and, by their absence, residents of North Cambridge—can seem "sinister" and "sterile" because it and they disconcertingly, even threateningly, produce nothing, go nowhere; they exist for nothing beyond themselves or the moment. Similarly, Eliot has such scenes "entreat" the eye, continuing the trick of turning things into people, in this case beggars. (I read *entreat* here to mean "to beg, implore.") Even more than the "minor considerations" in "First Caprice," however, these things qua people truly do command one's awareness, even sympathy. Together with the broken and used debris, including people, of a city, these entreaties "rack the mind" and "demand your pity" (5).

In the second stanza, however, Eliot undercuts that call to pity by remaking the scene into an essentially aesthetic one. Again, as William Carlos Williams will, Eliot here goes against the conventional wisdom to focus on the unexpected, unexplained, and perhaps unexplainable beauty of poverty. "Far from our definitions / And our aesthetic laws" (9–10), the slum allows this reconsideration; it allows "us" to "pause" (11) in the normal chain of considerations that follow on viewing such a scene and to see it, as it were, in a different light. By this reading, the parenthetical "What: again?" (13) seems to mark a definitive shift in the poem from ethics, a question of pity, to aesthetics. Returning to the "fields that hold and rack the brain" (12), a phrase that earlier led to demands on the observer's pity, the interjection "What: again?" pulls the speaker back from that pitying attitude, and what follows is not the language of ethics but of aesthetics. The fields now have "an unexpected charm / And an unexplained repose" (14–15)—they no longer demand our pity—and, freed from the ethical, the scene finally dissolves into the conventionally, even absurdly poetic. Eliot shifts to the pastoral (sunsets) but, even more ridiculously, does so in syntax so distorted—in order to rhyme "rose" (17) with "repose" (15)—that it recalls the nineteenth-century verse Eliot and Ezra Pound took turns ridiculing. Forced rhymes and too-clever syntax notwithstanding, though, the poem aims for an effect similar to that of the "First Caprice." Each turns a labor problem—the slum and its urban poor—into an occasion to track the awareness, aesthetic and reluctantly ethical, of an alienated, modern flaneur. It is not the slum, the poems suggest, but how we feel about the slum—and what we should resist feeling—that matters.

The final poem in the series, "Fourth Caprice in North Cambridge," later titled "Fourth Caprice in Montparnasse," may explain why Eliot risked expressing such callous indifference to poverty and sordidness.

We turn the corner of the street
And again
Here is a landscape grey with rain
On black umbrellas, waterproofs,
And dashing from the slated roofs
Into a mass of mud and sand.
Behind a row of blackened trees
The dripping plastered houses stand

Like mendicants without regrets
For unpaid debts
Hand in pocket, undecided,
Indifferent if derided.

Among such scattered thoughts as these
We turn the corner of the street;
But why are we so hard to please?

(1–15)

Though composed a year later than the other "Caprices," and generic enough to allow Eliot to later change the scene from North Cambridge to Montparnasse, the poem has much in common with the earlier North Cambridge "Caprices": the substitution of things for people, an emphasis on the inertness of the poor, and the language of aesthetics over ethics. The rain falls on black umbrellas and waterproofs, for example, not people holding or wearing them; "dashing" (5)—not people dashing—appears to be the subject of the fifth and sixth lines; and, trading metaphors for similes, the poem likens houses to beggars. As in the first and second "Caprices," too, the beggars qua houses are notable for their resignation. They have no "regrets / for unpaid debts" (9–10), they slouch with "hand in pocket" (11), and are "undecided" (11) and unmoved even when laughed at or scorned. As in those earlier caprices, too, the language of aesthetics both opens ("landscape" [3]) and closes the poem. Indeed, the poem shifts rather abruptly at the conclusion from "such scattered thoughts as these" to the question of pleasure. Viewing the street after turning a corner, the speaker wonders "why are we so hard to please?" (15), and "we" does not seem to include beggars or slum dwellers but, rather, those who visit slums. And while any number of things about the street could displease (or fail to please) the speaker—the sodden landscape, the houses, like beggars, that quietly accept their abjection—the remarkable thing about the poem is that the question of pleasure arises at all. As in "Second Caprice," what matters about slums, the poem implies, is not what should be done about them or for those who live in them but what they do or do not do to an admittedly dilettantish observer.

In short, the poems, especially the "Fourth Caprice," raise pitilessness and egotism to an art, and a few explanations, none necessarily exclusive of the other, may account for this peculiar choice: the speaker of the poem (and Eliot himself) may be so solipsistic that he can take an interest in nothing except his own experience; the poem may hold that solipsism up for judgment; or, and I think this one most likely, the poem may deliberately exaggerate its solipsism in order to distinguish itself from the conventional, earnest, reform-minded attitude many people in Eliot's class—including quite a few members of his immediate family—adopted toward slums and the poor. In other words, this poem and others may form part of Eliot's rather well-known rejection of the institutions and values of his class.

Biographers and critics have devotedly documented the many ways—religious, professional, sexual, geographic—in which Eliot broke with his prosperous, Unitarian family, but comparably less has been said about Eliot's political break with this class.[4] As Lyndall Gordon observes, many members of Eliot's family, especially the women, devoted themselves to social work. Gordon refers to "all those dutiful grandchildren of William Greenleaf Eliot who were settling into practical, public-spirited careers" (46). In a 1953 address, Eliot himself referred to "the law of Public Service" and the symbols of "Religion, the Community, and Education," which, as a child, he was "brought up to reverence" ("American Literature and the American Language" 44). In Saint Louis, for example, Eliot's mother, Charlotte C. Eliot, was the second vice president of the Humanity Club. In a 1903 article for *The Survey,* the national journal of the Charity Organization Society of New York, she described the Humanity Club as "an informal organization of ladies, whose object it is to aid in effecting legislation remedial of existing evils in the public institutions of St. Louis" (430). In addition to his mother, Eliot's older sister, Ada Eliot Sheffield, was a graduate of the New York School of Philanthropy (now the Columbia University School of Social Work) and "an eminent social work leader" (Tice 52), as a contemporary historian has called her, first as a probation officer in New York City and later as a leader of various charitable associations and social work bureaus in Boston. In 1909, as Eliot composed his caprices in North Cambridge, Sheffield was appointed a member of the Massachusetts State Board of Charity and published a book, *The Charity Director: A Brief Study of His Responsibilities.*[5]

In 1920, Sheffield published another book, *The Social Case History: Its Construction and Content,* which may clarify—if more by contrast than comparison—the far different attitude toward poverty and social ills that her brother adopts in his poetry. In her influential textbook, Sheffield argued that the social worker should expect "to concern herself with the clients' needs as to health, special training, diet, employment, and so on" (12) in order "to achieve the ultimate purpose of general social betterment" (6). Social workers could achieve that last goal by composing histories that would "illuminate the case problem by constantly relating the difficulties of the one client to defects or maladjustments in the social order" (15). Basically, Ada Eliot Sheffield asked social workers to develop "critical thinking," by which she meant the ability to connect individual case histories to "the typical combinations of character traits or of circumstance and character which make for various forms of dependency" (17). Such knowledge could aid legislators and reformers in their efforts to combat poverty (16).

At first glance, Eliot's "Caprices in North Cambridge" could not seem to depart further from his sister's view of the social order. Curiously, however, both Eliot and his sister seem to share the commonly held view that the poor—or, rather, the pauper—ultimately suffered from "dependency." Indeed, what seems to have struck Eliot about the slum is its static, nondialectical existence, an attitude closely related to what Gavin Jones calls the "rhetoric of pauperism" (86) that characterized turn-of-the-century thinking about poverty. According to the rhetoric of pauperism, the poor differed from the pauper in that, while the poor sought to resist their poverty, paupers surrendered to it, became almost pathologically torpid, and thus came to depend wholly on charitable relief. "There are in all large cities in America and abroad," the reformer Robert Hunter observed in his 1904 volume *Poverty,* in language that echoes Eliot's "Caprices" among the sordidly patient urban poor, "streets and courts and alleys where a class of people live who have lost all self respect and ambition, who rarely, if ever, work, who are aimless and drifting, who like drink, who have no thought for their children, and who live more or less contentedly on rubbish and alms" (3). "This is pauperism," Hunter concludes in a passage that again evokes the "undecided, / indifferent if derided" mendicants of Eliot's "Fourth Caprice." "There is no mental agony here; they do not work sore; there is no dread; they live miserably, but they do not care" (4).[6]

While Eliot may unconsciously draw on a similar rhetoric of pauperism to represent urban poverty, what separates him from his sister and social reformers like Hunter is that he is nowhere interested in legislation, preventative work, or the social betterment of paupers or the poor. Not only does he make little to no effort to concern himself with the health, special training, diet, or employment of slum dwellers, he barely registers the existence of slum dwellers at all. Rather than "social betterment," individual experience, more often his own—"why are we so hard to please?"—dominates Eliot's thinking about the slum. My point is not that Eliot should write case histories and not poetry, nor is my point even to judge him or his speakers for their solipsism; rather, my point is that his poetry of the slum marks a deliberate break with the conventional ways his social class and, even more closely, his family viewed poverty and, as Samuel Atkins Eliot put it, "the deplorable manifestations of the social life of modern cities" (150). "In care of the needy," Samuel Atkins Eliot brags, "Cambridge has been as much a pioneer as in education and religion," and the smugness rather understandably might tempt Eliot to sacrilege.[7] In any case, to belong to Eliot's social class required taking a charitable attitude toward the poor, if only to assure that they did not fall into the ranks of the pauper. Eliot, however, resists adopting such commonplace attitudes. By its constant and challenging return to the "scattered thoughts as these" of the observing, solipsistic self, Eliot's poetry mocks that social-minded attitude.

In its original form, "Fourth Caprice in Montparnasse" made this break with his class even clearer. At some point after transcribing the poem in his notebook, Eliot deleted two lines that had previously concluded the poem.

The world is full of journalists,
And full of universities.
(16–17)

Rhyming "hard to please," from the penultimate stanza, with "universities" is a job well done, but it suggests more than Eliot's ear for clever rhymes. Given its placement—and rhyme—the couplet appears to answer the question "why are we so hard to please?" While the answer, as ever, remains ambiguous, what is clear is the speaker's (and perhaps Eliot's) dissatisfaction with his own class. On the one hand, the speaker may be so hard to please because he cannot help looking at the slum through the eyes of "journalists" and "universities," that is, in ways that cast poverty as a pathology, that demand an ethical response to it, and that, in turn, guarantee that "we" will not, by definition, be pleased with the scene. In fact, our displeasure will be the measure of our misguided desire to change it. Conversely, the lines suggest that the world the speaker knows, that of journalists and, especially, universities, does not in fact please, and the failure of these individuals and institutions to please is what drives him to seek out something else, the slums, in the first place. To be sure, the speakers of Eliot's "Caprices" appear to find no more pleasure in North Cambridge than they do in, say, Harvard Square, but the absence of pleasure in those well-to-do places nevertheless precipitates a somewhat desperate if futile search for it among other classes. Even so, what drives those dissatisfied with their class to seek out pleasure in slums—the arid world of journalists and universities—is also what prevents them from realizing any pleasure once there. You can take the boy out of Harvard Square, but you can't take Harvard Square out of the boy.

As I argue below, that premise—that you cannot escape your social class no matter how little you think of it or how far among other classes you travel—would reappear in several of the poems Eliot wrote in the mid-1910s. In the meantime, Eliot continued his experiments in writing slum verse. Two of those poems, "Preludes" and "Rhapsody on a Windy Night," both written in the period between October 1910 and November 1911, would later appear in *Prufrock and Other Observations* (1917). Unsurprisingly, both poems, from their setting to their musical titles, share much with the "Caprices" of 1909 and 1910, especially the first two sections of "Preludes," which offer studies not of North Cambridge but of Roxbury, another down-at-the-heels neighborhood across the river from Cambridge. "Preludes," too, would give Eliot the chance to resume some of the ethical questions regarding poverty that he so cheekily dismisses in the earlier "Caprices." The latter two sections of "Preludes," however, and all of "Rhapsody on a Windy Night," differ from the "Caprices" in that they reflect the influence of two vastly dissimilar writers—the philosopher Henri Bergson and the novelist Charles Louis Philippe—whom Eliot discovered while in Paris in 1910–11. In very different ways, both Philippe and Bergson would lead Eliot to take a far greater interest in the consciousness—whether its presence or absence—of the poor and working class. Nevertheless, especially in "Preludes," he would arrive at a similar conclusion about the need to resist viewing the slum or its inhabitants with pity.

Because they date from roughly the same period, the first two sections of "Preludes" draw on the same reservoir of images and tropes that characterize the "Caprices."

The winter evening settles down
With smell of steaks in passage ways.
Six o'clock.
The burnt out ends of smoky days.
And now a gusty shower wraps
The grimy scraps
Of withered leaves around your feet,
And newspapers from vacant lots.

The showers beat
On broken blinds and chimney pots,
And at the corner of the street
A lonely cab horse steams and stamps.

And then the lighting of the lamps.
(1–13)

While most of the elements of the "Caprices"—vacant lots, expressive animals, the wreckage of civilization—also appear in this first section of "Preludes," this poem differs in the tension it cultivates between singular and recurrent action, between things that happen once and things that happen or are happening often, multiply. The opening line, for example, describes a single winter evening settling down. Yet it settles down with the smell of multiple people cooking multiple steaks in multiple passageways. Similarly, the next line names a specific time of day, "Six o'clock" (3), yet it—that time—represents the "burnt out ends" of all "smoky days" (4). It is not *a* time but the usual time. The following line, beginning "And now" (5), seems to describe an isolated incident of a gusty shower wrapping leaves and newspapers around "your feet" (7). (It is a shower, by the way, that threatens to entrap the speaker in the scene he would prefer merely to observe.) Yet by the following line this same shower is now plural, "showers" (9), which beat, habitually, on multiple "broken blinds and chimney pots" (10). Similarly, the penultimate image ("A lonely cab horse steams and stamps" [12]) seems to be singular, breaking the habitual action of showers that repeatedly beat, yet the "And then" (13) language of the final image makes the cab horse—and every previous incident in the poem—seem like one in a series of repeated, cheerlessly predictable events, so much so that it goes far toward robbing what should be a redemptive image ("the lighting of the lamps" [13]) of its redemption. If the lamps must be lighted every night, they cannot have done much—and will not do much—to dispel the darkness.

Even more clearly than in, say, "First Caprice in North Cambridge," then, Eliot depicts the slum as a static, repeating space where even incidents that seem to promise hope or development are instead revealed to be part of a recurring pattern. In the language of Prufrock, the speaker has known the slums already, known them all, because they do not change, they only repeat. The second section of "Preludes" depicts a similar relationship between incident and repetition.

The morning comes to consciousness,
Of faint stale smells of beer
From the sawdust trampled street
With its muddy feet that press
To early coffee stands.

With the other masquerades
That time resumes
One thinks of all the hands
That are raising dingy shades
In a thousand furnished rooms.

(14–23)

What starts out singular—the morning coming to consciousness—quickly turns multiple. Or, rather, part of what the morning (and the poem) comes to consciousness of is multiplicity: smells (plural) of beer and the many, muddy feet pressing to many, early coffee stands. Whereas the first section of "Preludes" describes what habitually happens in the evening, the second section describes what habitually happens in the morning, "the other masquerades / That time resumes" (19–20)—that time is always resuming. Furthermore, just as at the outset of the poem the morning comes to consciousness of multiplicity, in the final image of the poem "one thinks" as well of multiplicity, "of all the hands / That are raising dingy shades / In a thousand furnished rooms" (21–23). And while that powerful image—especially when it is framed as one of many "masquerades" (19)—suggests the loneliness and anomie of those who live in the thousand furnished rooms, much as the lonely cab horse concludes the previous section of the poem, that sense of loneliness seems to be overwhelmed by the aura of monotony, the habitual actions of an undifferentiated mass of slum dwellers resuming another day, anonymous and interchangeable as their furniture. As in "First Caprice in North Cambridge," then, Eliot seems to be impressed by the "sordid patience" of all those hands—not even people but dissociated hands—which rouse their owners to yet another round of raising dingy shades or delving in gutters.

Because of their strict focus on routine, on the undifferentiated mass, the first two sections of "Preludes" make the third section all the more remarkable. As many critics have noted, the section reflects Eliot's reading of the French novelist Charles-Louise Philippe, particularly his 1901 novel *Bubu de Montparnasse.* Philippe's novel tracks the lives of a syphilitic prostitute, her pimp, and a spiritually and sexually conflicted low-level clerk through the red light districts of turn-of-the-century Paris. In both the novel and Eliot's poem, a prostitute, Berthe, awakes late in a hotel room after a night of sex, alcohol, and "torpid-sleep" (49). "This bed of hotel rooms," Philippe writes, "where the bodies are dirty and the souls are as well" (49). While Philippe merely describes Berthe's sense of "disorder" and "degradation" as she wakes—"her thoughts lay heaped confusedly in her head" (49)—Eliot delves into her consciousness.

You tossed a blanket from the bed,
You lay upon your back, and waited;
You dozed, and watched the night revealing
The thousand sordid images
Of which your soul was constituted.
They flickered against the ceiling.
And when all the world came back
And the light crept up between the shutters
And you heard the sparrows in the gutters,
You had such a vision of the street
As the street hardly understands;
Sitting along the bed's edge, where
You curled the papers from your hair,
Or clasped the yellow soles of feet
In the palms of both soiled hands.

(24–38)

Almost a full year separates the composition of the third section of "Preludes" from the first two, and the difference is striking. When they do in fact concern themselves with people and not animals or vacant lots, the first two sections of "Preludes," as the previous "Caprices," are concerned with the parts of many people—feet, hands—and not whole or even individual people.[8] In the third section of "Preludes," however, Eliot unexpectedly takes up the soul of a single, discrete individual. Moreover, the soul he examines is capable of epiphanies that remain unavailable to the dismembered, consciousless slum dwellers whose appendages Eliot depicts in other poems. When the woman of the poem hears "the sparrows in the gutter," an image Eliot had previously used to represent the "sordid patience" of slum dwellers, she, unlike them, achieves "such a vision of the street / As the street hardly understands" (33–34). As Eric Schocket asserts, apparently forgetting this section of the "Preludes," "deeply intersubjective moments" with "the class Other" is "a road not taken" (165) in Eliot's poetry, but here Eliot decisively takes that road. Her case could be the exception that proves the rule: both of Eliot avoiding intersubjective moments with class Others and class Others having subjects and minds that Eliot could, however briefly, occupy. Still, it is a revealing exception. Indeed, this section of the poem suggests, as John T. Mayer aptly puts it, "that ordinary unpromising individuals may be touched to vision by suffering that releases them from the blindness of mechanical, routinized lives" (90). To be sure, the conclusion of the poem returns to a world where people are known by their parts—hair, feet, palms, hands—and not by their being, where they are known by their soles and not their souls, but that last pun distinguishes this instance of fragmentation from the typical Eliot dismemberment. By its end, the poem not only credits the woman with visionary insights into her soul unavailable to the street and its inhabitants but also with a desire for redemption. Instead of her sordid "soul," the woman clasps the "yellow soles of her feet / In the palms of both soiled hands" (37–38), praying, it seems, to be freed from the life that imposes so many sordid, soul-constituting images on her.

Crucially, this moment of intersubjectivity with the class Other, as Schocket might put it, threatens the emotional detachment the poem (and other poems) so carefully cultivates. In the final section of "Preludes," one can watch the speaker deliberately pulling back from the sympathy such a close identification with the soul and visions of another would demand. From the start, this final section of the poem returns to images of mechanical, routinized lives from which the soul of the previous poem had been released.

His soul stretched tight across the skies
That fade behind a city block,
Trampled by insistent feet
At four and five and six o'clock.
And short square fingers stuffing pipes,
And evening newspapers, and eyes
Assured of certain certainties:
The conscience of a blackened street
Impatient to assume the world.

I am moved by fancies that are curled
Around these images and cling:

The notion of some infinitely gentle
Infinitely suffering thing.

Wipe your hand across your mouth, and laugh;
The worlds revolve like ancient women
Gathering fuel in vacant lots.

(39–54)

Again, the poem returns to a dismembered world of feet and to the regular, clockwork return of workers from their jobs. So even though "His soul" (the speaker's?) is "stretched tight across the skies" (39), it still feels trampled by the insistency, the monotony of life among the urban working poor who periodically and predictably make their way home. Unsurprisingly, too, the poem resumes being bothered by multiplicity, in this case by the "short square fingers stuffing pipes" (43), "evening newspapers" (44), and "eyes /Assured of certain certainties" (44–45), a phrase that captures the fixed and even predetermined patterns of the slum. Nor does the street—or its inhabitants—seem to regret these "certain certainties." Unlike the previous section of the poem, in which a conscience suffering through a long night of the soul achieves a vision of the street the street hardly understands, here the darkened street is merely "Impatient to assume the world" (47), to take the world, that is, and its "certain certainties" for granted.

The final stanzas of the section, however, mark yet another shift in the poem, this time toward an acknowledgment of suffering and, albeit interrupted, an expression of sympathy, a shift that can be tracked in Eliot's use of pronouns. Throughout the previous sections of the poem, the pronouns drift closer and closer to the first person. The first section briefly occupies the second person ("a gusty shower wraps . . . leaves around *your* feet"), for example, while the second section settles for the impersonal "one" who "thinks." The third section abandons the impersonal for an identifiable "you," a real you, that is, and not an impersonal "you" or a "one," which elsewhere seems to mask the speaker. The fourth section gets to "his," and whether that soul belongs to the speaker or another "you"—the prostitute's companion, perhaps—remains unclear. In any case, by the final stanzas of the final section of the poem, the speaker of the poem at last assumes an "I," an "I," moreover, that is capable of being "moved" by what it sees in ways that its previous incarnation as a "you" or a "one" or a "his" was not—or would not admit to. (Eliot's original phrasing, "I am wrought" instead of "I am moved" [48], conveys even more strongly the sense that the speaker is created by what he witnesses.) This drift toward the personal suggests that the poem is finally ready to admit the claims such scenes might make on the observer's (or any observer's) sympathy. His use of the word *curled* (48), too, to describe the fancies around these images, recalls the woman from the third stanza who, in the moment of her epiphany, curls the papers from her hair. She, then, seems to be the "infinitely gentle, / Infinitely suffering thing" (40–41) that moves the speaker. (Christ on the Cross is another possibility.) Either way, the poem admits the existence of undeserved ("gentle") suffering, whether in the redeemer (Christ) or those (the woman from the previous poem) who desire redemption. In either case, the poem returns to the singular—*some* suffering and gentle thing—and not, say, the systematic loneliness that characterizes (and therefore minimizes) the suffering present in the thousand furnished rooms of the second section of the poem, rooms one rather dispassionately "thinks of" (44).

Yet the poem, even these same lines, does not settle for such a redemptive, humane reading. The speaker, for example, is not moved by suffering per se but by "fancies" (48), a word that seems to distance him from the suffering he imagines, as does referring to what he witnesses as "images." In other words, what moves him is not real: they are illusions, delusions even, and in any case merely images and not realities.[9] Furthermore, the speaker is not moved by some infinitely gentle, infinitely suffering thing, but by the "notion" (49) of such a thing. Needless to say, too, the speaker entertains a notion not of some infinitely gentle, infinitely suffering *soul* or *person* but instead of a "thing" (51). The poem, then, when it risks coming closest to the suffering it earlier acknowledges, retreats to abstractions.

Even so, these fancies, the notion of this thing, however abstracted, does, as in the "Second Caprice," seem to "demand your pity" (5). The final stanza of "Preludes," however, deliberately undermines that pity. The pronouns retreat to "you," the speaker seems to urge himself to abandon his pity for laughter, and in its final image, a somewhat forced simile, the poem returns to seeing the world in terms of multiplicity and habit. "The worlds"—plural—"revolve like ancient women / Gathering fuel in vacant lots" (53–54), and the image recalls the poem back to the "sordid patience" of slum dwellers, the inevitable, immutable, and literally cyclical routine of suffering. And while another poem, "Rhapsody on a Windy Night," will reveal Henri Bergson's influence on Eliot even more, this retreat from feeling to laughter at the conclusion of "Preludes" suggests his influence as well.

In his later years, Eliot admitted to "a temporary conversion to Bergsonism"

(*Sermon* 5) and stated, "I was certainly very much under Bergson's influence during the year 1910–11, when I both attended his lectures and gave close study to the books he had then written" (qtd. in Kumar 154). One of the books Eliot would have read, although few critics have noted it, was Bergson's *Laughter: An Essay on the Meaning of the Comic* (1900). In it, Bergson argues two points about laughter that bear on the conclusion of "Preludes." First, he suggested that laughter is accompanied by "the *absence of feeling*" (4, original emphasis); and, second, that laughter originates in, as he repeatedly puts it, "something mechanical encrusted upon the living" (39). As to the first, laughter and the absence of feeling, Bergson argues that "laughter has no greater foe than emotion" and, consequently, "indifference is its natural environment" (4). In other words, we cannot laugh at that (or those) with which we sympathize, at least not in the moment of our laughter. "Highly emotional souls," Bergson writes, "in tune and unison with life, in whom every event would be sentimentally prolonged and re-echoed, would neither know nor understand laughter" (4). "To produce the whole of its effect, then," he concludes, "the comic demands something like a momentary anesthesia of the heart" (5). The conclusion of "Preludes" takes this principle and assumes that effects will follow from causes, that laughter, rather than reflecting a "momentary anesthesia of the heart," will deliver that anesthetic. For an observer who feels too much, as the speaker of the final lines of "Preludes" does, the command to "Wipe your hand across your mouth, and laugh" may rescue the speaker from sentiment, may bring about the desired apathy. "Look upon life as a disinterested spectator," Bergson continues, and "many a drama will turn into a comedy" (5). Rather like the belief that smiling, regardless of one's mood, will make one happier, Eliot's speaker here assumes that laughing, regardless of one's feelings, will cultivate one's indifference, not because the scene has changed but because one's attitude toward it has. If I laugh at something, I cannot, by Bergson's definition, feel emotion about it.

But the poem does not settle for the dubious strategy of merely commanding one to laugh at suffering; rather, it recasts that suffering as something that should objectively inspire laughter, which, for Bergson, means showing that suffering to be essentially mechanical. For Bergson, laughter arises when something or someone exhibits what he calls "a certain *mechanical elasticity*" (10, original emphasis), when individuals fail to respond adequately to their environment. His example is "a man, who, running along the street, stumbles and falls," whereupon "passers-by burst out laughing" (8). They would not have laughed, Bergson supposes, if the man had chosen to sit on the ground. Rather, they laugh

> because his sitting down is involuntary. Consequently, it is not his sudden change of attitude that raises a laugh, but rather the involuntary element in this change,—his clumsiness, in fact. Perhaps there was a stone on the road. He should have altered his pace or avoided the obstacle. Instead of that, through lack of elasticity, through absentmindedness and a kind of physical obstinacy, *as a result, in fact, of rigidity or of momentum,* the muscles continued to perform the same movement when the circumstances of the case called for something else. That is the reason of the man's fall, and also of people's laughter. (8–9, original emphasis)

In sum, for Bergson, as the example of the clumsy runner suggests, "*The attitudes, gestures and movements of the human body are laughable in exact proportion as that body reminds us of a mere machine*" (29, original emphasis). In contrast, Bergson claims, "a really living life should never repeat itself" (34) and, it goes without saying, would also never be laughed at.

Eliot does not merely urge his observer to laugh at "fancies" that previously moved him, then, but, rather, he makes those fancies—that infinitely gentle, infinitely suffering thing—into something laughable. In order to do that, the speaker must make it into a thing in the first place, which a shift in diction accomplishes, but also emphasize that thing's mechanical inelasticity, highlight its similarities to a mere machine. Hence the simile that concludes the poem: "The worlds revolve like ancient women / Gathering fuel in vacant lots." The key words here seem to be *revolve* and *ancient.* The worlds revolve like ancient women walking around in a vacant lot and, like ancient women, do not stop because of anything as inconsequential as suffering, just as the ancient women have not stopped gathering fuel in all their lifetimes. Both women and worlds display a certain mechanical inelasticity, both repeat, fail to adapt, or fail to protest, and both, according to Bergson and, it seems, the poem, are therefore laughable. The world resembles a mere machine by resembling women who themselves act in machinelike ways. From a close-up view of some infinitely gentle, infinitely suffering thing, the poem pulls back to reveal worlds in motion, suffering multiplied but also as a result made routine, inevitable, and therefore unremarkable—except perhaps when it is funny. The laughter may seem forced, but that may also be the point. The poem is trying, a little desperately, to turn a tragedy into a comedy. And while the equation that allows it to do so only emerges at the conclusion of the poem, that equation has operated throughout. Individual things, and individuals, as in the third prelude, inspire pity, while anything that repeats, anything that is repeated, or both—that is, "short square fingers stuffing pipes" or "muddy feet that press / To early coffee stands"—does not. Such things—and they are mere things—in their very multiplicity and inelasticity actively repulse sympathy.

In addition to Bergson, here too Philippe seems to have influenced Eliot, not just in the content of the poem but in the tone of it as well. In 1932, Eliot contributed a preface to a new edition and translation of Charles-Louise Philippe's *Bubu de Montparnasse.* In the preface, Eliot praised Philippe's novel of the "prostitutes and mackerels of the Boulevard Sebastopol" in ways that may shed light on his own thoughts about how best to turn the slum and its dwellers into literary art. Philippe, Eliot observes, "had an intense pity for the humble and oppressed" (unpaginated); however, Philippe differed from other pitying novelists, like Dickens and Dostoyevsky, as Eliot puts it, "by the absence of any religious or humanitarian zeal: he is not explicitly concerned with altering things." He is, Eliot notes, in terms that seem to describe his own approach to the humble and oppressed, "both compassionate and dispassionate." "In his book," Eliot continues, "we *blame* no one, we blame not even a 'social system.'" Curiously, Eliot ascribes this desire to move beyond politics in Philippe and, presumably, his own poetry, not to any particular political sensibility but to a commitment to realism. In rejecting religious and humanitarian zeal, Eliot argues, Philippe "is perhaps the most faithful to the point of view of the humble and oppressed themselves, is more their spokesman than their champion." "It is not the sort of people that Philippe knew best," Eliot observes, "who become Christian zealots or revolutionaries; they simply toil and suffer, or take the easiest way out."

Whether the humble and oppressed in 1900 or 1910 or even 1932 had as little interest in altering things as Eliot here credits them with matters less than what Eliot thought Philippe had achieved and what he perhaps thought he had earlier achieved in his own poetry of the slum and its dwellers. For, like Philippe's novel, Eliot's poetry of the humble and oppressed is not explicitly concerned with altering things. In the early decades of the twentieth century, for example, when slums and prostitution were the peculiar obsession of most social reformers and middle-class women's magazines, Eliot does not use his poetic representation of those "problems" to advance any explicit social program. By presenting such "reality" without overt comment or "propaganda," Eliot could further taunt those in his class who could only see these "problems" through the lens of social reform. So Eric Schocket is right to insist that Eliot belongs to the school of "American modernists" who abstract the worker "from a sentimental system of affect" and, as Schocket says of "First Caprice in North Cambridge," disarticulate "working-class forms from their previous symbolic systems" in order "to vitalize new aesthetic structures" (152). Hence Eliot's infinitely gentle, infinitely suffering things, not to mention all the hands raising dingy shades in a thousand furnished rooms, whose perpetual toil and suffering, perhaps too conveniently, become the occasion to dismiss any thought—on their part, supposedly, or on the part of those who observe them—of altering things. What Schocket underestimates, however, is how reluctantly, and therefore awkwardly, Eliot undertook that abstraction and disarticulation from a sentimental system of affect. As in the conclusion of "Preludes," Eliot, it seems, had to laugh to keep from crying.

Having freed workers and the poor—and himself—from a discourse of pity and social reform, Eliot could put them to other uses. Specifically, they seem to have come in handy during the period of Eliot's most intense study of Henri Bergson and during his efforts to translate Bergsonian philosophy into poetry. One of the advances in Eliot scholarship over the last decade has been for critics to return to the explorations in American, British, and French philosophy Eliot began as an undergraduate at Harvard and continued through his deposited but undefended dissertation. One of the poems to benefit from that approach is "Rhapsody on a Windy Night," which scholars have now rather exhaustively shown to be stamped by Eliot's reading of Henri Bergson's *Matter and Memory* (1896) and *Creative Evolution* (1907) and his attendance at Bergson's lectures at the College de France in 1911. In relating Eliot to Bergson, however, critics of the poem tend to overlook the scene and dramatis personae that allow Eliot to translate seminar philosophy into slum poetry—they overlook, that is, how and to what end Eliot positions the poor and working class in the poem. As in "Caprices" and "Preludes," these figures represent the unconsciously, automatically lived life—a way of being that, Eliot discovered, Bergson had devoted much of his philosophy to describing. No longer objects of pity whose claims must be laughed off, dwellers of the slum instead embody what Bergson calls "the lowest degree of mind" (*Matter and Memory* 297), that is, a mechanistic, one-dimensional, purely adaptive consciousness. Yet while Bergson would speak of the automatically lived life as a more or less universal human condition, Eliot, as in "Caprices" and "Preludes" but especially in "Rhapsody on a Windy Night," would tend to cast it as a peculiar trait of the poor and working class. The problem for "Rhapsody on a Windy Night," then, is not, as it was in "Caprices" and "Preludes," to avoid pitying the poor but, instead, to avoid becoming like them.

Because of the density and occasional convolution of his thought, Bergson defies any easy summary. (As Bertrand Russell confessed in 1912 when discussing Bergson's concept of *duration,* "I do not fully understand it myself" [*History* 796].) Nevertheless, it is possible to reconstruct the principles in Bergson that would have the most influence on Eliot, both in "Preludes," as I have shown, and the more thoroughly Bergsonian "Rhapsody on a Windy Night." At bottom, for Bergson, reality is a process of continual change, of pure duration and pure time. However, in seeking to adapt human beings to their environment, what Bergson calls practical intellect divides that temporal existence into "the discontinuous and immobile" (*Creative Evolution* 165), into, that is, space and matter, or "objects excluding one another" (189).[10] Practical intellect, then, is both the making and the undoing of man. While it enables him to adapt to and thrive in his environment, it fundamentally distorts his perception of the actually existing world, turning the continuous into the discontinuous, time into space, and life—his own and the universe's—into matter. These distortions lead to the divisions in Bergson between past and present and between memory and perception. Practical intellect relies on what Bergson calls pure perception, which is absorbed in the present, capable of achieving an immediate and instantaneous vision of matter and therefore devoted largely if not exclusively to action, to adaptation. For the most part, pure perception remains firmly in the present—with the exception of habitual memory, which it uses in order to draw on past experiences and perfect certain recurring actions needed for the present, thereby making them into habits. In contrast, the past survives in memory, particularly what Bergson calls independent or pure memory, which stores images from the duration of our whole perceptive lives. Habitual memory, however, is far more common—and far more determinative of our actions—than independent memory. Our need for habitual movements, Bergson writes in *Matter and Memory,* "determine[s] in us attitudes which automatically follow our perception of things. . . . Thus is ensured the appropriate reaction, the correspondence to environment—adaptation, in a word—which is the general aim of life" (96). So in every decision we make, our choice is guided by perception, which is itself guided by habitual memory, all of which conspires to lead us to adapt, at times almost automatically, even mechanistically, our actions to our environment. Such a monomaniacal devotion to action, however, cuts us off from reality, the temporal flux of duration, imprisoning us instead in a world of matter and routine.

As he frequently does, Bergson illustrates these principles—the difference between memory and perception and the difference between habitual and independent memory—with an anecdote.

> When a dog welcomes his master, barking and wagging his tail, he certainly recognizes him; but does this recognition imply the evocation of a past image and the comparison of that image with present perception? Does it not rather consist in the animal's consciousness of a certain special attitude adopted by his body, an attitude which has been gradually built up by his familiar relations with his master, and which the mere perception of his master now calls forth in him mechanically? We must not go too far; even in the animal it is possible that vague images of the past overflow into the present perception; we can even conceive that its entire past is virtually indicated in its consciousness; but this past does not interest the animal enough to detach it from the fascinating present, and its recognition must be lived rather than thought. To call up the past in the form of an image, we must be able to withdraw ourselves from the action of the moment, we must have the power to value the useless, we must have the will to dream. (93–94)

For Bergson, humans, also caught up in "the fascinating present" and "the action of the moment," have more in common with dogs than they care to admit. Like dogs, humans sacrifice memory, the past, and the duration and in order to make their way in a perpetual present. For Bergson, our whole existence—consciousness, perception, memory—is ruled by practical intellect and tyrannically devoted to action, with perception and habitual memory steering us to the desired and appropriate response to our environment. Like dogs, we are machines for perceiving and doing, cut off equally from our pasts and the duration.

Bergson, however, believes—and earnestly desires—that human beings can transcend this mechanistic existence of practical intellect, pure perception, habitual memory, and automatic action. He argues that by relying on intuition and instinct, by drawing on independent memory, humans can bypass the regime of practical intellect and access the duration, can see, as Bergson puts it in the concluding paragraph of *Creative Evolution,* "the material world melt back into a simple flux" (369).

Inspired by Bergson's metaphysics, Eliot's "Rhapsody on a Windy Night" explores what living in the duration might entail. The poem as a whole is concerned with perception, memory, and habit—and, above all, with the difference between a doglike, mechanistic response to reality and a response to reality that has the will to dream, is informed by memory, and can offer a glimpse of the duration. All this is made clear in the first stanza of the poem, which readily suggests the influence of Bergson.

Twelve o'clock
Along the reaches of the street
Held in a lunar synthesis,
Whispering lunar incantations
Dissolve the floors of memory
And all its clear relations
Its divisions and precisions,
Every street lamp that I pass
Beats like a fatalistic drum,
And through the spaces of the dark
Midnight shakes the memory
As a madman shakes a dead geranium.
(1–12)

In *Matter and Memory,* Bergson sketches a series of cones that illustrate the geometrical relation among pure memory, habitual memory, and present perception, with each more or less interpenetrating the other but each also divided from the other. ("For, that a recollection should reappear in consciousness," Bersgon argues, "it is necessary that it should descend from the heights of pure memory down to the precise point where *action* is taking place" [197].) In "Rhapsody on a Windy Night," the "reaches of the street" (2), which whisper "lunar incantations" (4), all combine to "Dissolve the floors of memory / And all its clear relations / Its divisions and precisions" (5–7). In other words, as Donald J. Childs glosses these lines, in this first stanza, "memory as practical intellect threatens to dissolve into memory as pure memory" (55), although "threatens" does not quite capture the excitement such an eagerly sought after possibility would entail. In any case, just as in "Second Caprice in North Cambridge," in which the slum allows the speaker to pause from the influence of "our definitions / And our aesthetic laws" (9–10), a midnight stroll through a slum neighborhood offers the possibility of transcending practical intellect and achieving contact with pure time, pure memory, and an undivided unity. Thus, like infectious and rhythmic drums, the street lamps lead the stroller into the heart of slum darkness, where "midnight" further "shakes the memory" (11), potentially shaking loose all the memories that practical intellect and habitual memory normally suppress.

Eliot flirts with the possibility of achieving that transcendence in the remaining stanzas of the poem. In the second stanza, the street lamp, which acts like perception itself, orders the slumming flaneur to "Regard" a woman whose dress and presence on the street at this late hour mark her as a prostitute. The stanza ends with the rather striking (if ambiguous) comparison of the corner of her eye to a crooked pin, an image that suggests any number of things: her age, her immorality, a wink, or the profession—seamstress—she (and many other prostitutes) practiced previously or by day. Regardless, this encounter between perception (flaneur) and object (prostitute) inspires further memories. It "throws up" (23), as the third stanza has it, "high and dry / a crowd of twisted things" (23–24), and the "things" that the memory throws up ("a twisted branch upon the beach" [25] and "a broken spring in a factory yard" [30]) all relate to the twistedness of the prostitute's eye. Because these memories of twisted things relate so clearly to the immediate object of perception (the prostitute's twisted eye), most readers of Eliot's poem assume that the speaker of the poem fails to transcend habitual memory. Instead of matter connecting the speaker's memory to the duration of its past and present, memory can only produce associated images. Even so, while "memory" does "throw up, high and dry"—thus suggesting unexplored, submerged depths—images related to the prostitute's twisted eye, the sheer inventiveness and range of the images that memory throws up should suggest that the speaker is closer to the realm of independent rather than habitual memory.

This crowd of twisted things that memory throws up distinguishes the practical intellect of the poem, the observing "I" and "eye" who recollects these related images, from the automata that form the object of his perception and recollection. That difference becomes even clearer in the fourth stanza of the poem.

Half-past two,
The street lamp said,
'Remark the cat which flattens itself in the gutter,
Slips out its tongue
And devours a morsel of rancid butter.'
So the hand of the child, automatic,
Slipped out and pocketed a toy that was running along the quay.
I could see nothing behind that child's eye.
I have seen eyes in the street
Trying to peer through lighted shutters,
And a crab one afternoon in a pool,

An old crab with barnacles on his back,
Gripped the end of a stick which I held him.
(33–45)

As in the previous stanza, the original image—a cat—that the moon shows the speaker inspires a train of similar images: a child pocketing a toy, a voyeur, and a crab, each sharing with the cat an impulsive, "automatic" (38) existence. "I could see nothing," the speaker reports, "behind that child's eye" (40), and a similar nothing, the absence of thought, lies behind the actions of voyeur and crab. Donald J. Childs, referring to these lines, therefore draws a logical if limited conclusion: "Again, the images from memory seem to associate freely, but they are quite practical—translating the cat's movement into terms that the practical intellect, by means of memories of similar motives, can understand and assimilate" (58). The speaker of the poem, he concludes, thus shares movements and motivations with the objects he observes, namely, self-preservation. While Childs rightly notes that the images the consciousness recalls all relate to each other and the cat—marked by the "So" of line 38—what he underestimates is how profoundly *different* the speaker remains from the automata he observes, both in the stanza quoted here and at the conclusion of the poem. In *Matter and Memory,* for example, Bergson writes that "there are, we have said, two memories which are profoundly distinct: the one, fixed in the organism, is nothing but the complete set of intelligently constructed mechanisms which ensure the appropriate reply to the various possible demands" (195). ("The other," Bergson writes, "is pure memory" [195].) Someone who relies exclusively on the former kind of memory—the one that produces mechanisms that ensure appropriate replies—Bergson calls "a man of impulse" (198). Yet, in contrast to cat, child, voyeur, and crab, the speaker is no man of impulse. Rather, the poem carefully establishes a division between acting and reflecting, between suppressing and indulging memory, between creatures of impulse (cats, children, voyeurs, and crabs) and those (the speaker) who observe, reflect, and associate creatures of impulse in their memory.

The stanza that follows draws this line even more sharply.

Half past three,
The lamp sputtered,
The lamp muttered in the dark.
The lamp hummed:
'Regard the moon,

La lune ne garde aucune rancune,
She winks a feeble eye,
She smiles into corners.
She smooths the hair of the grass.
The moon has lost her memory.
A washed out smallpox cracks her face,
Her hand twists a paper rose,
That smells of dust and eau de cologne,
She is alone
With all the old nocturnal smells
That cross and cross across her brain.'
(46–61)

The moon, who "does not harbor ill feelings towards anyone," as line 51 translates, transforms into yet another prostitute; moreover, as the street lamp observes, the prostitute qua moon "has lost her memory" (55). She exists (like cat, child, voyeur, and crab) in a sensate but unreflective present. Not for nothing do prostitute and children get lumped together with cats and crabs; in terms of consciousness, they are interchangeable. "To live only in the present," Bergson writes in *Memory and Matter,* "to respond to a stimulus by the immediate reaction which prolongs it, is the mark of lower animals" (198). "Pure perception," he elsewhere writes, "is the lowest degree of mind" (*Matter and Memory* 297), so low a degree of mind that it no longer qualifies as mind. It is, instead, as in the stanza just quoted, characteristic of the brain, which "is not an instrument of representation," Bergson asserts, "but an instrument of action" (83).[11] For the speaker of the poem, then, the prostitute is a species of Bergson's lower mind, more animal than human, living only in the present (she "has lost her memory") and responding immediately to impulse, in this case a potential customer who automatically summons a wink from her. She has "a brain" (61)—but that brain is not a mind, nor, like the child, is there anything behind her winking eye that would indicate memory, self-consciousness, or intuition of the duration. The prostitute has not lost habitual memory, far from it, but she has "lost her memory" insofar as memory forms so little a part of her actions that it is all but useless to her. "All the old nocturnal smells" may "cross and cross across her brain" (60–61), but they leave no imprint or influence there because while she has a brain that can grasp the present, she lacks a mind that can indulge the past.

Note how deeply this conscious state contrasts with the stroller who, when confronted with the image of the prostitute qua moon, has a mind that considers nothing but memories.

The reminiscence comes
Of sunless dry geraniums
And dust in crevices
Smells of chestnuts in the streets
And female smells in shuttered rooms,
And cigarettes in corridors
And cocktail smells in bars.

(62–69)

In other words, while the prostitute qua moon may have lost her memory, the stroller entertains an excess of memories, an excess that may in fact inhibit an impulsive response to a prostitute. (I will take up this theme shortly.) Indeed, he reminisces about past encounters with other prostitutes and is sickened by the material and sordid recollections ("female smells" [66]) that cross and cross across the prostitute's brain with seemingly no effect on her ability to act but with an especially debilitating effect on his own impulses. Defeated by such memories, in the last stanza, the stroller returns to his rooms.

The lamp said,
"Four o'clock
Here is the number on the door.
Memory!
You have the key,
The little lamp spreads a ring on the stair.
Mount.
The bed is open; the tooth-brush hangs on the wall,
Put your shoes at the door, sleep, prepare for life."
The last twist of the knife.

(70–82)

By the end of the poem, "Memory"—here habitual memory—has guided the stroller to his disappointingly empty bed. Equally disappointing, it is in these rooms that he must have his shoes polished, brush his teeth, sleep, and, instead of transcending practical intellect, be ruled by it, by, as Bergson elsewhere puts it, the "requirements of practical life" (*Creative Evolution* 237). Thus Donald J.

Childs is surely right to claim of this last stanza that "'the last twist of the knife' is directed towards [the stroller] himself; the virtual quotation of *Matter and Memory* to the effect that practical memory is a 'blade' penetrating actual experience acknowledges the speaker's continuing subjection to the Bergsonian bogey-man—practical intellect" (62). However, Childs's emphasis on the speaker's return to practical intellect and habitual memory has to be supplemented by John T. Mayer's conclusions about the poem, which acknowledge (as Childs does not) the distance between the stroller and automatic slum dwellers he encounters on his stroll. "Yet this last twist of the poem," Mayer argues, "subtly subverts the engulfing automation: his very awareness sets him apart from the automatic creatures gripped by instinctive behavior patterns of which they are unaware" (84). The speaker of the poem may make a disappointed return to practical intellect, but unlike cats, crabs, and prostitutes, he knows it.

The point here is that in reconstructing Bergson's spectrum of consciousness, Eliot has allotted positions along that spectrum according to class, something Bergson never does. Contrasting the man "who should dream his life" with the man who "would be constantly acting his life"—that is, "the conscious automaton"—Bergson insists that "these two extreme states . . . are fully visible only in exceptional cases" (202). "In normal life," he observes, "they are interpenetrating," which I take him to mean (among other things) that few people are exclusively one sort of man (of action, of dreaming) or another, and certainly not that one class of men or another is one sort of consciousness or another. (In order to illustrate the pure expression of habitual memory and action-oriented consciousness, Bergson as often as not prefers animals.) With the intriguing exception of the third section of "Preludes," though, in which the prostitute has "such a vision of the street / As the street hardly understands," Eliot has made impulsive, automatic behavior the exclusive realm of the poor and working class; when, that is, it is not the realm of animals, which, as in "Rhapsody on a Windy Night" and "Caprices," are more or less interchangeable with the poor and working class.

The poem therefore stakes out three possible points along the mind-memory spectrum: the barely human life of habitual memory and mechanistic impulse, the somewhat unattainable duration of pure time and pure memory, and the life of practical intellect. The stroller may not have achieved the first, pure time and pure memory, but neither does he revert to the second state either, that of the automatic, mechanistic, and impulsive animals, prostitutes, and slum dwellers. (For Eliot, rather remarkably, these are all alike.) Instead, the speaker is mired in practical intellect, the name Bergson gives to the spatial, geometric, and mostly present-bound state of consciousness that adapts bodies and brains to their environments. Still, while the stroller fails to transcend the life of practical intellect and fails to experience—or fails to experience for long, anyway—Bergson's pure memory, he is nevertheless conscious of that failure, and thus quite separate from the mechanistic and automatic slum dwellers he encounters on his midnight stroll. As Mayer emphasizes, at some level the stroller in "Rhapsody on a Windy Night" suffers because of that consciousness of failure—a consciousness that the supposedly more impulsive slum figures do not share. Nevertheless, his frustration also arises from the fact that his life, the one he must assiduously prepare for, the life of practical intellect, perhaps shares more with the automatons he has witnessed than with the dream life of pure memory to which he aspires. Part of the pain of "the last twist of the knife," I take it, comes from its association with the "twisted" eye of the prostitute and the "twisted" images that vision throws up in the third stanza. In any case, Eliot makes clear the villains in the poem: the life of practical intellect and the life of sensory-motor existence to which the practical intellect tends.

Eliot's dissatisfaction with both states of consciousness complicates claims that he, like other modernists, engages in what Eric Schocket calls "an aesthetics of management," whereby modernists first "express a commitment to atomization and fragmentation" and then "reconnect these parts through an external system, logic, or, in more familiar terms, aesthetic technique" (148–49). According to this argument, modernists like Eliot—Schocket's other example is Gertrude Stein—deploy the literary equivalent of Frederick Winslow Taylor's scientific management techniques in order "to systematize bodies, labor, and the stresses and tensions of class conflict" (148). Modernists, including Eliot, therefore share, as Schocket argues, "a substructure that connects them to the social and economic processes of industrial modernization and to Taylor's mode of resolution through formal procedures" (148). To be sure, Eliot enlists most if not all the management techniques Schocket charges him with: atomization, fragmentation, fetishism, dismemberment. But here, too, Schocket underestimates how much of what Eliot represents in his poetry—the mechanization of the working class—also threatens him. In other words, Eliot seems to be less concerned with bringing off the mechanization of the working class than dealing with, in fact going in fear of, what he perceives as its a priori mechanization. Contrary to claims that Eliot scientifically manages the working class, Eliot would seem instead to be horrified by an already managed working class and horrified, too, at the prospect of coming to resemble that class.

In that horror, in rejecting the life of practical intellect and its culmination, the purely automatic life, Eliot places himself squarely in the tradition of romantic anticapitalism, which, as I argue throughout this book, is one of the defining attitudes of modern American poetry as it confronts the labor problem. In Eliot's case, this romantic anticapitalism revolves around questions of rationality. As Michael Löwy and Robert Sayre argue, summarizing the work of Marx, Weber, and Mannheim, rationalization is taken to be "at the heart of modern bourgeois civilization" (40). In contrast, "the Romantic opposition to rational abstraction," they argue, "can . . . be expressed as a rehabilitation of nonrational and/or nonrationalizable behaviors," including the "revalorization of intuitions, premonitions, instincts, feelings" (41), and one can observe this romantic opposition to rational abstraction in Bersgon and what Eliot makes of Bergson.[12] For Bergson—although this is less evident in Eliot's crabs, cats, children, voyeurs, and prostitutes—the mechanical, automatic working class suffers not from a lack of intellect but, as Bergson tells it, from a perfection of practical intellect. Their brains have perfectly adapted them to their environments but in so doing have cut them off from intuition, from the duration. Despite their outward thoughtlessness, the nothing behind their eyes, they have instead become so rational and reliant on practical intellect that they no longer require thought. Thought, rationalism, has calcified into action and habit. Paradoxically, given their mechanization, these workers and the poor nevertheless embody a purely rational—or rationalized—relation to the world.

In seeking to transcend practical intellect, Eliot also seeks to distance himself from the supposedly mechanical inhabitants of the slum, those who have perfected the life of practical intellect. In other words, Eliot seeks to distance himself from those creatures that have become perfectly rational, and he was not the only admirer of Bergson to share this suspicion of rationality. As many critics at the time noted, Bergson's popularity—among philosophers and nonphilosophers alike—owed in part to what Will Durant in his 1926 primer *The Story of Philosophy* described as Bergson's "revolt against materialism" (336). Bergson, Durant argues, showed that "it is ridiculous and shameful that men should be machines; and ridiculous and shameful that their philosophy should describe them so" (346). Before Bergson, Durant writes, "we were cogs and wheels in a vast and dead machine; now, if we wish it, we can help to write our own parts in the drama of creation" (350). Less enthusiastically, Bertrand Russell and Thorstein Veblen quietly ridiculed the antirational tendencies in Bergson. Russell observed that Bergson "exemplifies the revolt against reason which, beginning with Rousseau, has gradually dominated larger and larger areas in the life and thought of the world" (791). Writing of "this revulsion against thinking in uncoloured mechanistic terms" (*Instinct* 334), for his part Veblen complained, "Of all these latterday revulsionary schemes of surcease from the void and irritation of the mechanistic conception, that spoken for by M. H. Bersgon is doubtless the most felicitous, at the same time that it is, in its elements, the most engagingly naïve" (334).

At the time of "Rhapsody on a Windy Night," Eliot would seem to share Durant's appreciation for Bergson's antimaterialism and antirationalism rather than Russell or Veblen's contempt for the same. Nevertheless, and regardless of the attitude one ultimately took toward him, all would agree that Bergson articulates a horror at the "void and irritation of the mechanistic conception," as Veblen puts it. In the early decades of the twentieth century, that horror seems to have reached a crisis. As a later chapter on Carl Sandburg demonstrates, at just the moment when the United States was most fiercely contesting the ethics of scientific management, arts and crafts reformers and philosophers alike arrived to articulate a revulsion at the life (or the labor) lived automatically, mechanistically. (Taylor's *Principles of Scientific Management* and its attending debates and congressional inquiries, for example, appear in 1911, the same year as the English-language edition and unlikely popularity of Bergson's *Creative Evolution.*) Eliot, though already beginning to detach himself from the United States, nevertheless seems to have shared his culture's concerns. To those observing it, modernity, as Durant describes it, appeared to turn individuals—especially, for Eliot, the poor and working class—into "cogs and wheels in a vast and dead machine" (350). In contrast, and like other romantic anticapitalists, Eliot sought to keep alive what Bergson calls the "will to dream" (94). As "Rhapsody on a Windy Night" suggests, Eliot went in fear that such a life of cogs and wheels in a vast and dead machine might describe his own life—or worse, already did.

Except when he did not. Except, that is, when the mechanized, impulsive poor and working class did not seem to Eliot like a fate at all costs to be avoided but as an alternative, not altogether contemptible existence. Consider again the conclusion of "Rhapsody on a Windy Night." The sharpness and pain of "the last twist of the knife" come, as some critics have observed, from the speaker's return to the life of practical intellect and his knowledge of that return. In other words, while the speaker may suffer from his inability to transcend practical intellect for the higher order of pure time and pure memory, he also suffers from an inability to escape knowledge of his failure. The conclusion of the poem suggests that it is knowledge of his failure—as much as the failure itself—that bedevils him. One solution to that problem, of course, would be to escape that practical intellect for the duration and the life of pure memory but, failing that, one could also leave behind practical intellect for the decidedly lower and less taxing order of impulse and mechanism, to live the reckless, unconscious life of the prostitutes and slum dwellers whom the speaker encounters on his evening stroll. And in fact, at times, the speaker can seem envious of the life of impulse that the poor and working class seem to lead. Unlike them, he cannot act without getting enmeshed in recollections; unlike a crab, he cannot impulsively grab the end of a stick or, like an ordinary customer, answer a prostitute's wink in kind and not in memories. In short, the poem suggests, a little impulse may not be such a bad thing—especially when compared with the tooth brushing and the mounting of empty beds of the life lived by practical intellect.

In "Rhapsody on a Windy Night," this element, admittedly, remains in the background. In a series of poems Eliot wrote in the mid-1910s, however, beginning with "The Love Song of J. Alfred Prufrock," that trope—an impulsive, libidinous working class doing battle against an overcivilized, restrained, upper middle class—would increasingly govern both his poetry and his attitude toward the working class. Surprisingly, the impulsive, libidinous working class, from which Eliot previously recoiled, is now, metaphorically anyway, embraced.

Consider the opening stanza of "The Love Song of J. Alfred Prufrock," which begins with an explicit invitation to experience the pleasures of the slum and is motivated, as the remainder of the poem reveals, by displeasure with the speaker's own class.

Let us go then, you and I,
When the evening is spread out against the sky
Like a patient etherized upon a table;
Let us go through certain half-deserted streets,
The muttering retreats
Of restless nights in one-night cheap hotels
And sawdust restaurants with oyster shells:
Streets that follow like a tedious argument
Of insidious intent
To lead you to an overwhelming question . . .
Oh, do not ask, "What is it?"
Let us go and make our visit.

(1–12)

Unlike in the "Caprices," the streets here are only "half-deserted," yet they remain nearly as empty. Even so, they have much to offer. When Prufrock proposes to guide his reader (and the other half of his divided self), Virgil-like, through the city streets of cheap hotels and oyster bars, he draws on both the rhetoric and the images of fictional and nonfictional urban slumming narratives that were extremely popular at the turn of the century but which date back at least to the American publication of Eugène Sue's *The Mysteries of Paris* (1845) and George W. M. Reynolds's *The Mysteries of London* (1844) (Reynolds 82). Such works, David Reynolds notes, "reflected the profound fears and fantasies of an American population faced with rapid urbanization and industrialization" (82). They spoke to those for whom "the city was suddenly an overwhelming place, filled with hidden horrors and savage struggles as fascinating as they were appalling" (82). Regardless of whether these slumming narratives provide an explicit source for Eliot's "Prufrock," and there are enough overt borrowings to suggest they do, the genre at the least provided another rhetorical model—beyond musical tropes—for how Eliot could incorporate urban and working-class life into his poetry. For it is precisely those fears—and even more so the fantasies—of the fascinating and appalling city that Eliot first explored in the "Caprices" series and that Prufrock hopes to evoke with his "muttering retreats"; what George G. Foster, in arguably the most famous English-language slumming narrative, *New York by Gas-Light* (1850), calls "the festivities of prostitution, the orgies of pauperism, the haunts of theft and murder, the scenes of drunken debauch, and all the sad realities that go to make up the lower stratum—the underground story—of life in New York!" (69). In contrast to the private and paralyzing spaces of the speaker's chambers—and, later, the hyperarticulate rooms and kitchens where "women come and go / talking of Michelangelo" (13–14)—Prufrock imagines "retreating" to the public spaces of the lower stratum, the underground story of "one-night cheap hotels / And sawdust restaurants with oyster shells" (6–7).[13] However, perhaps to his regret, Prufrock is only passing through the festivities of prostitution and scenes of drunken debauch; that is, these slum "retreats" remain mostly unrealized possibilities. Instead, he is following streets that lead like a tedious argument back to this poem's version of "journalists" and "universities" or the rooms whose inhabitants "prepare for life" rather than live it: "the cups, the marmalade, the tea" (89)—that is, the rote signs of bourgeois civility and femininity. Nevertheless, the retreats linger as imaginative places where Prufrock can at least dream of escaping from the overcivilized and feminine spheres of parlors and kitchens or observe those who have escaped those places by luck of their birth and their lower social class. In other words, Eliot would seem to have traded horror at the impulsive, automatically lived life for something closer to envy.

T. J. Jackson Lears's influential study *No Place of Grace* (1981) underscores the importance of these unrealized but potential "retreats" to the American upper and upper middle classes of the late nineteenth and early twentieth centuries. Lears explores what he calls "Modernist anti-modernism": "the recoil from an 'overcivilized' modern existence to more intense forms of physical or spiritual experience supposedly embodied in medieval or Oriental cultures" (xiii). "For the educated bourgeoisie," Lears writes, "authentic experience of any sort seemed ever more elusive; life seemed increasingly confined to the airless parlor of material comfort and moral complacency. Many yearned to smash the glass and breathe freely—to experience 'real life' in all its intensity" (5). Lear's "airless parlors of material comfort and moral complacency" parallel the empty beds that bother the speaker of "Rhapsody on a Windy Night" or the kitchens and parlors that so aggravate Prufrock. In a 1918 essay on Henry James, Eliot called Boston society "refined beyond the point of civilization" ("The Hawthorne Aspect" 49). Prufrock thus imagines smashing out of these overrefined, "overcivilized" parlors and kitchens and breathing instead the dank but unrefined "free" air of oyster bars and cheap hotels. Instead of more intense forms of physical or spiritual experience embodied in medieval or "Oriental" cultures, then, for Eliot (as for many modern poets, especially William Carlos Williams) these forms of "real-life" experience are to be found in the urban primitive slums.[14]

Part of what makes the "real life" of the slum real, the poem implies, is its casual attitude toward sexuality, which sets it apart from the civilized parlors of the remainder of the poem, where alabaster women have to be revealed—as though it counted as a revelation—to be "downed with light brown hair" (64). This trope, the sexuality of the lower classes against the refinement of the bourgeoisie, introduced in "Prufrock," recurs in many, perhaps most of the poems Eliot subsequently writes about the poor and working class. It appears, albeit more satirically, in a series of poems Eliot composed and published in the mid-1910s and later included in *Prufrock and Other Observations.* "Aunt Helen," Eliot's sardonic elegy, revels in this imagined divide between bourgeois sexual and social propriety and working-class vitality.

Miss Helen Slingsby was my maiden aunt,
And lived in a small house near a fashionable square
Cared for by servants to the number of four.

Now when she died there was silence in heaven
And silence at the end of her street.
The shutters were drawn and the undertaker wiped his feet—
He was aware that this sort of thing had occurred before.
The dogs were handsomely provided for,
But shortly afterwards the parrot died too.
The Dresden clock continued ticking on the mantelpiece,
And the footman sat upon the dining-table
Holding the second housemaid on his knees—
Who had always been so careful while her mistress lived.

(1–13)

In the first parts of the poem, the symbols of Victorian refinement—the ticking of the Dresden clock, the considerate undertaker, the immaculate rugs, the well-kept pets—all join heaven and the fashionable street in silently (except for the clock) mourning Aunt Helen Slingsby's death. However, without the "careful" atmosphere that before Aunt Helen Slingsby's death restrained the footman and the second housemaid, randy servants (now to the number of two) can throw aside the serving trays and frolic on that icon of bourgeois respectability, the dining room table. In this upstairs-downstairs farce, the bourgeoisie plays superego to the unruly working-class id, and when the former withers away, the previously repressed sexuality can return. And while Eliot does not exactly celebrate the mischief Aunt Helen's servants manage to get into upon her death, their liberated playfulness does relieve the utter banality and propriety that seem to have characterized Aunt Helen's life, death, and social class.

Eliot also exploits this theme of bourgeois repression and working-class expression in "The *Boston Evening Transcript,*" whose title alludes to the now defunct but once "lively" newspaper that "covered in detail the slightest activity of Boston's leading families" (Kennedy 262).

The readers of the Boston Evening Transcript
Sway in the wind like a field of ripe corn.

When evening quickens faintly in the street,
Wakening the appetites of life in some
And to others bringing the Boston Evening Transcript
I mount the steps and ring the bell, turning
Wearily, as one would turn to nod good-bye to La Rochefoucauld,

If the street were time and he at the end of the street,
And I say, "Cousin Harriet, here is the Boston Evening Transcript."
(1–7)

Here Eliot rather sharply draws the binary that informs his symbolic use of the working class in this early, satirical poetry. For those in the street (i.e., for the working class and those lucky enough to cavort with them), "evening" and the end of the workday paradoxically "wakens" the "appetites of life" (4). For those in their homes, however, like Cousin Harriet and Aunt Helen Slingsby before her death, that same "evening" brings the *Boston Evening Transcript* and presumably puts to sleep whatever "appetites of life" they may have had. The speaker, however, stands on the ledge between these two worlds, although he will in all likelihood spend his evening with the *Boston Evening Transcript* and not with the appetites of life.

Eliot's own reflections on his Paris years—which would inspire "Preludes" and "Rhapsody on a Windy Night"—indicate just how deeply he resented these frustrated appetites. In a letter to Conrad Aiken in 1914, Eliot confessed that he had been going through "one of those nervous sexual attacks" and that "this is the worst since Paris" (*Letters* 75).[15] "One walks about the street with one's desires," Eliot writes, "and one's refinement rises up like a wall whenever opportunity approaches" (75). By "opportunity," of course, Eliot meant prostitutes, and just as he had in "Prufrock" and "Aunt Helen," he fingers a calcified, bourgeois refinement as a wall closing off his more youthful, primitive desire. (In "Rhapsody on a Windy Night," memory seems to play this role.) In another poem from this period, "Cousin Nancy," Eliot writes of bookshelves full of "Matthew and Waldo, guardians of faith, the army of unalterable law" that "kept watch" (11–13) over Miss Nancy Ellicot as she "smoked / And danced all the modern dances" (7–8). Eliot's poems from this period give the impression that those same guardians of faith and armies of unalterable law keep watch over Cousin Thomas's perambulations, inhibiting whatever desire he might have to take "opportunities" up on their offers and dance his own modern dance.

Not for nothing, then, does Prufrock, near the conclusion of his song, confess that he "should have been a pair of ragged claws / Scuttling across the floors of silent seas" (73–74). In an astonishing act of editorial exegesis, Christopher Ricks has proposed a source for the line in Eliot's copy of Charles Darwin's *Descent of Man.* In a passage on the "sexual characters" of crabs that Eliot underlined, Darwin writes that "The development of these hook-like processes has probably followed from those females who were most securely held during the act of reproduction, having left the largest number of offspring" (*Inventions* 187). Prufrock has other reasons for wishing to be a pair of ragged claws, but not the least of these is his desire to act impulsively, especially in the realm of sexuality, where he seems least capable of action without equally crippling reflection.

One can measure how far Eliot has traveled in his attitude toward the life of impulse and, indirectly, the supposedly impulsive life of the working class by comparing the crab in Prufrock to the crab in "Rhapsody on a Windy Night," which reflexively "gripped the end of a stick which I held him" (45). In both poems, crabs represent the same impulsive, habitual life. What differs is Eliot's attitude toward that life. In "Rhapsody on a Windy Night," its reflexive, adaptive impulse horrifies; in "The Love Song of J. Alfred Prufrock," it is enviable. What does not change is the crab, and by association the working class, which remains fundamentally habitual, impulsive, and reflexive. At times, in the earlier slum poems, for example, those mechanistic poor and working class would embody modernist rationality and the practical bent of civilization; at other times, the mechanistic but also impulsive poor and working class could paradoxically disrupt modernist rationality and propriety.

Strangely, but not altogether unexpectedly, Eliot would again change his attitude toward the supposedly bestial and mechanical existence of the working class. He would soon come to viewing working-class sexuality and impulsivity not so much as an "opportunity" denied or an escape hatch from bourgeois domestication but, as he did in "Caprices," "Preludes," and "Rhapsody on a Windy Night," as a pathology of modernity itself (Asher 11–34). Indeed, Eliot's portrait of a liberating or liberated working-class sexuality in "The Love Song of J. Alfred Prufrock," "Aunt Helen," and "The *Boston Evening Transcript*" does not at all square with how he represents working-class sexuality in the later, more canonical poems, including the "Sweeney" sequence and *The Waste Land.* In the former, over a number of poems ("Sweeney Erect," "Sweeney among the Nightingales," "Mr. Eliot's Sunday Morning Service") Eliot develops what some critics have called his "Sweeney Motif": the bed, bath, and bar adventures of "Apeneck" Sweeney. As might be gathered from his adventures, even the provenance of his name, Eliot usually invokes Sweeney to suggest a swarthy, hirsute manliness and an equally virile sexuality—no nervous attacks overcome Sweeney in the company of prostitutes.[16] In the poems where Sweeney figures, however, Eliot does not, as in the earlier notebook poems, celebrate working-class masculinity and sexuality as much as he trades on its sordidness.[17]

Sweeney also makes an appearance in *The Waste Land*, where he joins (to summarize all these moments from *The Waste Land*) the typist home at teatime, the young man carbuncular, and the cockney maids drinking pints in a pub threatening adultery and discussing their botched abortions, to embody Eliot's view of a symbolically sordid and debased working-class sexuality. To be sure, throughout *The Waste Land* Eliot locates the curse of sexuality in other bodies and other social classes, including the myth of Philomela and Mr. Eugenides' allusively homosexual invitation to one of the speakers of the poem, but the poem reserves its most explicit treatment of sexuality for working-class figures, and because of this the working-class figures appear to carry most of the symbolic burden of expressing aberrant and debased sexual energy.

That sexual energy reaches its heights of aberrance and debasement when the young man carbuncular, "flushed and decided," assaults the typist home at teatime. The published version of *The Waste Land* cleaned up this section considerably, while the original included the following telling quatrain. The young man carbuncular

> *—Bestows one final patronizing kiss,*
> *And gropes his way, finding the stairs unlit;*
> *And at the corner where the stable is,*
> *Delays only to urinate, and spit.*
>
> (47)[18]

Although, like Sweeney, the young man carbuncular is something of a class intermediary, one of the new lower-middle-class clerks less than a generation removed from a working-class background, like Sweeney his sexuality turns (and turns him) bestial: he not only urinates and spits but does so "where the stable is"—that is, with the rest of the animals. And while the poem offers some sympathy for the more explicitly working-class, pink-collar figure of the typist, it nevertheless reduces her (as Eliot had reduced prostitutes in "Rhapsody on a Windy Night") to an automaton, with a brain (not a mind—an important distinction for Eliot the student of Bergson) that allows only "one half-formed thought to pass" (251) before it numbs itself in the mechanically reproduced, mass cultural bliss of "a record on the gramophone" (256).[19] All the elements that first appear in "Caprices" thus return here: the poor and working class, when not acting like animals, are acting like automatons.

By the time of the Sweeney poems and *The Waste Land*, then, Eliot's view of the poor and working class had hardened into something far harsher: an impulsive working class no longer functioned as the imaginative liberator of bourgeois bedrooms but was, instead, the origin and expression of a discontented and fallen modernity. In the transition from envy to indictment, however, Eliot does not abandon his conception of the working class as existing at some lower level of consciousness, unbothered by "refinement" or any other check on its animalistic, autonomic impulses. Rather, as a reading of his earliest cityscape notebook poems through these later ones demonstrates, what does change is what Eliot makes of this animalistic, autonomic, impulsive working class. They are sordid, they must be pitied, they must not be pitied, they represent the lowest degree of mind, yet they also relieve the unrelieved propriety of the middle and upper middle class, when, that is, they do not represent a modern world gone wrong. In any case, the status of working-class "consciousness" (or lack thereof) is never in doubt; rather, it emerges as the central preoccupation of much of the poetry Eliot wrote in the 1910s and 1920s, and it constitutes his labor problem and his labor-problem poetry, just as it also allowed him to articulate an anticapitalism as romantic as it was antirational.

CHAPTER 4

"Starve, freeze": Edna St. Vincent Millay, Conspicuous Privation, and the Political Economy of Bohemia

I am awfully *broke.*

—EDNA ST. VINCENT MILLAY, letter to Harriet Monroe, March 1, 1918

Early on the morning of April 28, 1913, John Reed left his apartment in Greenwich Village for nearby Paterson, New Jersey, where, as I discuss in chapter 2, a colossal strike among immigrant silk workers had stalemated after nearly two months. At this point in his life, Reed was more prodigal bohemian poet than would-be Bolshevik hero, so his interest in Paterson and industrial strikes was somewhat novel, as was his waking up early enough to be in Paterson by seven in the morning. Once in Paterson, though, Reed observed from a worker's front porch the infamous cat-and-mouse confrontations between police and picketers that played out almost daily throughout the Paterson strike. Following a skirmish with striking workers in the streets, police ordered Reed and other observers to move from the porch, and when Reed refused he was arrested. After a few hours in jail, he was hauled before Recorder James Carroll, the local judge sympathetic to the mill owners and, according to the historian Graham Adams, "perhaps the most hated man in Paterson" (89). "What's your business?" Carroll asked Reed. "Poet," Reed replied, which may or may not have contributed to the twenty-day sentence Carroll gave Reed for disorderly conduct ("Writer Sent to Jail" 2).[1]

Labor historians of the Paterson strike and literary historians of American modernism love this story because it encapsulates their hopes for what Steve Golin has called "the moment of 1913," a moment characterized by "the sense of convergence . . . between art and socialism, the women's movement and the industrial labor movement, the personal and the political" (2)—the poet and the picket lines. More specific to Paterson, it was a moment that witnessed "the coming together of the silk workers, the [Industrial Workers of the World] organizers, and the Village intellectuals" (8).

Of course this "fragile bridge," as Golin describes it, between the stages, salons, and apartments of Greenwich Village bohemia and the jails, stoops, and silk mills of Paterson would soon collapse, destroyed (accounts differ) by the defeat of the Paterson strike; the onset of World War I and its hysterical, repressive patriotism; the Rockefeller bombing; the Russian Revolution and the split of the Communist from the Socialist Party; or, more generally and perhaps thus more accurately, the first Red Scare.[2] Regardless of how, though, labor and literary historians agree that the moment of 1913 was just a moment, its passing perceptible even to those at the time. In *Exile's Return,* for example, his chronicle of the 1920s, Malcolm Cowley separated Greenwich Village bohemians into a "they" and a "we"—that is, those who had arrived before 1917 and those, like Cowley, who had arrived after. "'They' had been rebels," Cowley wrote of the prewar bohemians, "they wanted to change the world, be leaders in the fight for justice and art, help to create a society in which individuals could express themselves. 'We' were convinced that society could never be changed by an effort of the will" (72).

In 1917, four years after the Paterson silk strike concluded, Edna St. Vincent Millay arrived in Greenwich Village from Vassar College. Millay thus belongs somewhere between Cowley's "they" and "we," between prewar idealists and postwar cynics. Within a year or two of her arrival, however, Millay quite simply *was* bohemia. "If Jack Reed was the Golden Boy of Greenwich Village," Ross Wetzsteon has concluded, "its Golden Girl was Edna St. Vincent Millay" (240). Claimed by pre- and post-1917 Villagers alike as "the emblem of waning bohemian authenticity" (Miller 18), Millay's reputation as the Golden Girl of Greenwich Village brightened still further with the publication of *A Few Figs from Thistles* in 1920, her collection of daring lyrics that articulated for a wider audience than ever before the bohemian ethos of free love and prodigal merrymaking.[3] "One may as well admit," a contemporary reviewer wrote of *A Few Figs from Thistles,* "that Edna St. Vincent Millay is just now the most interesting person in American poetry," even if, that same reviewer regretted, a "great many started reading her verse not because they were seeking good art, but because . . . of her frank professions of impropriety" (35). Echoing that anonymous reviewer, Elizabeth Atkins wrote in 1936 that "To say that [*A Few Figs from Thistles*] became popular conveys but a faint idea of the truth. Edna St. Vincent Millay became, in effect, the unrivaled embodiment of sex appeal, the It-girl of the hour, the Miss America of 1920" (70). "It seemed there was hardly a literate young person in all the English-speaking world," Atkins added, "who was not repeating, *ad nauseam,*" Millay's gloriously insouciant poem, "First Fig" (70).

To date, most discussions of Millay's poetry have focused on reviving her place in the modern American poetry canon, unearthing the reasons for her disappearance from it, and, as part of both efforts, recovering the peculiar set of gender politics and, later, political commitments that inform her poetry. In contrast, in this chapter I examine Millay and one of her best-known works, *A Few Figs from Thistles,* against the backdrop of the events that opened this chapter—that is, the relation between Greenwich Village bohemia and the nexus of concerns about poverty, exploitation, and alienation that came to a head in Paterson and that contemporaries of Millay called, simply, "the labor problem." At first glance, this may seem like a strange way to read Millay. Unlike the other poets in this collection, who, I argue, started writing modern poetry when they started writing about workers and the poor, Millay only occasionally reaches out to include such figures in her poems. Nevertheless, many of her poems reveal a quiet obsession with economics, with, that is, the production, distribution, and consumption of wealth. As a result, one can read the poems collected in Millay's *A Few Figs from Thistles* as evidence of a sophisticated if largely unspoken attitude toward poverty and labor, one that would, because of the popularity of the text, resonate with readers throughout the interwar period.

In brief, I argue that as post-Paterson bohemian poetry like Millay's becomes increasingly anticapitalist—dismissive of the work ethic, contemptful of the cash nexus—it nevertheless risks, admittedly somewhat counterintuitively, also becoming increasingly indifferent to the problems of labor and poverty. Reading Millay's bohemian poetry in this light, I hope to give one answer to the question of whether voluntary poverty, and other varieties of antimaterialism common to the nineteenth and twentieth centuries, suppresses or marginalizes, as Laurence Buell puts it, "the hard realities of poverty" (663). I believe that it does—and then some. I argue not only that voluntary, bohemian poverty, at least Millay's version of it, suppressed or marginalized "the hard realities of poverty" but that the bohemian, voluntarily poor sought to distinguish themselves from the actually existing poor. In which case, the bohemian poor would function less like heroic challengers to capitalist hegemony, a role historians and lay historians alike have occasionally cast them in, and more like yet one more class formation in that economy. They would constitute a class formation, too, that, at least in their attitudes toward labor and poverty, seems to share more with a conventional leisure class than with the poor and working poor with whom they commonly shared urban space and, superficially anyway, with whom they shared their poverty. To put it bluntly, if a bridge had in fact spanned Greenwich Village and the neighborhoods of the poor and working class in the "moment of 1913," by, say, the moment of 1920, that bridge had collapsed. Following that collapse, the two groups seem, at best, to approach each other as convenient foils, and, at worst, as one of Millay's Greenwich Village poems, "Macdougal Street," suggests, to stare at each other across a wide gulf of mutual recriminations and hostility.

Millay's bohemian poetry thus offers a case study in the perils of romantic anticapitalism. Indeed, few social formations challenged the tenets of industrial capitalism as fiercely as bohemianism. In celebrating free love, leisure, and poverty, bohemianism made public its break with the capitalist ethos. Yet, as with other forms of romantic anticapitalism, bohemianism and the poetry it inspired could oftentimes seem indifferent to the working and living conditions of the poor and working poor, those who also, and perhaps more intensely, suffered capitalism's affronts.

When, as Elizabeth Atkins wrote in 1936, all the "literate young people in all the English-speaking world" were reciting "First Fig," what exactly were they saying? And why did they choose this poem to say it for them? On the surface, the proem to *A Few Figs from Thistles* offers, as Jane Stanbrough writes, an "image of liberation and self-assurance" (213), one that Millay would cultivate for herself and that other young people, especially the New Women of the 1920s, were eager to assume. Its brevity, which made it almost epigrammatic, also contributed to its popularity.

My candle burns at both ends;
It will not last the night;
But ah, my foes, and oh, my friends—
It gives a lovely light.

(1–4)

Despite its evident fame, few critics have explored Millay's poem in much detail, beyond noting, as Jane Stanbrough observes, that it, and the collection from which it comes, is "dominated by a narrative voice that irreverently mocked public opinion and public morality, that scorned imposed values and prescribed behavior" (213). This conventional reading of the poem, however, leaves unstated exactly what opinions and morality, what values and behavior, the poem is supposed to have mocked and scorned.

Some have offered that, as JoEllen Green Kaiser puts it, the poem marks "Millay's break with sentimentality," and that is likely true even if still vague, not least about what everyone, beside Millay, was being sentimental about. In any case, any reading of the poem must start with the idiom at its core, burning the candle at both ends. The modern sense of the phrase, of course, is "to do more than one ought to" (Hirsch 62), to not sleep enough because you stay up late every night and get up early every morning. In other words, one burns the candle at both ends of the day, working or carousing late into the night only to begin again before the sun has risen the next day. Yet, as many other poems in *A Few Figs from Thistles* demonstrate, while bohemians may have stayed up late, they slept scandalously late, too, and this habit ought to be reason enough to doubt that the speaker is proudly burning her candle at both ends of her day, especially early in the morning. No self-respecting bohemian would wake up before the sun rose—the only way one would see the sun rise, in fact, as a later poem will show, is if one stayed up all night.

More likely, then, is that the poem relies on the original meaning of the idiom, in which to burn the candle at both ends did not mean to burn the candle in the morning and evening but, rather, to burn the candle at both of *its* ends, which meant, effectively, to waste it. As late as the early twentieth century the phrase carried this implication of excessive, wasteful consumption, especially of money. As an American railway journal in the late nineteenth century complained about a railway line that mismanaged its finances, "they had been 'burning the candle at both ends,' and instead of holding in reserve a portion of their easily acquired earnings, they had been spending with a lavish hand" (Ackerman 533). Or, as a 1905 article in the *New York Times* titled "Living beyond Our Means" put it while discussing the city's deflated bond price, "The truth is that New York is burning the candle at both ends. It is adding to its expenses and reducing its taxable base" (8).

From a certain perspective, the difference in meaning is slight. Whether the candle is a metonym for one's financial resources or, more generally, one's strength or health, burning those resources, whether from both ends or at both ends of the day, is sure to lead to ruin. That, doubtless, is why the poem invited so many literate young people to recite it. The poem articulates a certain devil-may-care attitude that almost certainly fit the mood of the early 1920s. So, too, did its celebration of unchecked individuality. The speaker has acquired foes as well as friends but remains equally unbothered by the concerns of both. Rather than conserve her resources or heed their advice, she sacrifices everything for beauty, the "lovely" light the candle gives off before it or she expires. Essentially, the poem offers the belief that "It's better to burn out than to fade away," as the aging rocker Neil Young sang while trying to revitalize his career.

Yet the difference between burning a candle at both of its ends and burning a candle at both ends of the day does matter. In the former, one burns through one's material resources; in the latter, one burns through one's health. If the resources one squanders are merely physical, though, one loses the equation that is at the heart of the poem specifically and of Greenwich Village life circa 1920 more generally: the deliberate sacrifice of money—not only or even especially health—but money for beauty.

The deliberate sacrifice of money for beauty is the only way to make sense of the second poem in *A Few Figs from Thistles,* called, appropriately enough, "Second Fig." By reworking a few sentences from Christ's Sermon on the Mount, the poem sets in motion a nearly identical economy.

Safe upon the solid rock the ugly houses stand;
Come and see my shining palace built upon the sand.
(1–2)

In Matthew 7:24–26, Christ tells his disciples,"Everyone then who hears these words of mine and acts on them will be like a wise man who built his house on rock." In contrast, Christ says, "[E]veryone who hears these words of mine and does not act on them will be like a foolish man who built his house on sand" (*The New Oxford Annotated Bible*). Millay's poem accepts that wise and foolish men may be known by the foundations of their houses, but it reverses Christ's parable by valuing foolishness far more than wisdom. If one builds a house with safety uppermost in mind, Millay implies, her house will be ugly, not because the house is inherently ugly but because of its context, because it is so safely built on solid rock. Even a palace built on solid rock would be ugly. Just as form follows function, ugliness follows safety. In contrast, the "shining" palace of the second line is worth seeing not just because it is a shining palace but, rather, because it is "built upon the sand" (2) and, come high tide, will be washed out to sea. In other words, its beauty is ephemeral and prodigal; indeed, it is beautiful *because* it is so ephemeral and prodigal, because it squanders resources.

Here, then, in as concise a form as one is likely to find it, is the bohemian economy, in which what is scarce and thus dear are not resources, whether money, candles, or houses, but beauty. As such, one does not attempt to maximize one's resources but, rather, one's experience of and contact with beauty. Moreover, in the bohemian economy, one may produce or experience beauty only (or, it certainly helps) by wasting—or renouncing—otherwise precious resources. Indeed, this economy pervades bohemian life and the Village in the first few decades of the twentieth century. As John Reed wrote in the Harvard *Lampoon* in 1909, "It all comes down to this. Happiness and experience, or money and a rut" (qtd. in Rosenstone 59). Or, as Floyd Dell, managing editor of *The Masses* during that magical year 1913, would put it, "It was, for all of us, a life that was quaintly enriched by our poverty. How otherwise, except by being very poor, should we ever have learned to make the most of those joys that are so cheap, or that cost nothing at all, the joys of comradeship and play and mere childlike fun?" (33). Confirming Reed's and Dell's economies, in 1935, the sociologist Caroline Ware observed that "almost without exception, the various types of Villagers agreed in setting a relatively low social value on money for its own sake" (110). Among the "basic common qualities" that all Villagers shared, Ware wrote, was "a disregard for money values and for prestige based on either income or conspicuous expenditure" (236).

In both Reed's and Dell's formulations, money leads to a rut and closes off happiness and experience; poverty, by contrast, which is the cousin of waste in this economy, opens up a world of joyous opportunity—not least of which is the opportunity for beauty. That formula would inform another Millay poem from *A Few Figs from Thistles,* "To Kathleen," which Millay dedicates to her younger sister, who had followed the poet first to Vassar College and then to Greenwich Village.

Still must the poet as of old,
In barren attic bleak and cold,
Starve, freeze, and fashion verses to
Such things as flowers and song and you;

Still as of old his being give
In Beauty's name, while she may live,
Beauty that may not die as long
As there are flowers and song and you.
(1–8)

Given that some critics have read "First Fig" and much of Millay's poetry as a break with sentimentality, it may seem odd to encounter such a seemingly sincere poem about "flowers and song and you" (8). Yet, if Millay occasionally wrote or is supposed to have written mockingly of love—and even that is not always true—"Beauty," as evidenced by its capital letter here, is usually spared such ironic treatment. To be sure, the "Still" of the first line (and the "Still as of old" of the fifth) suggests how well Millay knows her and other Villagers' belatedness in bohemian popular history. Henri Murger's 1851 collection *Scènes de la Vie de Bohème*—and, better known to Millay and her contemporaries, the opera it inspired, Puccini's 1896 *La Bohème*—first circulated the tropes of bohemians starving and freezing in attics and garrets for love, art, and beauty, so much so that by 1920, and well before that date, for that matter, one could not live a bohemian life in Greenwich Village without being conscious of following, even repeating, somewhat shopworn conventions.[4] Nevertheless, the poem asserts that these conventions must "still" go on. And what goes on, as in "First Fig" and "Second Fig," is the deliberate sacrifice of resources—food, warmth, comfort—for "Beauty." True, the poet behind "To Kathleen" may view these conventions from an anthropological distance, but by repeating and recirculating them, by "fashioning" her own "verses" on the subject, Millay herself becomes one of these poets "as of old," one who admires beauty at whatever cost to health and wealth—indeed, the costlier the better.

Nor did this economy of poverty and beauty unfold only in Millay's poetry; it drove her decision to move to and remain in Greenwich Village in the first place. In a long letter home to her sister and mother in August 1917, shortly after she had moved to New York City from Vassar, Millay reported:

> Mrs. Thompson, a lovely woman who helped put me through college wants me to come & be her secretary for a while—she believes in me as a poet & would even pamper me in order not to interfere with my writing & she would pay me a salary & her place is out in the beautiful country & everything would be lovely & Aunt Calline is exceedingly anxious to have me do it—but I just *don' wanna!* (*Letters* 77)

As her somewhat childish outburst at the conclusion of this passage suggests, Millay could not bear even a salaried sinecure for fear that it might interfere with writing poetry. "Of course, I feel like the underside of a toad," she continues, "not to do what she wants me to do—but I can't make up my mind to address envelopes & make out card catalogues all fall—& then if I had time to write—which I know she intends me to have—nevertheless be always conscious that I may be called on to answer the telephone & make appointments &

reject invites" (77). In sum, Millay concludes, one could not "his being give / In Beauty's name" if one also had to answer the phone. Moreover, one could not "starve, freeze," the conditions seemingly necessary for the creation of beauty, while on a salary. "I might have been governess to the Aults," Millay writes, referring to another family, "except for a similar feeling about my independence" (77).

Millay's principal concern for her "independence" is all the more remarkable because unlike many Villagers, who came from solidly middle class or better families, Millay grew up extremely poor in rural Maine. Her father divorced her mother when Millay was eight years old, and her mother worked for most of Millay's childhood as a nurse, which called her away from the Millay home for extended periods of time. The letters between her and the Millay girls during their childhood are filled with anxieties about money, about whether dollars arrived in time to pay for various overdue household or schooling expenses. As her reference to Mrs. Thompson, the "lovely woman who helped put me through college," demonstrates, too, Millay could not have afforded to attend Vassar without considerable financial help, from Mildred C. Thompson, her history professor and mentor at Vassar, but primarily from Caroline Dow, "Aunt Calline" in the letter, who "discovered" the young poet while vacationing at a resort in Camden, Maine, near where the Millays lived and where Millay's sister waited tables.[5]

After she left Vassar, neither her nor her family's poverty abated. Millay would dutifully send to her mother and sister back home in Maine a portion of whatever she earned by selling poems and, later, stories to magazines. The letter wherein she rejected the position of social secretary, for example, concludes with Millay reporting that she is "sending you [her mother] a dollar 'cause have feeling you may need it" (77). A few years earlier, in 1913, after a windfall of twenty-five dollars for publishing two poems, Millay made the check over to her mother and in an accompanying letter instructed her, "Promise me, please, that with some of this you'll do something to make something easier for yourself. Shoes, dear,—or have your glasses fixed if they're not just right. Please, please do something like that" (37). The letter and others imply how fine the line between necessities (shoes, glasses) and luxuries had become—and had been—for the Millays.

These details from Millay's biography—her childhood poverty, her college financial aid in the form of a wealthy patron, her continuing need to support her mother at home from the sale of poetry and short stories, her rejection of a steady job—suggest how much of a mask Millay had to assume in order to appear so carefree about burning her candles at both ends, building palaces on the sand, and starving and freezing for beauty. (They also suggest that, despite the limited opportunities available to women, Millay's college education and social connections could have freed her from poverty essentially whenever she chose.) Two of these poems, for example—"First Fig" and "Second Fig"—would appear together (with three others also from the later collection) in the June 1918 edition of *Poetry.* In March, Millay wrote Harriet Monroe, the editor of *Poetry,* to say, "Spring is here—and I could be very happy, except that I am broke" (85). Millay asked Monroe if she could pay her "*now* instead of on publication for those so stunning verses of mine which you have," noting that she had become "very very thin, and have taken to smoking Virginia tobacco." In a postscript, she added, "I am *awfully* broke. Would you mind paying me a lot?" (85). Millay signed the letter "wistfully," which, together with the tone of the letter, suggests, as with Floyd Dell's recollection of his Village years, a lighthearted poverty, but it is a poverty all the same—made all the more remarkable because Millay is requesting payment for poems that in some sense celebrate poverty. Millay was, as she wrote in a letter home in 1917, constantly thinking of "the business end of it"—that is, poetry—claiming that "more than the disgusting money," she wanted "to be read," but adding, revealingly, "the dirty necessary money!" (77).

As that postscript suggests, these economies would influence her writing. Later critics have made much of Millay's appropriation of traditional forms, especially the sonnet, but in the days before the modernist revolution in form had taken hold, the sonnet and traditional forms were the only ones that paid, especially in the mass circulation magazines—*Vanity Fair, Ainslee's*—that paid the most and where Millay published the bulk of her poetry during the late 1910s and early 1920s.[6] In other words, poverty, the "dirty necessary money," as Millay described the need to publish salable poetry, may have had as much or more to do with the forms Millay chose to work in as any loftier motive. The "dirty necessary money" may also account for the separation between form and content in these poems: poems that extol poverty are written in forms designed to keep Millay and her family out of poverty.

If, as John Reed put it, money leads to a rut, and poverty, as Dell put it, to joy, it would follow that the Village sensibility would hold work, especially in the service of making money, in as little regard as money itself, and many poems in *A Few Figs from Thistles* do just that. In "Portrait by a Neighbor," for example, Millay adopts a persona outraged by the careless life of her bohemian neighbor.

While references to gardening and lawns likely place the poem outside Greenwich Village proper, the poem nevertheless offers a quintessential bohemian attitude toward labor—or, that is, offers a portrait of an observing neighbor who values everything about labor that bohemians would treat so indifferently.

Before she has her floor swept
Or her dishes done,
Any day you'll find her
A-sunning in the sun!

It's long after midnight
Her key's in the lock,
And you never see her chimney smoke
Till past ten o'clock!

She digs in her garden
With a shovel and a spoon,
She weeds her lazy lettuce
By the light of the moon.

She walks up the walk
Like a woman in a dream,
She forgets she borrowed butter
And pays you back cream!

Her lawn looks like a meadow,
And if she mows the place
She leaves the clover standing
And the Queen Anne's lace!

(1–20)

In the first stanza, the observed neighbor forgoes labor—sweeping the floor, doing the dishes—for "A-sunning in the sun" (4), a phrase that in its recursiveness perfectly captures the languor of the inaction. Moreover, decidedly not burning her candles at both ends of the day (in the modern sense of the phrase), the neighbor, according to her observer, is late to bed and equally, scandalously late to rise; one never sees "her chimney smoke / Till past ten o'clock" (7–8). Nor does she follow the conventional workday, as likely to weed her lettuce by moonlight as by sunlight—lettuce that she has infected, somehow, with her laziness. Likewise, what work she does she does carelessly. She does not have the right tools for the job, digging in the garden with a shovel and a spoon instead of a trowel. She does not keep sufficient groceries in the house and must borrow from neighbors, and she does not care enough to remember what she has borrowed or does not bother to distinguish between one borrowed thing and another. Finally, and in keeping with poems like "First Fig" and "Second Fig," she cares more for beauty than utility, so that when she does mow her lawn, which "looks like a meadow," she spares the clover and Queen Anne's lace—weeds, essentially—because they have some slight, redeeming charm. In short, the poem delights in the scandal that bohemian attitudes toward labor would cause for the conventional middle class.

Yet another of Millay's pithier, more easily recited poems, "Grown-up," suggests that it is not just any labor that this bohemian homesteader abjures but, rather, domestic labor: sweeping floors, washing dishes, gardening, cooking, weeding, or, as in "Grown-up," serving more generally.

Was it for this I uttered prayers,
And sobbed and cursed and kicked the stairs,
That now, domestic as a plate,
I should retire at half-past eight?

(1–4)

At first glance, the poem offers the attitude purportedly on hand in "First Fig." In other words, it implies that it is far more exciting to stay up late—doing things one might regret—than to be "domestic as a plate" (3).[7] That phrase, however, "domestic as a plate," also captures some of the skepticism toward traditional forms of domesticity—and domestic labor—current in the other poems. In addition to remaining closed up in cupboards, plates also serve—something the speaker of the poem is anxious to avoid doing. (Millay famously said of Freud that his was "a Teutonic attempt to lock women up in the house and restrict them to cooking and baby-tending" [qtd. in Wetzsteon 258–59].) Read by the light of aversion to domestic labor, then, the shining palaces in "Second Fig" may be superior not just because they are more aesthetically interesting than the ugly houses built safely on solid rock but, rather, because those ugly houses will need to be cleaned, in perpetuity given their solid foundation, while one does not have to keep the shining palace shining since it will not last on its foundation of sand long enough to lose its gleam.

The aversion to domestic labor that informs some of the poems in *A Few Figs from Thistles* may help explain what would otherwise seem so out of place in the collection, namely, all the love poems. Surely a poet skeptical of domesticity would bring a similar skepticism to bear on love since love could rather easily lead to, to cite Millay on Freud again, "cooking and baby-tending." Yet in *A Few Figs from Thistles* one finds many poems like "The Philosopher."

And what are you that, wanting you,
I should be kept awake
As many nights as there are days
With weeping for your sake?

And what are you that, missing you,
As many days as crawl
I should be listening to the wind
And looking at the wall?

I know a man that's a braver man
And twenty men as kind,
And what are you, that you should be
The one man in my mind?

Yet women's ways are witless ways,
As any sage will tell,—
And what am I, that I should love
So wisely and so well?

(1–16)

Critics seeking to rescue Millay as a feminist poet have rarely discussed poems like "The Philosopher," for probably obvious reasons. While the speaker of the poem acknowledges that the object of her love is nothing special, she nevertheless wallows in her inexplicable love for him. "And what are you," she repeatedly demands of her lover, but the better question, which she eventually arrives at, is what is *she* that she should love neither the bravest nor the kindest man when there are so many brave and kind men to be loved. The answer, that "women's ways are witless ways" (13), will satisfy no one, but the point of the poem is not that women are witless but that love trumps wisdom and, all things considered, that is not always regrettable. Like burning one's candles at both ends, building a shining palace on sand, or gardening with a spoon, the poem celebrates inutility and irrationality. As in "Second Fig" and its remixing of Christ's parable of the wise and foolish builders, loving wisely and well is boring; it is what sages do—the same sages who build safe, ugly houses or take secure, well-paying jobs as social secretaries. In other words, for Millay, love, like beauty, is something worth starving and freezing for; its very irrationality and waste testify to its value.

Similarly, one also finds in *A Few Figs from Thistles* and throughout Millay's other volumes poems like the sonnet "I shall forget you presently, my dear," which, as Jo Ellen Green Kaiser has written—inaptly of "First Fig" but appropriately of that sonnet—"rejoices in love's impermanence" (33). "Thursday," while not quite so joyous, nevertheless also speaks plainly about love's impermanence.

And if I loved you Wednesday.
Well, what is that to you?
I do not love you Thursday—
So much is true.

And why you come complaining
Is more than I can see.
I love you Wednesday,—yes, but what
Is that to me?

(1–8)

Poems like "Thursday," with its insistence that love is fleeting and lovers fickle, provide a safety net for poems like "The Philosopher." In the latter poem, love conquers all, especially wisdom. To a point, too, this is a conquest that one can happily indulge. If indulged too deeply, though, such unreflective love might lead one to wake up one Thursday morning with a husband and a baby and the prospect of cleaning a safe, ugly house and monitoring neighbors for their scandalous departures from bourgeois proprieties and ethics of work. In sum, Millay can make room for losing oneself in love, but she resists strenuously any relationship that might turn a woman lover into something "domestic as a plate."

For the most part, then, these poems celebrate free love, that slogan of the late nineteenth and early twentieth centuries, and do so in two senses. The first, more obvious sense, as the Victorian feminist and labor reformer Victoria

Woodhull put it in 1871, is that women have, as Woodhull claimed to have, an "*inalienable, constitutional* and *natural* right to love whom I may, to love as *long* or as *short* a period as I can; to *change* that love *every day* if I please, and with *that* right neither *you* nor any *law* you can frame have any right to interfere" (23–24, original emphasis). Marriage, obviously, would interfere with that right to free love—hence the relatively low opinion Millay's poems hold about love that lasts any longer than a week or month or, at most, a season.

Yet free love was free in a second sense, not just because by practicing it women could remain free from the prison of marriage but, literally, because it cost nothing. It was, as Floyd Dell put it, one "of those joys that are so cheap, or that cost nothing at all, the joys of comradeship and play and mere childlike fun" (33). Both senses of free love, then, guarantee one's freedom from labor. On the one hand, free love kept women out of marriages, thus keeping them out of "cooking and baby-tending." On the other hand, falling in and out of love also kept one from other sorts of nondomestic labor. As Millay put it in "To Kathleen," "Still must the poet as of old" "Starve, freeze, and fashion verses"—in other words, the poet must fall in love and write hymns to beauty, not marry or take jobs as private secretaries.

All of these bohemian elements—the correlation between poverty and beauty, the aversion to labor, domestic or otherwise—come together in "Recuerdo," one of Millay's most frequently anthologized poems and, for the purposes of my argument, one of the most revealing. The title of the poem is Spanish for "remembrance," as in a "souvenir," and the poem itself fittingly immortalizes an ideal bohemian evening spent doing, seemingly, nothing.

We were very tired, we were very merry—
We had gone back and forth all night on the ferry.
It was bare and bright, and smelled like a stable—
But we looked into a fire, we leaned across a table,
We lay on a hill-top underneath the moon;
And the whistles kept blowing, and the dawn came soon.

We were very tired, we were very merry—
We had gone back and forth all night on the ferry;
And you ate an apple, and I ate a pear,
From a dozen of each we had bought somewhere;
And the sky went wan, and the wind came cold,
And the sun rose dripping a bucketful of gold.

We were very tired, we were very merry,
We had gone back and forth all night on the ferry.
We hailed, "Good morrow, mother!" to a shawl-covered head,
And bought a morning paper, which neither of us read;
And she wept, "God Bless You!" for the apples and pears,
And we gave her all our money but our subway fares.

(1–18)

The poem purportedly commemorates an all-night ferry trip to and from Staten Island that Millay, Floyd Dell, and the poet Arthur Davison Ficke took following the announcement that World War I had ended. (In the poem, Millay collapses those two men into one "you.") Unlike John Reed and other Greenwich Village artists and intellectuals during the moment of 1913, who took ferries across the Hudson to see the strike in Paterson, the Villagers of Millay's poem take the ferry to no particular place, or, rather, take a ferry to and from somewhere to somewhere else for no obvious reason. Without a biographical context, a reader of the poem would not even know where the ferry goes once it leaves Manhattan—or even if it embarked from Manhattan at all. Yet the absence of any location seems to make the point. What matters in the poem is something very much like the Futurist's obsession with movement in and of itself—although, to be sure, a ferry moves considerably more slowly than Fillipo Marinetti's object of obsession, the automobile. Be that as it may, the lack of any fixed destination, as well as other details in the poem, makes the poem more than just a fascination with movement; the poem becomes a parody of purposeful movement itself, in this case the morning commute, one of the reasons for the Staten Island Ferry in the first place, and, implicitly anyway, a rejection of the work those commuters do once they get where they are going.

The morning commute in this poem, for example, takes place at night. Like most commuters, the "we" of the poem are "very tired," but instead of the ordinary listlessness or anomie of workers traveling to work, the "we" of the poem are also "very merry." According to the logic of the poem, "very tired" is not a condition to redress or regret but the very source of merriness. As Nina Miller has pointed out, "[T]he ordering of the phrases implies that 'we were merry' *because* 'we were tired.'" In other words, in a perfectly recursive economy, tiredness produces merriness, which produces more tiredness and on and on, which the repetition of the opening couplet at the outset of each stanza reinforces. "If in the conventional world," Miller adds, "'merriness' produces 'tiredness,' in bohemia merriness is the *effect* of tiredness; the way to a bohemian temperament is constant emotional expenditure" (32).

If to be tired (and merry) is to refuse the call to sleep, so, too, do the ferry-goers refuse other calls to action. The whistles, for example. Whistles blow to announce the imminent arrival or departure of the ferry—and thus instruct passengers to prepare to disembark or embark. Whistles are thus meant to be heard once, at most twice. Yet, as at the end of the first stanza, the speaker observes that the whistles "kept blowing" (6). For the speaker of the poem to hear the whistles repeatedly, the travelers must be indifferent to a schedule. They have nowhere to go. It does not matter if they get there on time—or remain to hear otherwise urgent whistles blow again and again.

Moreover, the poem does not so much conclude with an arrival at an anticipated destination as it implies more traveling, now by subway. Presumably, the speaker and her companion leave themselves enough money to get home, but, as with the ferry ride, a destination is never named, only the means of more traveling (the subway), perhaps even more back-and-forthing. If the speakers do intend to travel home, though, they will only further reverse the direction of most morning commuters, who travel from home to work. The commuters in the poem, though, will travel from work, such as it is, to home.

Earlier in the poem, the travelers will buy "a morning paper" that neither will read. In addition to completing the parody of the morning commute, buying a paper and not reading it is an act of pure waste—not unlike burning a candle at both ends. The act also confirms the poem's complete indifference to the public world of work, commerce, and exchange. In keeping with this indifference to the public world, the public space of the ferry is turned into a perfectly squalid bohemian garret. "It was bare and bright, and smelled like a stable" (3), the speaker notes but—or, rather, and—the speakers pass their time staring into a fire and leaning across a table, acts of intimacy that belie their public setting. Moreover, while the apple and pear the speaker and her companion eat necessarily involve them in a market economy, their vagueness about having bought the fruit "somewhere" (10) suggests how little such details matter. What matters about apples and pears is not their production or distribution but their consumption.

The image that follows, the sky turning wan, returns to the spirit of the opening couplet. Like the "we" of the poem, the sky goes from pallid and weary ("wan") to "very merry" when "the sun rose dripping a bucketful of gold" (12). In other words, the sky was very tired, the sky was very merry. Despite her many insights into the poem, Nina Miller seems to misread this image when she argues that when the sun "rose dripping a bucketful of gold," it suggests something vital about "the speaker's psyche," namely, "an unconscious preoccupation with opulence beneath her willed frugality" (32). Perhaps. But it seems just as likely that the sun rising like a "dripping bucketful of gold" is yet one more example of what Floyd Dell, supposedly a passenger on this ferry ride to nowhere, called "those joys that are so cheap, or that cost nothing at all," that are only open to those who are "very poor" (33).[8] As in other poems from *A Few Figs from Thistles,* beauty costs nothing, but it also costs a lot since one must relinquish everything one has in order to be in a position to experience it. The rising sun is a bucketful of gold only for those who have rid themselves of real gold or the habit of making gold—that is, rid themselves of the habit of working. Only those who do not work during the day can stay up until dawn to watch a brilliant, beautiful sunrise from the bow of a ferry. It is beauty for free only for those who are themselves free from labor. Instead of being paid with real gold, their bucketfuls of gold come in the currency of sunrises.

In any case, the poem is the ideal bohemian idyll, celebrating in three stanzas waste, inutility, beauty, free love, and freedom from labor. It is so ideal, in fact, that even the manifestation of real poverty in the form of a "shawl-covered head" (15) in the final stanza only confirms its idyllic charms. Like the moment of 1913, the poem climaxes with an encounter between bohemia and hardscrabble immigrant poverty—and, despite its outward optimism, ends with equally mixed results. The "mother" (15) who rears her shawl-covered head in the conclusion of the poem does double duty. On the one hand, her reduction to a metonymy—"a shawl-covered head"—places her firmly in the category of tradition, which provides a useful contrast to the ferrygoers' modernity. That she believes in a God with which to bless them underscores this still further. Moreover, and while there is a danger in taking the commonplace greeting "mother" too seriously, it nevertheless further divides dependent immigrant motherhood from the bohemian free lovers. But the immigrant mother serves a final, more important purpose as well. When the bohemian couple makes the shawl-covered head an object of their charity—by giving her the fruit of their nonlabor as well as their money—they effectively win for losing. The "shawl-covered head" (15) pays them back by enabling the ferrygoers to demonstrate their detachment from worldly concerns—rather like buying a newspaper and not reading it does earlier. I will have more to say of this in a moment, but, as Nina Miller is surely right to observe, the "tearful gratitude" of the immigrant woman "only serves to highlight their own transcendence of material need—the difference of their bohemian poverty" (32).

While Miller goes on to focus on what she calls the "resource management" implied by this exchange, I want to focus on all that the ferrygoers give away and not the little that they retain. Or, rather, focus on what they get in return for almost all that they give away. Before doing so, though, it is worth pausing to appreciate the pull that bohemia held in the first decades of the twentieth century, including the challenge it posed to the Protestant and capitalist work ethic.[9] It is also worth pausing to consider how much the bohemian contempt for work shares with earlier traditions, and, for that matter, the problem of what, if anything, to do about poverty.

In *Bohemians: The Glorious Outcasts,* Elizabeth Wilson argues that "the myth of the bohemian represents an imaginary solution to the *problem* of art in industrial Western societies" (3, original emphasis). In medieval society, Wilson argues, somewhat wistfully, "art had been seamlessly integrated into the social institutions of religion"; it "was produced collectively as a craft," and, at least by the seventeenth century, its modes of production, distribution, and consumption were solidly organized around a patronage system. After industrialization, though, all that is solid—including art—melts into air, and "these changed circumstances," as Wilson calls them, "resulted in the construction of a new definition of 'artist' or 'writer'" (17). "Art," she observes, "was becoming just another commodity," and as such "the artist not only had to prostitute his art to the logic of profit, but was expected to entertain an audience, which (or so at least he felt) lacked discrimination" (17). The result, in addition to elevating the previously socialized, craft-oriented artist to the figure of the isolated, Romantic genius, was an artist "set against the bourgeois 'philistine'" (17).

Crucially, however, the figure of the artist, and especially the bohemian artist, came to oppose not just bourgeois taste and the commercial art market but the bourgeoisie and modernity more generally. For "members of the educated classes [who] felt a deep ambivalence" about modernity, Wilson adds, "art gave spiritual meaning to life," and the figure of the bohemian artist, regardless of whether these bourgeois semimalcontents took up that life or not, allowed them to express their ambivalence toward what Max Weber called "the Protestant ethic," the virtues of "thrift, restraint, and the work ethic" that "favoured the development of capitalism" (19). Bohemia, then, represented a powerful imaginary escape from what Weber called the "iron cage" of modern capitalism, which, as he put it, "to-day determine[s] the lives of all individuals who are born into this mechanism, not only those directly concerned with economic acquisition, with irresistible force" (181). "Perhaps," Weber speculated, "it will so determine them until the last ton of fossilized coal is burnt" (181)—or, a bohemian might have added, until people dismiss economic acquisition altogether and devote their lives to beauty, love, and art. That bohemians opposed bourgeois culture as much as they did at least in part explains why they developed into such a beloved myth of bourgeois culture.

Bohemians, then, like the "gypsies" after whom they were named, occupied a "marginal, yet challenging" place in modernity. One of the sharpest challenges they made, as Millay's poetry demonstrates, came against the valorization of work. In their rejection of honest toil and thrift, though, the figure of the bohemian dovetails with a long tradition of thought in the West that vilifies work and the work ethic. As an ancient Greek commentary on the *Iliad* supposedly written by the lyric poet Alcaeus put it, "This I know for certain, that if a man moves gravel, stone not safely workable, he will probably get a sore head" (379). Similar, and even pithier, is the proverb credited to Sappho: "don't move gravel" (159). In *Politics,* Aristotle advanced the notion that "The citizen must not live the life of mechanics or shopkeepers, which is ignoble and inimical to goodness. Nor can those who are to be citizens engage in farming: leisure is a necessity, both for growth in goodness and for the pursuit of political activities" (271). One could go on and on in this vein, but the examples would all confirm what Herodotus first observed about the Greeks—as well as "the Thracians, Scythians, Persians, Lydians, and well-nigh all foreign nations"—in his *Histories,* which is that "men who learn trades and their descendants are held in less regard than other citizens, whilst any who need not work with their hands are considered noble" (159). As for the Romans, "no workshop can have anything liberal about it," Cicero asserted in *De Officiis* (153).

With the arrival of industrialization, these doubts about work (and workers) begin to multiply, and, unlike the examples from antiquity, specifically challenge the approbation of work and the work ethic that characterized the advent and consolidation of industrial capitalism. In *Walden,* Henry David Thoreau documents his attempt to get out from under what Philip Larkin would famously call "the toad work" (1). In a passage that resonates with Millay's "To Kathleen," Thoreau observes, "This spending of the best part of one's life earning money in order to enjoy a questionable liberty during the least valuable part of it reminds me of the Englishman who went to India to make a fortune first, in order that he might return to live the life of a poet. He should have gone up garret at once" (30). As my chapter on Carl Sandburg explores, too, William Morris distinguished between "Useful Work and Useless Toil," as the title of one of his more famous essays has it, seeing, in his survey of life under industrial capitalism, far more of the latter than the former. Around the same time as Morris (the 1880s), Karl Marx's no-good son-in-law, Paul LaFargue, published a pamphlet, "The Right to Be Lazy," which reprimanded workers for "proclaim[ing] as a revolutionary principle the Right to Work" (16). "Shame on the proletarians!" LaFargue scolds (17). They should demand instead, as his title offers, "The Right to Be Lazy."[10] Several decades later, Bertrand Russell's "In Praise of Idleness" made much the same point as LaFargue. Like LaFargue, Russell regretted the "great deal of harm . . . being done in the modern world by the belief in the virtuousness of WORK" and argued instead that "the road to happiness and prosperity lies in an organized diminution of work" (3). "Leisure is essential for civilization," Russell argues, and unlike the ancients, who preserved leisure "for the few," "with modern technique it would be possible to distribute leisure justly without injury to civilization" (5). "The morality of work," Russell observes, by way of contrast, "is the morality of slavery, and the modern world has no need of slavery" (5). Even within the last decade, Tom Hodgekinson's journal *The Idler* and his book, *How to Be Idle,* recycled these critiques of the work ethic for contemporary readers, while Timothy Ferris's gimmicky *The 4-Hour Workweek* (2007) remained on the Advice and How-To best-seller list for months and months.

Again, one can go on for pages citing these sources, and I have left out exponentially more than I include, but, presumably, for anyone who entertains the slightest doubts about industrial or postindustrial capitalism and its regimes of work, these critiques will ring true. If so, then Millay's bohemians, tiring themselves out merrily on ferries to nowhere, will seem like glorious, even enviable outcasts indeed. As Elizabeth Wilson notes, "Even those most committed to the status quo experienced the ennui of the 'iron cage' of modernity, and envied the rebels who seemed to have escaped" (56).

For humanists trained to abhor capitalism, all these bohemian attitudes toward consumption and labor will seem especially compelling. And speaking as someone who once memorized quite a few passages from the "Economy" chapter of Henry David Thoreau's *Walden,* I, too, find the poems heartening. But I nevertheless want to register some misgivings about these critiques, and Thorstein Veblen's *Theory of the Leisure Class* may help to articulate them. In the end, I fear that these bohemian attitudes toward labor and poverty entail rather conventional—and worrisome—attitudes toward workers and the poor.

In his most famous work, Veblen starts from the premise that economists err when they assume that "a struggle for wealth" is "substantially a struggle for subsistence"—that is, that as people and their communities grow wealthier, the better off in that community consume more goods out of a desire "for an increase of the comforts of life" (25).[11] Rather, Veblen argues, "the motive that lies at the root of ownership is emulation" (25)—basically, that the accumulation of wealth does not reflect a desire for more comfort but for more status in a given community; the desire, as he puts it, "to excel everyone else in the accumulation of goods" (32). In other words, it's not what you have that matters but what you have that someone else lacks.

For Veblen, an individual—one of Veblen's "leisure class"—could adopt two strategies to display his greater relative accumulation of wealth: conspicuous consumption and conspicuous leisure. Of conspicuous leisure, Veblen observes, a leisure class—almost by definition—must not engage in any industrial employment or "any effort directed to enhance human life by taking advantage of the non-human environment" (10). In other words, the leisure class cannot make anything useful, nor grow food, nor clean nor prepare what has already been made or grown. Such employments are "drudgery," the occupations of women and the poor, and least likely to bring a leisure class the aura of exploit it requires. Conversely, of course, such labor will bring ignominy to those who must perform it. Such attitudes, he notes, express themselves most forcibly in a "habitual aversion to menial employments" (8) and "abstention from productive work" (36). Therefore, "conspicuous abstention from labour," Veblen writes, "becomes the conventional mark of superior pecuniary achievement and the conventional index of reputability; and conversely, since application to productive labour is a mark of poverty and subjection, it becomes inconsistent with a reputable standing in the community" (38).

Yet a leisure class does not abstain from all labor, only, as Veblen calls it, "useful employment" (40). That is, some occupations are judged to be sufficiently useless, unproductive, or "immaterial" (45) that a self-respecting member of the leisure class could undertake them. Among other things—government, war, sports, and religious observances—these include "quasi-scholarly and quasi-artistic accomplishments and a knowledge of processes and incidents which do not conduce directly to the furtherance of human life" (45). Above all, leisure must involve the "non-productive consumption of time," which one undertakes out of a sense that "productive work" is unworthy, and because the nonproductive consumption of time provides evidence of, as Veblen puts it, a "pecuniary ability to afford a life of leisure" (43). In fact, one way to demonstrate your wealth is to show that you do not have to work to secure it and can instead devote yourself to useless tasks. "The abiding test of good breeding," Veblen offers, "is the requirement of a substantial and patent waste of time" (51).[12]

Veblen's other, better-known leisure class strategy, conspicuous consumption, perhaps requires less explanation. As with conspicuous leisure, conspicuous consumption requires consuming—or, in the case of wives, children, and servants, having others consume on one's behalf—"excellent goods" (food, drink, and clothing but also "immaterial goods" like scholarship and art) in order to demonstrate wealth, which, again, is done in order to generate honor and repute. Conversely, failure to consume excellent goods—to be poor or poorer than others—brings dishonor and ill-repute.

So where do Millay and bohemia figure in all of this? On the surface, bohemia and the voluntarily poor would seem to share little if anything with Veblen's leisure class. Yet, at least in their attitudes toward labor, they may in fact share something important. "Recuerdo," for example, revels in its freedom from productive labor—and, as I will show in a moment, takes pains to distance itself from the conventionally poor and the productive labor of begging. Moreover, poems like "Grown-up" and "Portrait by a Neighbor" suggest that labor, especially domestic labor, is irksome and degrading, and perhaps it is. Nevertheless, bohemia, like a leisure class, requires and maintains a sharp distinction between, as Veblen puts it, "exploit and drudgery," wherein exploit entails the creation of art or the deliberate wasting of time while drudgery involves all other productive labor, including and especially domestic labor. To take an example from Millay's life, being a social secretary is marginally productive, useful anyway, and therefore dishonorable, especially compared to what Veblen would call the "immaterial" and therefore honorable labor of starving and freezing to produce poetry. My point is not that the world needs social secretaries more than it does poets—the former are far more superfluous than the latter—but, rather, to suggest that while bohemia supposedly breaks with the work ethic that drives capitalism, so, too, do other class formations in that economy. Of course, just because something (bohemia) resembles something else (a leisure class) does not make them identical formations. Nevertheless, bohemia does seem to share with a leisure class a "habitual aversion to menial employments," and my concern is that this contempt for menial employments risks, as it does for a leisure class, drifting into contempt for menial employees.

Of course what separates bohemians from a leisure class proper is bohemian poverty, and bohemia, whether as depicted in Millay's poetry or more generally, could not seem to have less to do with conspicuous or honorific consumption or, for that matter, with the desire to excel others in the accumulation of goods. It is quite the opposite, to judge from their garrets and poverty. When Millay orders poets to "starve, freeze," that injunction not only validates the production of art and beauty but also implicitly rejects concerns about status and invidious distinctions between individuals. In bohemia, everyone is equally poor; "*awfully* broke" as Millay wrote Harriet Monroe. Moreover, as Millay's letter to her mother attests, that poverty is not necessarily something to be embarrassed by but, rather, a mark of "independence."

Yet this poverty may also bear with it a sort of contempt. In fact, the political economy of bohemia seems to require not conspicuous consumption but—and here I need to coin a term—conspicuous privation. The point of conspicuous consumption, as Veblen describes it, is not to secure the comforts of life but, rather, to secure honor and status in the eyes of "transient observers." In conspicuous consumption, one earns honor and status by demonstrating how much wealth one has, which one can do by spending that wealth on luxuries. While any spoon will move food from a bowl to your mouth, only a silver, handcrafted spoon—Veblen's famous example—will allow one to waste resources on superfluities and in so doing receive the honor and repute that attaches to conspicuous displays of wealth. Conversely, bohemians must deliberately renounce the accumulation of wealth; they must devote little thought and even fewer resources to their utensils.

In both cases, however, the consumption or privation must be conspicuous—demonstrable. But demonstrable to whom? In the case of conspicuous consumption, a leisure class makes invidious, visible distinctions between itself and the less wealthy. In the case of conspicuous privation, however, bohemians seem to have a different audience in mind. Conspicuous privation allows them to distinguish themselves from a conventional leisure class and its habits of consumption, as well as workers trapped in the iron cage of capitalism, as Weber put it, who work in order to consume. But also, and perhaps equally if not more important, conspicuous privation allows bohemians to distinguish themselves from the poor qua poor, who by definition cannot accumulate excess resources nor indulge in wasting them.

In short, a bohemian could not just be plainly poor, and their particular mode of poverty, oddly enough, may represent their grab for honor and repute. For bohemians, one must choose one's poverty voluntarily—and publicize the fact that it is so chosen. Hence conspicuous privation. If poverty is not voluntarily chosen, then one risks losing one's repute by being associated with the grasping, hoarding, involuntary poor. Conspicuous privation thus solves the problem of how to make what would otherwise seem disreputable—poverty, lack of wealth—reputable. The lines that distinguish bohemians from the conventionally poor are drawn both in their attitude toward accumulating resources *and* in their ability to do so. In other words, the poor would acquire resources if they could; bohemians can but they mustn't.

It follows, then, that conspicuous privation (or voluntary poverty) does not make conventional poverty in and of itself reputable. Just the opposite: it remains as disreputable and regrettable as ever, so much so that one must take care to distinguish oneself from it. Conspicuous privation may also explain why poverty must be treated as lightheartedly as it is in these and other bohemian poems. For poverty to be a burden is to admit that one regrets it, that it is unavoidable. Bohemian poverty, though, must publicize the fact that one fails to accumulate resources not because it is difficult or impossible but because one chooses not to. But it must be a choice.

Consider again the final stanza of "Recuerdo." As in "First Fig," what matters throughout this stanza is one's capacity to waste resources, whether by not earning them in the first place (conspicuous leisure), spending them frivolously (buying a newspaper and not reading it), or giving them away to people whose desperate need for them will highlight one's own indifference to them (conspicuous privation). The real poor, however, cannot indulge in these displays of waste. Indeed, what distinguishes the ferrygoers from the "shawl-covered head" is the latter's desire for resources, as shown in her weeping gratitude for the cast-off fruit and money. The ferrygoers, meanwhile, aspire to be just as poor as the shawl-covered head, but they must also demonstrate that they have no desire for resources, that their food and money, like their time, are easily expendable. By neither working nor begging, they demonstrate their commitment to art, beauty, and frivolity—callings considerably higher and more independent than the irksome labor of poverty.

Crucially, poetry thus plays a key role in making privation conspicuous. Poverty without poetry—or poverty without publicity—is just plain old poverty. In addition to offering one a useless but reputable task to devote oneself to, poetry, and art more generally, thus serves as a way to ensure bohemian status, publicize poverty, and therefore stabilize the invidious distinctions between the voluntarily and involuntarily poor.

My point is not that bohemians are hypocritical or insincerely poor or even that they are merely playing at poverty but, rather, that their attitudes toward the poor and working class are considerably more complicated—and more hierarchical—than their poverty, geography, and anticapitalist politics might suggest. In addition to the theoretical approach offered by Veblen, there is considerable historical evidence for this proposition. In its attitude toward workers and the conventionally poor, it may be that Millay's poetry does not depart from so much as give voice to the mutual hostility and contempt between bohemians and the mostly Italian immigrant poor who also called Greenwich Village home. In her foundational work of urban sociology, *Greenwich Village, 1920–1930* (1935), Caroline Ware documented the enmity between "Villagers" and "local people," as they somewhat dismissively referred to each other. Through interviews, statistics, and direct observation, Ware described a "gulf [that] was and had always been wide and virtually unbridgeable" between "'local people' and 'Villagers.'"[13]

To be sure, one reason for this "unbridgeable gulf" is race or, more accurately, ethnicity in that bohemian Greenwich Village is mostly white while Italian Greenwich Village hovered in some racial and ethnic no-man's land of not quite white enough. But these questions of race and ethnicity seem to confirm the larger point about class, which is that the immigrant poor provided a convenient and picturesque backdrop against which bohemians could announce their contempt for the bourgeoisie at the same time as they confirm their difference from the conventionally—and ethnically or racially marked—poor.

Many of the intellectuals, artists, and professionals who first colonized Greenwich Village prior to World War I seem to have thought of the Italians and their neighborhood as "picturesque"—a view that comes through to some extent in Millay's "Recuerdo." More and more, however, the Villagers came to view the local Italians with a combination of contempt and disgust. For their part, the local Italians matched the Villagers' contempt, but it is clear that they also viewed Villagers with dismay and not a little envy.

All told, Villagers and local Italians were strictly divided along lines of education, wealth, and attitudes about sex and family. In terms of education, Villagers, for whom "literature, art, and music constituted their principal vocation or avocation," as Ware puts it, tended to see the not infrequently illiterate Italians as "ignorant" (106). And while the local people assumed "that all Villagers, except the out-and-out bohemians, were 'wealthy,' the Villagers, in turn, equally undiscriminatingly, assumed that all the local people were poor" (108). To be sure, many of the local Italians were poor, well over half if Ware's estimates are correct (36), and the slums they lived in were for real—and far less romantic than the imagined attic garrets of bohemian poems. Even so, Villagers tended to blame the Italians themselves—rather than their poverty—for those slums. "The Villagers," Ware writes, "condemned their neighbors wholesale for living in squalor—i.e., in the only houses which the incomes of most of the local families could encompass" (108). Not surprisingly, given poems like "Recuerdo" and the bohemian ethos more generally, Villagers and Italians diverged most in their attitude toward money. As Ware writes, "Almost without exception, the various types of Villagers agreed in setting a relatively low social value on money for its own sake" (110). "For the local people," Ware notes, "in direct and violent contrast, the money drive was the great outstanding drive of life" (110). In sum, as Ware describes their mutual suspicion, "To the Villagers the Italians were 'grasping'—to the Italians the Villagers were 'crazy' "(111).

Much the same could be said about their differing attitudes toward sex and the family. On the one hand, the local Italians were dismayed by Villagers, especially women, who practiced free love or remained single. "The local people," Ware reports, "regarded the Villagers as a menace to the decency of their neighborhood and to the morals of their children" (112). And while Villagers gave less thought to the sexual lives of their Italian neighbors, they were nevertheless dismayed by the numerous offspring of that sexual life. While the local Italians viewed Villagers as "living only for themselves," Villagers believed the Italians' attitude toward child rearing was "evidence of ignorance and of economic irresponsibility" (112–13). Village bohemians economic irresponsibility, but not all economic irresponsibility, was alike. In particular, breeding indiscriminately may have taken irresponsibility too far. Villagers believed that "child-bearing was a matter of choice," and, thus, "parents had no business having children unless they could afford to rear them, and that the low-class, poor people like their neighbors had no business having a large family" (112). In short, as Ware writes, "The Villagers condemned their tenement neighbors because they had 'too many children' " (112). Villagers complained endlessly about the local neighborhood children: their play, their noise, their vandalism. One correspondent for the *New York Times,* Helen Bullitt Lowry, reported mournfully to the rest of the city in a June 13, 1920, article, "Then there are the Italian children." "When you're inside Greenwich Village looking out," Lowry observed in sketching the view from her Greenwich Village apartment, "you see a lot of children, because they are looking in." "They climb up on the window sill," she added, "as cats used to do in the Murray Hill district" (66).

To leave Millay for a moment, this bundle of attitudes that Villagers took toward local Italians surfaces in John Reed's *The Day in Bohemia* (1913), his self-published, mock-epic "Account of the Life led by Geniuses in Manhattan's *QUARTIER LATIN*." In the "Forty-two Washington Square" section of the poem, Reed sketched the scene he and his Village roommates could see from their "Third Floor, Hall-room and Black, Elysian bower."

The high sun-parlor, looking South and East,
Whence we discerned a million cats at least
Commuting in the tenement back-yards,
And hove at them innumerable shards.
There spawn the overworked and underpaid
Mute thousands;—packed in buildings badly made,—
In stinking squalor penned,—and overflowing
On sagging fire-escapes. Such to-and-froing
From room to room we spied on! Such a shrill
Cursing between brass earringed women, still
Venomous, Italian! Love-making and hate;
Laughter, white rage, a passionate debate;
A drunken workman beating up his wife;
Mafia and Camorra,—yelling strife!
The wail of children,—dull, monotonous,
Unceasing,—and a liquid, tremulous
High tenor, singing, somewhere out of sight
"Santa Lucia!" in the troubled night.

(15–16).

Reed's sketch comprises roughly equal parts mythologizing of, sympathizing with, and contempt for the Lower East Side Italians with whom Villagers shared tenements and streets. On the one hand, the Italians are "overworked and underpaid" (15); on the other hand, the "overworked and underpaid" "spawn," breeding uncontrollably and, given their confined space, unwisely. Like the "million cats at least," such spawning has produced "Mute thousands," as well as, less mutely, the "wail of children,—dull, monotonous, / Unceasing" (16). Even the Mafia makes its dutiful appearance—as does a "High tenor" singing "'Santa Lucia!' in the troubled night" (16).

While Reed does activate rather hoary stereotypes of Lower East Side life, the more relevant point is how Villagers like Reed used their perception of the local Italian poor to construct and test their own bohemian identity. One can see this more clearly in Millay's "Macdougal Street," one of the few poems in *A*

Few Figs from Thistles that makes plain its Village setting, and one that offers a similar portrait of Lower East Side Italian immigrants. Titled after the street that runs through the heart of Greenwich Village (it turns into Washington Square West), the poem has a somewhat disorienting structure. A speaker lies awake at night recalling an aborted romantic encounter earlier in the day. In addition to being a slightly unconventional love lyric, the poem makes plain what some Villagers thought about their Italian neighbors.

As I went walking up and down to take the evening air,
(Sweet to meet upon the street, why must I be so shy?)
I saw him lay his hand upon her torn black hair;
("Little dirty Latin child, let the lady by!")

The women squatting on the stoops were slovenly and fat,
(Lay me out in organdie, lay me out in lawn!)
And everywhere I stepped there was a baby or a cat;
(Lord God in Heaven, will it never be dawn?)

The fruit-carts and clam-carts were ribald as a fair,
(Pink nets and wet shells trodden under heel)
She had haggled from the fruit-man of his rotting ware;
(I shall never get to sleep, the way I feel!)

He walked like a king through the filth and the clutter,
(Sweet to meet upon the street, why did you glance me by?)
But he caught the quaint Italian quip she flung him from the gutter;
(What can there be to cry about that I should lie and cry?)

He laid his darling hand upon her little black head,
(I wish I were a ragged child with ear-rings in my ears!)
And he said she was a baggage to have said what she had said;
(Truly I shall be ill unless I stop these tears!)

(1–24)

From the outset, the speaker of the poem adopts a language of leisure ("to take the evening air" [1]), and as the poem continues that line between leisure—unrequited love and its torturous recollection—and the "grasping" immigrant poor is strictly maintained. That that line might dissolve is the poem's chief concern. More than love, though, the poem is about class—or, rather, where love (and sex) intersect with class. The class distinctions are established at the outset by the division the man makes between "Little dirty Latin" children and ladies (4) and the assumption that the former must make way for the latter. Later, too, the man will walk "like a king through the filth and clutter" (13), extending the antiquated language of aristocracy ("lady") spoken earlier. And while describing the child as "Latin" rather than "Italian" may attempt to make the scene seem picturesque, that attempt fails horribly in the two stanzas that follow when the speaker describes, with nose held, the decidedly unpicturesque degradations of the slum. The speaker complains that the "women squatting on the stoops were slovenly and fat" (5), and "everywhere I stepped there was a baby or a cat," echoing Lowry's *New York Times* article (or Reed's poem), which likened innumerable children to innumerable cats. These visions of the slum even cause the speaker to trade bohemian antimaterialism for conspicuous consumption, or, at least, the desire for consumption. "Lay me out in organdie, lay me out in lawn" (6) the speaker exclaims on seeing the local women "squatting upon the stoops" (5). Both organdie and lawn are sheer, crisp fabrics used for dresses and blouses, and the pun on "lawn" suggests that the speaker also wants to dress not in the slums but the suburbs, "in lawn" (6). Perhaps, the line seems to suggest, one should not volunteer for poverty quite so quickly.

Ironically, though, given her desire for organdie and lawn, the speaker seems to object the most to the sordid operations of capitalism and bartering. Unlike in "Recuerdo," the speaker here must confront the market, at least in the form of the distribution of goods, and the workings of the market are not a pretty sight. Fruit, as "Recuerdo" describes it, is to be bought "somewhere," not, as it is here, by "dirty Latin" children who haggle "from the fruit-man his rotting wares." Equally repulsive, "The fruit-carts and clam-carts" are "ribald as a fair" (9), and by "ribald" the speaker seems to mean something more like coarse and vulgar than an earthy, liberated treatment of sex, although both definitions are clearly meant, especially as the sexual elements of the poem emerge in the later stanzas. In any case, the neighborhood makes plain the operations of the market, which, if Ware's interviews with Villagers and bohemians are right, was what one came to Greenwich Village to avoid.

In general, then, the speaker seems less charmed by the picturesque scene and more repulsed at intrusive capitalism and intrusive bodies, whether the fat and slovenly women or their brood of children and cats. Curiously, these stanzas and their complaints match, almost word for word, the description Villagers commonly gave to Ware about how Italians affected the "attractiveness" of the

Village. As with their objection to slums, bohemian tolerance for squalor apparently had its limits. Villagers, Ware reports,

> objected to dirt and smell—to the dregs of the wine barrel on the sidewalk; the banana peels hurled out of the window, the odor of garlic; the litter habitually tossed on the streets where, in warm weather, people lived out-of-doors and where there was rarely a rubbish can; grimy children whose play space was the gutter. Almost more strongly, they disliked the noise—the children at play, the scolding of the women, the vendors peddling their wares—all the human sounds characteristic of congested living. The adults were too gregarious, always congregating on the stoops and chattering. The children were frightful. (114)

Nor is this attitude especially surprising given the principles of free love. If Millay and other Villagers celebrated free love for keeping women out of the prison of cooking and baby tending, the local Italian immigrants provided them with something very near its opposite: women tied to their homes and their streets by too many children and babies.

In the poem, though, the slum children are "frightful" for more than just the noise they make or the space they take up; rather, they—or, in this case, this one dirty Latin child—is frightful because she erotically interferes with the "lady" and her "king." Either because of her shyness, his shyness, or his indifference to her, the man neglects ("glance me by" [14]) the speaker of the poem, even though, as the speaker relates at the outset, it is "Sweet to meet upon the street" (2). (She will quickly change her mind—at least about the street.) Worse yet, while the man does not directly address the speaker of the poem, he does casually touch the dirty Latin child on her hair. (Why her hair must be "torn" [3] remains a mystery, except perhaps to highlight its lack of care.) The speaker never reveals what the "quaint Italian quip" (15) is that the Latin child "flung him from the gutter" (15) in response to his order, but it violates the assumed class hierarchy of the encounter, and, even if it is not explicitly sexual, it is treated so by the speaker of the poem and even by the man himself. Indeed, his response to her quip—to call her "a baggage" (23)—is strange but ultimately revealing. One definition of *baggage* is "a saucy, impudent, lively girl," which would seem most apt here, but that definition shares its etymology with a second definition, in which *baggage* means "prostitute" or "whore."[14] Just as earlier the dirty Latin child trades her money for fruit, to call her a "baggage" suggests that she is trading her precocious sexuality for money or, at least, notice.

The upshot of all this is that the poem paints the immigrant poor as something like the evil twin of the bohemian. If bohemia eschews the market and labor, both work and the labor of pregnancy, the immigrant poor seem to embrace all three. It is the market itself—its haggling and rotting wares, as well as its teeming fecundity—that ruins the beauty of the scene and the lovers' rendezvous. Worse still, assuming that the "king" (13) of Macdougal Street is not in fact Italian, the possibilities of cross-class and cross-ethnic sexuality are interrupting the possibilities of free but temporary love.[15] In other words, the immigrant poor threaten to out free love the free love bohemians, even if (or as) the presence of all those babies and children recall—in addition to their fat and slovenly mothers—the risk that free love may result in a condition that is anything but free. In sum, nothing could be further from "beauty," further from free love, than the "filth and clutter" (13) of the slum and its teeming inhabitants.

Despite their differences, though, or perhaps because of them, the speaker nevertheless "wishes" that she, too, were a "baggage," "were a ragged child with ear-rings in my ears!" (22), presumably so that she and not the dirty Latin child would be the object of the man's affection and flirting. As the chapter on T. S. Eliot suggests, one can see this wistful identification with the immigrant poor and working class quite frequently in modern poetry. And in fact this poem's "pink nets and wet shells trodden under heel" (10) does share something with Eliot's "Prufrock," both in that poem's "restless nights in one night cheap hotels / And sawdust restaurants with oyster shells" *and* in its desire to assume slum sexuality in order to escape bourgeois propriety or, in the case of both poems, the speakers' shyness and hesitancy. By contrast, the dirty Latin child suffers from no such inhibitions, nor does the man, who seems far freer with a "baggage" Italian child than he does with his class and possibly ethnic equal, the speaker of the poem. Unlike Eliot's "Prufrock," though, "Macdougal Street" reveals what that cross-class sexuality might have looked like to the well-to-do women excluded from it, those left in the kitchen talking of Michelangelo, as it were. They, too, apparently, could envy the supposedly "uncivilized" licentiousness of the immigrant poor. The speaker of the poem both resents the Italian girl for her liberality and at the same time desires to be her because that liberality opens erotic possibilities with members of her opposite sex but identical class.

In terms of the relation between bohemia and the poor and working class, I would argue that "Macdougal Street" is both representative and an aberration. It is an aberration in that bohemians—in contrast to Villagers—seem to have approached the local Italians as picturesque rather than, as here, repulsive. Similarly, the poem almost certainly overdraws the lines that divided bohemians from the immigrant, ethnic poor. In Millay's case, for example, she would heroically come to the defense of Sacco and Vanzetti, the two Italian-born laborers and anarchists who in 1927 were convicted and eventually executed for the murder of two payroll clerks. Far from any repulsion from their ethnicity, Millay seems to have come to their defense out of concern that prejudice against their ethnicity and immigrant status, as well as their politics, might have led to injustice. In short, one should not associate Millay with the speaker of the poem nor the speaker of the poem with all of bohemian Greenwich Village.[16]

In other words, it may be that "Macdougal Street" is not entirely fair to bohemians' attitudes toward the immigrant poor. Far more representative is a poem like "Recuerdo," wherein the immigrant poor provide a convenient and picturesque backdrop against which bohemians can announce their contempt for the bourgeoisie at the same time as they confirm their difference from the conventionally poor. Nevertheless, "Macdougal Street" is representative in that it reveals what otherwise remains latent in the political economy of bohemia—that is, its foundation in an occasional disgust for but at the least a need to keep a measured distance from the immigrant and involuntarily poor.

If that is the case, then such a conclusion casts doubt on Laurence Buell's defense of voluntary poverty against critics, especially Gavin Jones, who view the politics of voluntary poverty with considerable skepticism. Buell acknowledges that writers like Thoreau, who dramatize "the positive virtues of antimaterialism," cannot avoid suppressing or marginalizing "the hard realities of poverty." Nevertheless, Buell defends "the downwardly mobile for conscience sake" because those who "set a high value on personal limits and restraints" would be less "likely to tolerate uncritically a culture of capitalist exploitation" (663). In other words, those who recognize the virtues of simplicity are more likely to object to the vices of exploitation. Buell calls this formulation "obvious," and there is doubtless something to it. Still, Millay's poetry and bohemia more generally demonstrate that the relation between voluntary poverty and attitudes toward involuntary poverty are far more complicated than obvious. Briefly, as in Jack Reed's ferry ride to Paterson in 1913, it seemed like the two groups might join forces. Yet as a collection like *A Few Figs from Thistles* suggests, a real, occasionally even insurmountable divide existed—and perhaps exists—between the voluntarily poor and the involuntarily poor, despite their mutual poverty.

CHAPTER 5

"Yes, sir!": Langston Hughes, Claude McKay, and the Poetics of Serving

Claude McKay became famous because he waited tables, Langston Hughes because he bused them. By this I do not mean that these writers became famous *as* busboys or waiters instead of as poets. (Has there ever been a famous busboy?) Nor do I mean that Hughes and McKay supported themselves as busboys and waiters while they wrote the poems that would make them famous—although that is true enough. Rather, I mean that both of these poets' first brush with poetic fame came while serving and clearing food—and as a more or less direct result of doing so.

McKay's example is better known. In the spring and summer of 1919, he was a dining-car waiter on the Pennsylvania Railroad line. Moving from one hub to the next on the railroad's northeastern and midwestern routes, McKay witnessed many of the twenty-odd racial riots that consumed cities throughout the country during the Red Summer of 1919. As he remembered in his autobiography, *A Long Way from Home:*

> Our Negro newspapers were morbid, full of details of clashes between colored and white, murderous shootings and hangings. Traveling from city to city and unable to gauge the attitude and temper of each one, we Negro railroad men were nervous. We were less light-hearted. We did not separate from one another gaily to spend ourselves in speakeasies and gambling joints. We stuck together, some of us armed, going from railroad station to railroad station to our quarters. We stayed in our quarters all through the dreary ominous nights, for we never knew what was going to happen. (29–30)

These "clashes between colored and white"—and McKay's anxious proximity to them—would inspire his signature poem, "If We Must Die," which urged its readers to "like men . . . face the murderous, cowardly pack, / Pressed to the wall, dying, but fighting back!" (13–14). The ambiguous "we" of that poem, which famously goes racially unmarked, ultimately refers to African Americans in general, especially African American men. More locally, though, given the context, the "we" of the poem is also the "we" of Negro railroad men, who, as McKay tells it, and as the poem instructed other African Americans to do, "stuck together" and went "armed" during this tumultuous period. More than just a potentially original "we" of the poem, though, Negro railroad men also constituted its first "you," that is, McKay's first audience. As McKay writes, "It was the only poem I ever read to the members of my [dining-car] crew," who, after hearing it, McKay reports, were "all agitated" (31–32). Printed in Max and Crystal Eastman's *The Liberator* in July 1919 and then in Negro newspapers across the country, the poem quickly found a much larger audience. Nevertheless, and despite its later, wider fame, the inaugural poem of the New Negro was at least in part written by, for, and about waiters—and only because its author happened to be a waiter.

Strangely enough, Langston Hughes's public debut as a poet would also emerge from waiting—or, in his case, setting and clearing—tables. His "first publicity break," as Hughes put it in his autobiography, *The Big Sea* (1940), came during the winter of 1925 while working as a busboy at the Wardman Park Hotel in Washington, DC. In addition to various Washington politicos, the dining room at the Wardman also attracted celebrated poets, including, in late November, Vachel Lindsay, then at the height of his chanting fame, who stayed at the hotel while in town to give a reading. Hughes, eager to drum up publicity for his forthcoming first book of poems, *The Weary Blues* (1926), waited for his chance to engage the prominent poet. Spying Lindsay eating dinner alone, Hughes delivered three of his poems—"Jazzonia," "Negro Dancers," and "The Weary Blues"—to Lindsay's table, hastily telling him,"I liked his poems and that these were poems of mine" (169). (In doing so, Hughes took quite a chance. As he later told a reporter, "I couldn't talk to him or wait. Busboys aren't allowed to talk to the guests" ["Langston Hughes, 'Busboy Poet'"].) Later that evening, unbeknownst to Hughes, Lindsay read all three poems to his Washington audience and announced that he, in Hughes's words, "had discovered a Negro bus boy poet!" (169).

Hughes discovered Lindsay's discovery of him in a newspaper the next morning, and when he arrived at the Wardman, he writes, "[T]he reporters were already waiting for me" (169). Appearing first in the Washington papers, the story was soon picked up by the Associated Press, and, as Arnold Rampersad tells it, "[T]he item about the Negro busboy poet and Vachel Lindsay made its way into newspapers from Maine to Florida" (117). Hughes had to leave for Harlem shortly thereafter, but when he returned to Washington in early December he milked the incident for all its worth. He arranged to have his picture taken in full busboy regalia, with a tray of dishes on his shoulder, and enlisted Josephine Tighe Williams, a journalist for the *Washington Star,* to write the story up for the newspapers (Rampersad 119).

The story of Langston Hughes, busboy poet, is truly bizarre, not least because it counted as news at all. But poets were not thought to be busboys, nor were busboys thought to write poetry. (It was a shock, Hughes observed, first experienced by the Washington black bourgeoisie, who could not believe that the man whose poems appeared in *Crisis* and *Opportunity* made his living bussing tables.) In any case, because of the publicity, Hughes became a curiosity. He reports in *The Big Sea* that the "incident was certainly good for my poetic career, but it was not good for my job, because from then on, very often the head waiter would call me to come and stand before some table whose curious guests wished to see what a Negro bus boy poet looked like" (170). However annoying or degrading, the publicity did help Hughes sell books. In fact, it gave reporters and reviewers a ready-made lead. "Langston Hughes, 'Busboy Poet' and Writer of 'Weary Blues,'" the *Pittsburgh Courier* reported in a long-winded and metaphorically promiscuous headline, "Tells How a Long Shot First Gave Him Chance to Scale Height." As a result, one of the most famous volumes of Harlem Renaissance poetry, Hughes's *The Weary Blues,* was to many a novelty act: the cries from the heart of a Negro busboy poet.

But my opening claim—that McKay's and Hughes's reputations as poets came in part from serving and clearing food—is true in another sense that neither of these anecdotes quite capture, namely, that both poets would write poems *about* serving and clearing food. McKay's "If We Must Die," for example, first appeared in *The Liberator* alongside six other poems, among them "A Capitalist at Dinner," which explores the irony that such an unremarkable specimen—a fat, bald-headed capitalist—should command so much labor and service. As I explore below, McKay would write many more poems about serving.

Or consider the poems Hughes did and did not offer Lindsay. "Jazzonia" celebrates "a Harlem cabaret" where "Six long-headed jazzers play" and "A dancing girl whose eyes are bold / Lifts high a dress of silken gold" (3–7). Similarly, the speaker in "Negro Dancers" brags that "Me an' ma baby's / Got two mo' ways / Two mo' ways to do de buck" (1–3), leaving "white folks" to "laugh" and "pray" at their audacity (11–12). "The Weary Blues," of course, is the would-be elegy of a Negro bluesman "play[ing] / Down on Lenox Avenue" (3–4), for which Hughes had earlier won first place in the 1925 literary contest sponsored by *Opportunity.* One can imagine why Hughes would choose these poems to deliver to Lindsay's table. He had a stake in publicizing the poems that would soon appear in his collection, as each of these would, and Hughes no doubt calculated that the poems he chose would appeal to Lindsay's racialist poetic tastes.[1] Nevertheless, and however shrewd his choices, Hughes could have offered Lindsay any one of several poems—"Porter," "Brass Spittoons," "Song to a Negro Wash-woman"—about serving the likes of Lindsay and other whites that Hughes was then writing.[2] To be sure, showing Lindsay these poems would not have advanced Hughes's poetic career—nor, in all likelihood, his busboy career. Rather, showing Lindsay these service poems would have called attention to the emotions and hierarchies of serving, which, as several Hughes and McKay poems on the subject make clear, is just what one is forbidden to do. In other words, Lindsay would not have likely read Hughes's service poems at his reading, claimed to have discovered a Negro busboy poet, or engineered the first big break of this then largely unknown poet. Hughes would have been lucky to keep his job.

Unlike Hughes at Lindsey's table at the Wardman Park Hotel or Lindsay at his reading later that night, this chapter takes up the poems Hughes and McKay wrote about service. Like the other poets in this book, Hughes and McKay both illustrate the principle that, in terms of content, modern poetry often enough meant poetry about workers and the poor. Nor was this without controversy. Indeed, debates within the New Negro intelligentsia about poetry tended to replicate earlier debates between the genteel poets and the moderns, with some editors and critics championing the rarified work of Countee Cullen and Jessie Fauset while others, fewer in number, took up the working-class literature of writers like Hughes and McKay. One sees this debate most pointedly in the reception given Langston Hughes's 1926 collection *Fine Clothes to the Jews.* Some critics, like Margaret Larkin, praised Hughes for giving "voice to the philosophy of men of the people," in contrast to other young African American poets who "want to write about nicer emotions than those of the prize fighter" (52). Others, however, were not so kind. As one reviewer cuttingly—it was not a compliment—put it, Hughes was the "poet low-rate of Harlem" ("Review of *Fine Clothes to the Jew,* by Langston Hughes"). Or consider the headlines that greeted Hughes's collection in a couple of the most prominent black newspapers in the country, each of which picked up on the garbage and cesspool metaphors that modernists and critics of modernism alike found so useful. The *Pittsburgh Courier* wrote, "LANGSTON HUGHES BOOK OF POEMS TRASH," while New York's *Amsterdam News* offered "LANGSTON HUGHES—SEWER DWELLER" (*The Big Sea* 203).[3]

Despite this reception, neither McKay nor Hughes was alone in making his living serving—or in writing poems about the way he made his living. As William J. Maxwell points out, "a greater percentage of the [Harlem] renaissance's talented tenth than is usually acknowledged . . . earned [their] rent money working at some of the unskilled labor and service jobs that then occupied around seven out of ten Harlem men" (38).[4] With the exception of Maxwell, however, this body of service literature has attracted little attention.[5] Moreover, that so many of the leading lights of Harlem's renaissance, including its two most famous poets, either served, wrote about serving, or both makes the critical silence on this body of literature all the more curious.

In any case, a careful study of these service poems is long overdue, and so in what follows I survey the poetics of serving, how, to put it as plainly as possible, Hughes and McKay represent service labor. Taken as a whole, I argue that the poems Hughes and McKay wrote about service labor constitutes what Ann Cvetkovich calls "an archive of feelings" (7). Although it was rarely mentioned in various textbooks of the late nineteenth and early twentieth centuries, for those subject to it, serving, as McKay and Hughes both suggest, constituted a serious labor problem. For both poets, serving seems to demand as much emotional as it does physical labor, although the physical labor, as many of these poems' references to tiredness and weariness suggest, is not to be underestimated. Even so, it is the emotional labor that proves most damaging. For Hughes and McKay, serving entails the regulation and management of emotions, the suppressing of one's most urgent feelings—of anger, resentment, bitterness—beneath a show of outward servility. This management of emotions, however, had potentially dire consequences for the server's pride and autonomy, especially when the racial dynamics of serving bore all too close a resemblance to the racial hierarchy of slavery. In addition to describing its emotional costs, though, Hughes and McKay also explore the various strategies—indulging fantasies of revolution, cultivating reveries of quitting, finding solace in religion, and, most controversially, dancing in cabarets—that workers deploy in order to ease the constant emotional regulation and management compelled by service work.

If the Harlem Renaissance poetry of service work has not attracted much scholarly attention, one of the strategies—jazz and cabaret life—that Hughes and McKay depict service workers drawing on in order to manage its emotional degradations decidedly has. Since at least the publication of Houston J. Baker's influential *Blues, Ideology, and Afro-American Literature* (1984), a growing body of scholarship has made the blues and, equally, jazz the Rosetta stones for decoding African American literature and culture.[6] And to be sure, both poets, though Hughes much more than McKay, offer the cabaret scene and its jazz soundtrack as possibly restoring a basic integrity to a self divided by the labor of its day jobs. More important, however, both poets frequently doubt and in the final analysis reject the redemptive promises and possibilities of cabarets and jazz. Even so, in entertaining the possibility that jazz and the cabaret could be cures for what ails service workers, Hughes and McKay join other modernist poets (and some contemporary critics) in the romantic anticapitalist belief that the past—in this case, jazz and its rhythmic echo of African wholeness—could redeem the fallen present and, in particular, alleviate the urgent labor problems of that capitalist present. As I argue below, however, that belief requires some suspension of disbelief about the effect that noneconomic and cultural solutions can have on essentially economic and material problems. To their credit, McKay and Hughes both manage to check this faith in the utopian, anticapitalist possibilities of the cabaret scene. Scholars of these poets, however, and scholars more generally, have not always joined McKay and Hughes in their doubts, and in closing I argue why they might, as both poets ultimately did, approach the jazz and cabaret backdrop of the Harlem Renaissance with more skepticism than they have thus far.

In his biography of McKay, Wayne Cooper places "A Capitalist at Dinner" in "the best cartoon tradition of the period" because of its somewhat clichéd portrait of "the capitalist" as a "disgustingly fat man with a pimply bald head" (102). McKay in fact could have borrowed his capitalist from a *Liberator* cartoon, where, as mentioned earlier, the poem appeared in July 1919, but too much focus on the cartoonlike capitalist obscures the real subject of the poem, the servants of this capitalist in particular and the servants of capital more generally. I start with the poem because it offers two of the principal themes of Harlem Renaissance service poetry: the unworthiness of those served and the turbulent emotions inspired by serving them. The poem also offers one of the principal imaginative strategies McKay invents in response to that situation, namely, revolution. Indeed, as the poem gradually reveals, the possibility of revolution profoundly alters the interplay of emotions between servers and served.

As the poem opens, McKay portrays the capitalist as the ultimate consumer of goods and men.

An ugly figure, heavy, overfed,
Settles uneasily into a chair,
Nervously he mops his pimply pink bald head,
Frowns at the fawning waiter standing near.
The entire service tries its best to please
This overpampered piece of broken-health,
Who sits there thoughtless, querulous, obese
Wrapped in his sordid visions of vast wealth.
Great God! if creatures like this money-fool,
Who hold the service of mankind so cheap,
Over the people must forever rule,
Driving them at their will like helpless sheep—
Then let proud mothers cease from giving birth;
Let human beings perish from the earth.

(1–14)

While the opening lines of the poem admittedly sketch a rather cartoonish capitalist, certain details redeem the whole from being merely cartoonish. In a poem about serving capitalists and capital, for example, it is a delightful irony to have this capitalist "mop" his own "pimply pink bald head" (3)—a gesture of self-service that anticipates the conclusion of the poem when the capitalist will find himself servantless. By the sixth line of the poem, however, the capitalist seems less like a cartoon and more like a helpless baby: hairless, not just coddled or pampered but "overpampered," and, most revoltingly, swaddled ("wrapped") in "visions of vast wealth" that are "sordid" (8), filthy. In other words, having eaten of his vast wealth, McKay's capitalist-baby now wallows in the filth of it, completely dependent on others, in this case, his waiter-parents.

However, if being served infantilizes, McKay suggests, then serving dehumanizes. By the fifth line of the poem the capitalist is no longer waited on by a "waiter" or even "servants" but "service," their being reduced to mere action. They devolve into instruments of "pleas[ing]" (5). Reduced to instruments of serving, the servants soon lose their humanity altogether. They are cringing, flattering, "fawning" (4) waiters, an adjective said as often of dogs as humans. Later in the poem, the entire "service of mankind" (10) is driven like "helpless sheep" (12), a simile that plays on the sense of servants as "help," only now, as sheep, driven and isolated, lacking solidarity, they are, as it were, the helpless help.

These animal motifs recall the "we" of "If We Must Die," who must not die "like hogs" (1) but "like men" (14), and as with the dining-car origins of that poem, "A Capitalist at Dinner" struggles to assert the dignity and humanity of servers. To that end, the closing sestet functions as both curse and prophecy. It begins, unlike most accounts of industrial capitalism, by casting service—and not production—as the essential capitalist relation. (Workers, even production workers, serve capitalists.) Having established the centrality of service to capitalism, the poem then imagines the destruction of both. It calls down a curse from God: if "creatures like this money-fool" (9) are allowed to rule over humanity, then "proud mothers" should "cease from giving birth" (13). In other words, if humans continue to allow themselves to be reduced to instruments and animals, they have surrendered their right to existence. They have befouled God's creation, humans. Yet the curse is also prophecy, its vengeance directed as much at capitalists as at the workers qua servants who allow themselves to be treated like sheep. If "proud mothers cease from giving birth" and "human beings vanish from the earth" (14), no one will survive to serve or be driven like sheep, leaving the capitalist at dinner and capitalists more generally, as at the beginning of the poem, to do their own mopping, as well as every other form of labor. By asserting control over birth, humanity—specifically here women—also asserts its control over labor. The poem thus ends in a fantasy of a worldwide general strike, withholding reproductive labor and consequently productive and service labor as well. The capitalist as dependent child would, in the poem's fantasy, be undone by men and women refusing to make more men and women. If capitalism is, as Marx characterized it, a definite social relation between men, then removing the men, the poem suggests, ought to solve the problem of capitalism and capitalists (*Capital* 165).[7]

In addition to sounding a revolutionary call to arms, the poem reveals a great deal about the relation between emotion and class. As in other Harlem Renaissance service poems, "A Capitalist at Dinner" tracks a series of emotional responses to serving: from disgust (at the capitalist's bloated, consumptive body) to betrayal (due to the capitalist's ingratitude) to anger and ultimately vengeance. Moreover, the poem implies, as more recent theorists of emotions have argued, that emotions are not strictly biological or neurological phenomena but very much social ones. That is, emotions are not only hardwired responses to external stimuli but derive, at least in part, from relations among individuals, particularly as those relations are ruled by status.

As Aristotle, one of the first and still one of the most influential theorists of emotions, recognized, individuals have different social standings and, thus, more or fewer claims to having certain emotions and more or fewer claims to having those emotions recognized and honored. Consider indignation, one of Aristotle's canonical emotions and one very much alive in McKay's poem. Aristotle defined *indignation* as "being pained at undeserved good fortune" and "those who [undeservedly] fare well" (*On Rhetoric* 155). In short, one feels indignation when good things happen to bad or undeserving people. Moreover, Aristotle argued that "people [who] are prone to feel indignant" are those who have themselves acquired things virtuously. So too those who "are ambitious and desirous of certain things and, especially, are ambitious in regard to things that others are really unworthy of" (158). If so, it follows, Aristotle observes, that "the servile, the worthless, and the unambitious are not given to indignation; for there is nothing of which they regard themselves as worthy" (158). In other words, the servile cannot experience indignation, Aristotle holds, since they lack the social standing, the worthiness, needed to begrudge another's undeserved good fortune. If I deserve nothing, am worthy of nothing, I lack the grounds to resent others' success, however ill-deserved.

By contrast, McKay's "A Capitalist at Dinner" assumes that those lower down the social hierarchy also experience emotions and, moreover, that those emotions matter. That assumption may seem unremarkable today, but as the example of Aristotle or the attitude of a capitalist at dinner suggests, it was not always so.[8] As late as 1875, for example, William Smith, editor of a hotel trade journal, wrote that "everything goes to prove that the colored men are the best" waiters because "[t]hey are naturally subordinates, and where white men take the position only as a matter of convenience and aspire to higher positions . . . the height of the negro's ambitions is a rush of good-feeling patrons" (qtd. in Cocks 89). As McKay's poem makes clear, however, the servile are servile in name only, and they have much grander, even revolutionary, ambitions than to please white patrons. Unlike Aristotle's servants or Smith's fantasies, that is, they are not only capable of feeling indignant but *are* in fact indignant at the good things that have befallen this very bad, this very undeserving capitalist.

A similar process informs other emotions in the poem—that is, McKay appropriates for workers emotions usually reserved for the elite. For example, the speaker of the poem is angered because the capitalist, sticking with Aristotle's canonical emotions for a moment, belittles the waiters. Belittling, for Aristotle, occurs when someone acts from the assumption that someone or something is worthless. The capitalist, for example, belittles the waiters because, as Aristotle puts it, "[P]eople have contempt for those things they think of no account" (125). "Lack of sensitivity," he observes, "is a sign of belittling," since "what we care about does not escape our notice" (129)—and, conversely, what we do not care about does. Except for his frown at the outset of the poem, the capitalist for the most part does not notice the waiters. As Aristotle has it, he is not sensitive to them because they do not matter. (Or, as McKay describes the capitalist's attitude toward his waiters, he "hold[s] the service of mankind so cheap" [10].) He does so because, as Aristotle writes, "[P]eople think they are entitled to be treated with respect by those inferior in birth, in power, in virtue, and generally in whatever they themselves have much of" (126). In other words, the capitalist feels his power entitles him to the waiters' service. As such, he cannot imagine that his belittling of them—his holding them of no account—will anger them. Only those who have been unjustifiably slighted can feel anger—and the capitalist has treated the waiters with as much consideration as he imagines they might justifiably expect, that is, none at all.

The speaker of the poem, of course, undermines all these assumptions. In response to the capitalist's belittling, the speaker is angered because he believes himself the equal—if not the better—of the capitalist. Indeed, the speaker of the poem grows angriest because the capitalist does not acknowledge the gift of solicitude that the waiter and other laborers have bestowed on the capitalist, who, to reiterate, "hold[s] the service of mankind so cheap" (10). The capitalist assumes that because of his elevated social position, the gift of service is a well-deserved tribute to his power and does not need to be acknowledged, whereas the speaker assumes that both capitalist and waiter are more or less equals. To overlook the service one performs for the other, then, implies—infuriatingly—that the two are not equals.

Yet what this poem and others demonstrate is not that McKay democratizes emotions—that is, shows that even inferiors and the servile have them—or that there is no such thing as a truly servile person. Rather, it shows that McKay, like Marx, believed that all value comes from labor, and this belief enables him to keep intact the hierarchy (and emotional hierarchy) between superior and inferior but reverse the class positions of that hierarchy. As Aristotle noted, anger at being belittled is directed "against those who have no right to do it, and inferiors have no right to belittle" (129). Against expectations, the speaker of the poem agrees, but he implies that it is the dependent capitalist who is inferior, physically inferior but also economically inferior. His wealth, as his person, is dependent on others. His value comes from labor. As a result, inferior capitalists have no right to belittle superior waiters, the real creators of value and wealth. In McKay's poem, then, informed as it is by a labor theory of value, it is workers who "are vexed by their sense of their [ignored] superiority," as Aristotle describes the causes of anger. It is waiters who "think they are entitled to be treated with respect" by capitalists since capitalists are inferior in virtue and only temporarily and contingently superior in power. Slighted, belittled, and held in unjustified contempt, these wronged workers express their anger in visions of revolution, a general reproductive strike, taking pleasure, as Aristotle argued the angered did, in "the hope of getting retaliation" and "the image"—a helpless capitalist—"that occurs" (125).

In two related poems included in his 1922 collection *Harlem Shadows,* McKay focuses less on the dialectical synthesis of serving—that is, as in "A Capitalist at Dinner," the play between emotion and revolution—and more on the competing emotions of servers and served, as well as the strategies servers develop in order to manage the usually losing outcome of that battle. The first poem, "Alfonso, Dressing to Wait at Table," was, as William J. Maxwell notes, "inspired by McKay's employment as a sonnet-writing headwaiter on the Pennsylvania Railroad" (*Complete Poems* 316). The opening stanzas of the poem describe "Alfonso," "a handsome bronze-hued lad" and how "down in the glory hole"—that is, a small, enclosed space—Alfonso "sings an olden song of wine and clinking glasses" (6). The song "thrills" his fellow waiters' "swaying forms and steals [their] hearts with joy" (9–10). From this climax of joy, however, the closing stanza of the poem predicts a devastating low.

But, O Alfonso! wherefore do you sing
Dream-songs of carefree men and ancient places?
Soon we shall be beset by clamouring
Of hungry and importunate palefaces.
(11–14)

The theme of the poem seems simple enough. McKay's antiquated diction ("wherefore," the several kennings) and the poem's balladlike quatrains may struggle to keep the spirit of Alfonso's song alive, but it cannot survive the demands of waiting tables. Unlike work songs, which are traditionally invented and sung in order to accompany and set the pace of labor, Alfonso's song cannot follow these waiters to their work.[9] It is not just that the song does not fit the mood—waiters are not "carefree men," just the opposite, and a dining car is not an "ancient place"—but that the song would be drowned out by other voices, by the "clamouring" noise of "hungry and importunate palefaces" (14). McKay's martial metaphor ("beset") and racialized lingo ("palefaces") cast waiters as the colonized, conquered by the desires and demands of encroaching diners. What these dining-car colonizers colonize, though, is not continents—although they do take over the dining car—but emotions. In the first stanza of the poem, Alfonso's moods "are storms that frighten and make glad" (3); by the conclusion of the poem, those moods—and the songs they inspire—have been quelled. The gaiety of dream songs and the impulsive moods of waiters are displaced by the exigencies of serving and the insistent emotions of those served.

A similar contest between the emotions of server and served informs a second poem from *Harlem Shadows*, "On the Road." In the opening octet, emotion functions as a contagion, with the waiters taking on the "ugly mood" of their patrons.

Roar of the rushing train fearfully rocking,
Impatient people jammed in line for food,
The rasping noise of cars together knocking,
And worried waiters, some in ugly mood,
Crowding into the choking pantry hole
To call out dishes for each angry glutton
Exasperated grown beyond control,
From waiting for his soup or fish or mutton.
(1–8)

In Walt Whitman's "Out of the Cradle Endlessly Rocking," which McKay's first line invokes, the title phrase becomes the occasion for the poet to "sing" "a reminiscence" (22) of the formation and coherence of his bardic self. In McKay's version, however, the "Roar" (1) of the rushing train, its fearful rocking, "The rasping noise of cars together knocking" (3)—the whole scene in fact—conspire against such poetic recollections or subject formations. As McKay represents it, waiting tables has its own time, that of a suspended and chaotic present, as well as its own subject, a subordinate one. The opening octet is a fragment, built out of gerunds ("rushing," "rocking," "knocking," "crowding," "choking") that subordinate subjects ("worried waiters" [4] but also "impatient people" [2]) to the onrushing and chaotic scene. Instead of emotions recollected in tranquility, McKay offers a vision of emotions—"exasperated," "angry gluttons" and the "ugly mood" of "worried waiters"—forming in pandemonium.

In the sestet that closes the poem, subjects (and predicates) return, even though entirely different fates await waiters and travelers.

At last the station's reached, the engine stops;
For bags and wraps the red-caps circle round;
From off the step the passenger lightly hops,
And seeks his cab or tram-car homeward bound;
The waiters pass out weary, listless, glum,
To spend their tips on harlots, cards, and rum.
(9–14)

After the jamming, crowding, and chaos of the octet, the poem begins to slow down. The train stops, the engine ceases, and while the porters ("red-caps"), engaged in their own service labor, may "circle round" (10), they leave the passengers at the stable center of the action. And after the confined quarters and ugly mood of the first half of the poem, the passengers' "lightly hop[ping]" (11) off the train comes as a liberation. The waiters, in contrast, "pass out" (13): a pun that describes their exit from the train, the result of what (drinking) they will leave the train to do, and what, in effect, their labor on the train has driven them to. Unlike passengers, they are not bound for home but "harlots, cards, and rum" (14). Presumably, as is evident in several McKay and Hughes poems with similar themes, these "worried waiters" pursue "harlots, cards, and rum" because they allow for the relief of the "ugly mood" generated by serving. Instead of serving, waiters will now, at least in the case of harlots and rum, be served. Their "tips"—the wages of serving—will become others' wages ("harlots'" and perhaps other waiters', depending on where they do their drinking and gambling). The poem thus builds and at the same time mourns an economy of service: the labor of one set of workers (dining-car waiters) becomes the occasion for the physical (and emotional) labor of others, harlots and barkeeps. What *these* workers spend their tips on one can only guess, but only the passengers, who set off this economy in the first place, get to exit fully from it.

Elsewhere in *Harlem Shadows*, however, McKay represents waiters and service workers developing other strategies than the somewhat class-defeating "harlots, cards, and rum" to handle the emotional repercussions of their work. In one such poem, taken up below, workers simply quit or stay away. Imagining a less final strategy, another poem, "The Tired Worker," celebrates the end of the workday.

O whisper, O my soul! The afternoon
Is waning into evening, whisper soft!
Peace, O my rebel heart! for soon the moon
From out its misty veil will swing aloft!
Be patient, weary body, soon the night
Will wrap thee gently in her sable sheet,
And with a leaden sigh thou wilt invite
To rest thy tired hands and aching feet.
The wretched day was theirs, the night is mine;
Come tender sleep, and fold me to thy breast.
But what steals out the gray clouds like red wine?
O dawn! O dreaded dawn! O let me rest
Weary my veins, my brain, my life! Have pity!
No! Once again the harsh, ugly city.

(1–14)

In the opening quatrain, the end of the workday signals relief from workaday passions. One can imagine the poem being uttered by any of the speakers of the previous poems about service. Instead of, presumably, shouting, the tired worker's soul is invited to whisper, and the "rebel heart" (3)—the same one that imagines vengeance against capitalists, palefaces, and angry gluttons—is calmed. The night, as the speaker observes, "is mine"—after the "wretched day" that "was theirs" (9). In addition to offering physical rest, the night also promises the return of unity and identity. In contrast to the revolutionary militancy and fervor of a poem like "A Capitalist at Dinner," the tired worker here assumes a childlike dependence on the night: it will serve him, "wrap [him] gently in her sable sheet" (6)—instead of, as in "Alfonso," being beset by the whiter sheet of "importunate palefaces"—and "invite" the worker "To rest [his] tired hands and aching feet" (8).

Of course the poem does not end here. Dawn returns like a slave driver, pushing the speaker back to the "harsh, ugly city" (14) of work. A companion poem, "French Leave," which, as William Maxwell glosses the title, refers to "a Francophobic eighteenth-century British term for taking leave without notice or permission" (337), offers a similar yet more permanent strategy for dealing with this pitiless call to work.

No servile little fear shall daunt my will
This morning. I have courage steeled to say

I will be lazy, conqueringly still.
I will not lose the hours in toil this day.

The roaring world without, careless of souls,
Shall leave me to my placid dream of rest,
My four walls shield me from its shouting ghouls,
And all its hates have fled my quiet breast.

And I will loll here resting, wide awake,
Dead to the world of work, the world of love,
I laze contented just for dreaming's sake
With not the slightest urge to think or move.

How tired unto death, how tired I was!
Now for a day I put my burdens by,
And like a child amidst the meadow grass
Under the southern sun, I languid lie

And feel the bed about me kindly deep,
My strength ooze gently from my hollow bones,
My worried brain drift aimlessly to sleep
Like softening to a song of tuneful tones.

(1–20)

The heavily alliterated last line of the poem may ruin the effect, but the poem, especially its charged first line, reveals much about the emotions and consolations of serving. The "servile little fear" of the opening line lacks a referent—fear of what, one asks. Presumably, the speaker fears the consequences of not showing up for work: being fired, going jobless, and all—lack of money for rent and food—that goes with this condition. In other words, the speaker's servile fear keeps him enslaved to work. Nevertheless, the poem—especially when read next to other service poems—seems to speak much more specifically about escaping service labor and its "servile" fears. In place of the "driving" of "A Capitalist at Dinner" or the chaos of movement and voices in "On the Road"—or the conquering diners of "Alfonso, Dressing to Wait at Table"—the speaker in "French Leave" vows to be "conqueringly still" (3). In the third stanza, he resolves to neither "think [nor] move" (12), thereby conquering those, namely, the clamorous diners, who would urge him to do their bidding or adopt their emotions. Similarly evocative of these service poems, in the second stanza the "shouting ghouls" (7) bear a striking resemblance to the "importunate pale-faces" of "Alfonso," as do the "hates" (8) that here flee the speaker's breast in contrast to the "rebel heart" of "Tired Worker," which must be appeased. In short, in addition to the myriad other strategies—fantasies of revolution, "harlots, cards, and rum," rest—that McKay describes waiters deploying to survive the physical but essentially emotional ordeal of their labor, "French Leave" offers a final, decisive one of staying away altogether. Although at best a temporary solution to the problem, and not the collective staying away of a general strike, as imagined in "A Capitalist at Dinner," the poem does offer a radically scaled down and ideologically similar version of that fantasy.

I take up Langston Hughes and his service poetry in the section that follows, but one of his poems, "Elevator Boy," is especially relevant to this discussion of managing the emotions of service labor by simply staying away. Instead of tired workers generally or tired waiters specifically, Hughes focuses on tired elevator operators, although he notes the similarity of their working conditions to those of other service workers.

I got a job now
Runnin' an elevator
In the Dennison Hotel in Jersey.
Job ain't no good though.
No money around.
    Jobs are just chances
    Like everything else.
    Maybe a little luck now,
    Maybe not.
    Maybe a good job sometimes:
    Step out o' the barrel, boy.
Two new suits an'
A woman to sleep with.
    Maybe no luck for a long time.
    Only the elevators
    Goin' up an' down,
    Up an' down,
    Or somebody else's shoes
    To shine,
    Or greasy pots in a dirty kitchen.

I been runnin' this
Elevator too long.
Guess I'll quit now.
(1–23)

As both Hughes and McKay represent them, service jobs do not for the most part require special training or skills, just deference and a capacity to manage chaos, which makes workers for these jobs (as their employers know) for the most part interchangeable. But the unskilled nature of the work also makes the jobs more or less interchangeable too. "Jobs are just chances," Hughes's elevator boy observes, "Like anything else" (7), and the rewards (or lack thereof) for such work—money, "Two new suits an' / A woman to sleep with" (12–13)—are more a matter of luck than skill or ambition.[10] As such, workers, in lieu of other strategies, could, like McKay's tired workers, simply stay away. If a service job grows tiresome, in most economic climates an identical one is easily available. "Guess I'll quit now" (23), Hughes's speaker concludes, and the casualness of the sentiment reveals how little is at stake in the decision—yet how important the always available strategy of quitting was to making service work manageable.

Thus far, I have focused on the poetry of various service jobs—waiting tables, bussing tables, running elevators, shining shoes—and the strategies (revolution, "harlots, cards, and rum," leisure, and quitting) that McKay (and, briefly, Hughes) describes workers taking in response to this labor. Throughout, I have referred to the emotional work of service labor and suggested that these poems constitute an emotional archive of serving. But the emotional aspects of service labor require a far more deliberate look. McKay's frequently anthologized poem "The Harlem Dancer" is a good place to start. Though perhaps more glamorous than the other service work taken up thus far, cabaret dancing, as McKay sketches it, involves just as much emotional labor as waiting tables.

Applauding youths laughed with young prostitutes
And watched her perfect, half-clothed body sway:
Her voice was like the sound of blended flutes
Blown by black players upon a picnic day.
She sang and danced on gracefully and calm,
The light gauze hanging loose about her form;
To me she seemed a proudly-swaying palm

Grown lovelier for passing through a storm.
Upon her swarthy neck black shiny curls
Luxuriant fell; and tossing coins in praise,
The wine-flushed, bold-eyed boys, and even the girls,
Devoured her shape with eager, passionate gaze;
But looking at her falsely-smiling face,
I knew her self was not in that strange place.

(1–14)

While much can be made of the Harlem dancer's body and its consumption ("Devoured" [12]) by "Applauding youths" and "young prostitutes" (1), the poem is also a drama of emotions. Even the dancer's body, which is what the people paid for, is nevertheless engaged in eliciting emotions. As McKay describes it, the job description of a Harlem dancer requires using her body and voice to inspire a consumptive desire in her audience. In other words, she must cultivate their lust, and an audience pays for the cultivation of their emotions at least as much as for a glimpse of her body. (The two are, of course, related.) Thus the material—her body, her voice—is used to bring about an emotion, arousal. The final focus of the poem, however, is not on the audience or even the Harlem dancer's body but on her self, her absence or presence in the scene. "But looking at her falsely-smiling face," the speaker concludes, "I knew her self was not in that strange place" (13–14), and what seems to make the place "strange" is not just the behavior of the audience but the place's estranging effects on the self, where one is a stranger to oneself and one's emotions. By making her smile when she would rather not—when she is anything but happy—the job and the place divide actual from expressed emotion and thus internal from external selves.

As it happens, falsely smiling faces and estranging places also inspired Arlie Hochschild's neglected but powerful study of flight attendants, *The Managed Heart: Commercialization of Human Feeling* (1984)—a study that helps to show what might be at stake emotionally in Harlem Renaissance poems of service. As Hochschild defines it, drawing on Charles Darwin and other theorists of emotion (William James, Erving Goffman), an emotion is a "bodily orientation to an imaginary act" (28). By "imaginary act," Hochschild means, following Darwin, that emotion is a "protoaction," "what occurs instead of or before an action" (219). Thus anger, for example, is "the preact or prelude to killing," and emotion, more generally, "is our experience of the body ready for an imaginary action" (220). As such, she notes, an emotion "has a signal function: it warns us of where we stand vis-à-vis outer or inner events" (28). Yet emotions are not a purely biological phenomenon. Social factors—who, as Aristotle noted, has the right to be insulted by whom—partly determine emotions. Moreover, individuals are not wholly subject to their emotions but intervene to manage them. Through various degrees of acting, individuals regulate their emotions according to rules about which feelings are appropriate to given social situations. If someone you secretly hate dies, for example, you do not express your exhilaration to his widow at his funeral—such emotions, however sincere, would not be fitting.

The problem, however, is when that capacity to manage emotions is "transmuted" (119), as Hochschild puts it, from a purely private or social act into a market or commodified one. The result, she argues, based on her study of flight attendants, is a radical estrangement from one's emotions and thus a radical estrangement from one's self.

Compare, as Hochschild does, the labor of a factory worker and a flight attendant. For a factory worker, output is measured in strictly material ways: how many widgets one produces or contributes to producing. As such, factory work requires mostly physical labor. While perhaps damaged as a result of his body being turned into an instrument of labor or from being alienated from the commodities he produces, a worker's emotions do not strictly or necessarily enter into the production of goods. If emotions did factor into production, workers could not so easily lose their jobs to automation. In factories, the input (labor) and output (product) are largely material. As Hochschild points out, drawing on an example from Marx, "loving or hating wallpaper is not a part of producing wallpaper" (5).[11]

In contrast, Hochschild asks, and it is a question that applies to dining-car waiters, porters, and Harlem dancers as well, how do we measure the output—and the labor—of a flight attendant? The flight attendant produces not goods but services, a service documented, in this case, in terms of emotions: satisfied passengers. "In processing people," Hochschild writes, "the product is a state of mind" (6). A flight attendant produces this state of mind—this emotion—in others by managing and deploying her own emotions: smiling, appearing solicitous, flirting, and absorbing abuse without becoming angry (or revealing anger). "This [emotional] labor," Hochschild observes, "requires one to induce or suppress feeling in order to sustain the outward countenance that produces the proper state of mind in others—in this case, the sense of being cared for in a convivial and safe place" (7). In other words, unlike factory workers, flight attendants—and other service workers who deal mainly in states of minds and states of bodies—must enlist and regulate their own emotions in order to produce the appropriate countenance in themselves and thus the appropriate emotions in others. "The [airline] company," Hochschild notes, "lays claim not simply to [a flight attendant's] physical motions—how she handles food trays—but to her emotional actions and the way that they show in the ease of a smile" (7–8). For Hochschild, however, this emotional labor poses a real, almost existential risk to those who undertake it, namely, that in manipulating or managing one's emotions for others' benefit and still others' profit, one becomes radically estranged from the self. "Beneath the difference between physical and emotional labor," she argues, "there lies a similarity in the possible cost of doing the work: the worker can become estranged or alienated from an aspect of self—either the body or the margins of the soul—that is *used* to do the work" (7, her emphasis).[12]

In the case of McKay's Harlem dancer, as I have noted, her performance enlists both body ("her perfect, half-clothed body" [2]) and emotions (a "falsely-smiling face" [13]) in order to produce a state of mind (lust, desire) in her audience. That the Harlem dancer has turned both body and emotions into an instrument and thus a commodity is evident, of course, from the "coins" that are tossed her way "in praise" (10). Yet even without these coins one would know that the dancer is working, is managing both body and mind, since the speaker of the poem claims to perceive a true self behind "her falsely-smiling face." As Hochschild points out, "[I]n order to survive in their jobs, [workers] must mentally detach themselves—the factory worker from his own body and physical labor; the flight attendant from her own feelings and emotional labor" (17). In the case of the Harlem dancer, she has detached herself from both body and emotion: the smiling face is a false one; it belies the supposedly true face beneath.

As opposed to her alienated laboring body and emotions, the poem idealizes the natural and spontaneous, which is figured as things black or African. Her voice is like "blended flutes / Blown by black players upon a picnic day" (3–4); later she is a "a proudly-swaying palm / Grown lovelier for passing through a storm" (7–8), and later still "black shiny curls" luxuriantly fall down her "swarthy neck" (9–10). ("Swarthy" comes from *swart,* "black.") Here, as in so many other McKay and Harlem Renaissance poems—"Outcast" perhaps most famously—Africa functions as the source of an original authenticity and intact identity in contrast to Western alienation from body and emotion.[13]

As many of McKay's and Hughes's poems suggest, though, absent an African supplement, service labor devolves into the merely alienating. Consider Hughes's poem "Porter," which articulates the divisions—between physical and emotional labor, between internal and external selves—that inform so many Harlem Renaissance service poems.

I must say
Yes, sir,
To you all the time.
Yes, sir!
Yes, sir!
All my days
Climbing up a great big mountain
Of yes, sirs!

Rich old white man
Owns the world.
Gimme yo' shoes
To Shine.

Yes, sir!

(1–13)

On the one hand, the poem's title—"Porter"—describes the physical labor that characterizes the work. (*Porter* derives from a Latin verb, *portare,* "to carry.") And, indeed, near the end of the poem, the porter will carry and shine the rich old white man's shoes. Yet in the first stanza, and then again in the last, the labor that the speaker must perform is not physical but emotional. Specifically, he must "say / Yes, sir" (1–2) all his days. While this may not seem taxing, it in fact requires fairly constant emotional management. In recent centuries *sir* has become a general term of respect, but its etymology—it is the shortened form of *sire,* "man of rank, lord"—recalls its deeply inegalitarian origins. In other words, part (and the most onerous part, it would seem) of the porter's labor is to abase himself, to recognize the authority and superiority of others when—as in "A Capitalist at Dinner"—the other may have no special claim to that honor. In addition to fetching and carrying things, then, this porter must accomplish the Sisyphean task of fetching and carrying himself "up a great big mountain / Of yes, sirs!" (7–8). In which case, the actual physical labor—shining shoes—is not primarily what porters do; rather, at least from their perspective, and perhaps even the patron's, it is the material embodiment of the emotional service they provide, namely, deference. In the course of this labor, they, like the

Harlem dancer, must manage their emotions and thus run the risk of losing their true selves in that strange place of service. That the service resembles the hierarchy of slavery only adds insult to its emotional injury.

In many ways, of course, these falsely smiling face poems rearticulate the problem of African American doubleness—whether W. E. B. Du Bois's double consciousness or "the mask that grins and lies" of Paul Laurence Dunbar's hypercanonical "We Wear the Mask" (1895). An inner state—in Dunbar's poem, "tears and sighs" (7)—is belied by a carefully cultivated superficial state, again, in Dunbar's case, smiling (10) or singing (12). In contrast to Dunbar's general statement of divided African American selves, though, McKay's and Hughes's poems of service reveal how that division is expressed in, exacerbated by, and perhaps even born from labor. The poems thus lend force to Stuart Hall's assertion that race is the modality in which class is lived—although the poems show how that logic can be reversed as well (341). The hierarchies and inequalities of race are also very much lived through the hierarchies and inequalities of class and service labor.

In one of the most celebrated service poems of the Harlem Renaissance, Hughes's "Brass Spittoons," first published in *New Masses* in 1926 and later included in his 1927 collection *Fine Clothes to the Jews,* the poet explores one of the strategies workers develop to mend these divisions. Despite its relative fame (it appears in a number of anthologies, unlike most of the poems I have discussed) and all the scholarship on Hughes in recent years, the poem has attracted remarkably little attention. That is curious given the ambiguity behind its seeming simplicity, which would seem to compel commentary. The poem starts with a summons to work, turning the poem, as in so many Hughes poems, from a monologue into an implied dialogue—this time between boss or patron and worker.

Clean the spittoons, boy.
    Detroit,
    Chicago,
    Atlantic City,
    Palm Beach.
Clean the spittoons.
The steam in hotel kitchens,
And the smoke in hotel lobbies,
And the slime in hotel spittoons:
Part of my life.

Hey, boy!
A nickel,
A dime,
A dollar,
Two dollars a day.
Hey, boy!
A nickel,
A dime,
A dollar,
Two dollars
Buys shoes for the baby.
House rent to pay.
Gin on Saturday,
Church on Sunday.
My God!
Babies and gin and church
and women and Sunday
all mixed up with dimes and
dollars and clean spittoons
and house rent to pay.
Hey, boy!
A bright bowl of brass is beautiful to the Lord.
Bright polished brass like the cymbals
Of King David's dancers,
Like the wine cups of Solomon.
Hey, boy!
A clean spittoon on the altar of the Lord.
A clean bright spittoon all newly polished,—
At least I can offer that.
Come 'ere, boy!

(1–40)

The recitation of cities in the opening lines of the poem ties the working conditions of porters and spittoon cleaners to, broadly speaking, hotel life—that is, the need to create homes away from home for businessmen ("Detroit / Chicago" [2–3]) or vacationers ("Atlantic City / Palm Beach" [4–5]).[14] In the lines that follow, the speaker is obscured by the various waste products of that life: steam from washing dishes, smoke from cigars, and slime from men spitting tobacco. These form, the speaker asserts, "Part of my life" (10), and from that point forward the poem becomes less concerned with the totality of relations between travelers and workers than with the totality—or seeming totality—of relations among parts of a worker's life. As in McKay's "On the Road," Hughes constructs an economy of service. The speaker's tips ("A nickel, / A dime, / A dollar" [12–14]) add up to his daily wages, which pay for the other parts of his life: "Babies and gin and church / and women and Sunday" (26–27). Yet these parts are "all mixed up," as though they do not logically belong together, an effect, perhaps, of the irony that his daily subjection at work, where he is infantilized as "boy," underwrites the remainder of his adult life of fatherhood, leisure, and worship.[15]

Just as the speaker is most overwhelmed with how mixed up his life is, though, the poem takes a religious turn that leaves its final meaning somewhat unsettled. It is not clear, for example, how sincerely one should take the poem's proclamations that "A bright bowl of brass is beautiful to the Lord" (32) and "At least I can offer that" (39). It is not even clear who paints cleaning spittoons in a religious radiance. In line 31, for example, who calls out, "Hey, boy!"? The indented line—and absence of quotation marks—suggest that the worker is adopting the persona of those who would hail him as "Hey, boy!" If so, does he continue to speak in their voice in the next line, ventriloquizing them, as it were? Or has he switched to his own voice? In other words, does he sincerely believe that a bright bowl of brass is beautiful to the Lord, or is this merely what he has been told, what, perhaps, his boss or tobacco chewers would like him to believe? The answers to these questions matter because whether implanted there or native to him, unlike Hughes's poem "Elevator Boy," in which service jobs are largely meaningless and interchangeable, the speaker here seems to believe that cleaning spittoons is meaningful work, a calling, even—as in the penultimate line of the poem where he decides "At least I can offer that" (39). However degraded and submissive his work may seem, he implies, it is still necessary labor, and more than that, labor that produces beauty, a beauty that supposedly pleases the Lord.

Yet that reading seems to be belied by the fact that the speaker does not only offer his "bright bowl of brass" to the Lord but, in this world, to white travelers who, far from treasuring his tribute, as the Lord might, will soon and casually befoul it. At this point in the poem, then, Hughes may invite readers to doubt the justifications the speaker invents—or has had invented for him—to make his labor more meaningful or less degraded than it actually is. In that case, some parts of his life, especially church, are indeed "all mixed up with" the other parts, including his labor. These parts may confuse his perception of the other parts—that is, what gets said in church on Sunday may influence how the speaker thinks about work on Monday. In other words, to put it as a Marxist might, the speaker may be falsely conscious of the actual value and meaning of his labor, perceiving his degraded and degrading labor (remember he is cleaning up other people's spit) through an ennobling lens of religion, even martyrdom. If that is the effect Hughes is after, then the final lines of the poem become especially charged. In the penultimate gesture of the poem, a "clean bright spittoon" (38)—the speaker's offering—is deposited "on the altar of the Lord" (37). However, altars—as Abraham's son Isaac nearly discovers—are also sacrificial places. In which case, the speaker is more like Isaac than he might know. Just as Isaac, accompanying his father to the altar, naively wonders, "[W]here is the lamb for a burnt offering?" (*New Oxford Annotated Bible,* Genesis 22:7)—he is in for a big surprise—so, too, may the speaker of the poem, in carrying his offering to the Lord, be the lamb ultimately sacrificed to the Lord. If so, the final command of the poem, when the "boy" is again summoned, is suddenly made much more sinister. The summons to "clean the spittoons" is also a summons to death, just as the speaker routinely sacrifices his self, his emotions, and his labor to the other parts of his life. As in McKay's "A Capitalist at Dinner," service work is here represented as a repeated tribute to some higher power, whether God or patron. As in that poem, too, the gift goes unappreciated. Instead of resorting to anger, though, the speaker of "Brass Spittoon" responds by making his work sacred.

To be sure, "Brass Spittoons" ends ambiguously, and far from an aberration, many Hughes's poems about labor during this period end in ambiguity or outright silence. These silences and ambiguities perhaps owe to the tight political corner Hughes had painted himself into in the 1920s. Having left behind a youthful enthusiasm for socialism and Bolshevism but years away from his Communist internationalism of the 1930s, Hughes in the mid-to-late 1920s is perhaps best described—as several critics, including Onwuchekwa Jemie and Anthony Dawahare have—as a literary black nationalist, albeit one with a particular interest in the black working class.[16] While those politics enabled him to pay tribute to the oppressed lives and defiant culture of working-class blacks, they frequently left him with few ways to talk about exploitation per se or to resolve the deepest contradictions of workers' lives—hence the ambiguity or silence.[17] An early poem like "Johannesburg Mines," for example, published in *The Messenger* in 1925, is deliberately silent before the fact of exploitation.

> *In the Johannesburg mines*
> *There are 240,000*
> *Native Africans working.*
> *What kind of poem*
> *Would you*
> *Make out of that?*
> *240,000 natives*
> *Working in the*
> *Johannesburg mines.*
>
> (1–9)

To the rhetorical question Hughes poses—what kind of poem would you make out of that?—the answer is merely a reassertion of the fact. To be sure, it is a reassertion of the fact with a difference. As Rebecca Walkowitz observes, a poem *is* made out of this fact. "The last three lines," she writes, "at once reiterate the staggering, stuttering fact and 'make' it poetic by reshaping the first three into two rough tetrameters (the second line is divided over the last two lines). The reiteration suggests that the poem cannot be made, while the reshaping makes it" (508). In addition to altering the meter, the "poem" of the last three lines also shuffles the syntax of the opening fact. In the first iteration, the sentence begins with "In the Johannesburg mines"; in the reiteration, the sentence begins with "240,000 natives," thus shifting the emphasis from workplace to the workers themselves. Part of making a poem out of this fact, Hughes suggests, if one can be made out of it, would involve, perhaps as a gesture of Atlantic triangle, Pan-African solidarity, giving priority to the 240,000 natives as opposed to where or for whom they work.

But finding the poem within the avowedly nonpoetic may involve more cleverly reading than Hughes intends. It is at least as likely that Hughes does not want his readers to make a poem out of the fact and that the altered syntax merely offers another, differently worded attempt to grasp and convey the incomprehensible but profound fact. That reading is supported by a similar silence in another Hughes poem about exploited labor from roughly the same period, "A Song to a Negro Wash-woman" (1925). In the opening stanza, repeated as the final stanza, the speaker invokes the "wash-woman" of the title.

Her arms, "elbow-deep in white suds," leave her "Soul washed clean" just as the clothes are "washed clean" (2–4). "I have many songs to sing you," the speaker tells her, "Could I but find the words" (5–6). His inability to invent words or songs is echoed, as the poem continues, by his confusion in apprehending the washwoman's comings and goings. "Was it four o'clock or six o'clock on a winter afternoon," the speaker asks in the next stanza, "I saw you wringing out the last shirt in Miss White / Lady's kitchen?" (7–8). But this confession of confusion is momentary, for soon the speaker knows her comings and goings exactly, vividly recalling her "one spring morning on Vermont street with a bundle in your arms going to wash clothes" (11) and again "in a New York subway train in the late afternoon coming home from washing clothes" (12). These sightings add up, in the speaker's mind, to a perfect knowledge, and the poem concludes with a paean to her work, one that is nevertheless punctuated by another confession of silence.

> *Yes, I know you, wash-woman.*
> *I know how you send your children to school, and high-school and even college.*
> *I know how you work and help your man when times are hard.*
> *I know how you build your house up from the wash-tub and call it home.*
> *And I know how you raise your churches from white suds for the service of the Holy God.*
>
> *And I've seen you singing, wash-woman. Out in the back-yard garden under the apple trees, singing, hanging white clothes on long lines in the sun-shine.*
> *And I've seen you in church a Sunday morning singing, praising your Jesus, because some day you're going to sit on the right hand of the Son of God and forget you ever were a wash-woman. And the aching back and the bundles of clothes will be unremembered then.*
> *Yes, I've seen you singing.*
>
> *And for you,*
> *O singing wash-woman,*
> *For you, singing little brown woman,*
> *Singing strong black woman,*
> *Singing tall yellow woman,*
> *Arms deep in white suds,*

Soul clean,
Clothes clean,—
For you I have many songs to make
Could I but find the words.
(13–30)

With its long lines and slightly awestruck admiration for the working class, the poem reveals Carl Sandburg's influence on Hughes—an influence the latter readily acknowledged (*The Big Sea* 28–32). Unlike Sandburg, though, who had few qualms about attacking organized religion, at this point in his career Hughes betrays much more ambivalence about the subject, as this poem, "Brass Spittoons," and the sequence of Gospel lyrics at the end of *Fine Clothes to the Jew* all attest. In "A Song to a Negro Wash-woman," as well as "Brass Spittoons," "churches" (17) and the "service of the Holy God" are built up from a foundation of service labor. As in "Brass Spittoons," too, Christianity offers a way to make sense of otherwise tedious service work that is also born of racial inequalities. The washwoman sings in church on Sunday, the speaker reveals, "praising your Jesus, because some day you're going to sit on the right hand of the Son of God and forget you ever were a wash-woman. And the aching back and the bundles of clothes will be unremembered then" (19).

For the most part, the speaker adopts an ethnographic attitude toward these beliefs, describing rather than judging. But he cannot remain completely detached. On the one hand, as in "Brass Spittoons," religion clearly provides solace and a way to make sense of labor. On the other hand, and as the "your Jesus" aside suggests, it is a sense (and solace) that the speaker—and Hughes himself—does not share or endorse.[18] Moreover, the rhetoric of a poem like "Goodbye Christ" (1932), which famously bids farewell to "Christ Jesus Lord God Jehova" (18) and welcomes "a guy with no religion at all—/ A real guy named / Marx Communist Lenin Peasant Stalin Worker ME—" (20–22), would not be available to Hughes for several more years. So whatever misgivings he may have about the religious songs rooted in her Jesus, the speaker has, as he acknowledges in the closing stanza, no songs to offer her in their place. All he can do, as in "Johannesburg Mines," is acknowledge the fact. "Yes, I've seen you singing" (20)—as though singing alone is a triumph, and perhaps it is. But as in "Johannesburg Mines," the poem surrenders to the fact, in this case religion's value to exploited and racially oppressed workers, about which poetry can do or say little, except to note it. Religion may help workers make sense of their labor, but the poem implies that Hughes would prefer that she sing, or at least hear, other, less compromised but as yet unknown and, given his politics, perhaps unknowable songs.

Another poem from this period, however, "Negro Servant," does find a song for its tired workers that Hughes can perhaps more readily celebrate. The poem appeared in *Opportunity* in December 1930, slightly later than most of the poems I have included here, but it offers a way to read the potential incongruities of Hughes's earlier collection, *Fine Clothes to the Jews* (1927). That volume famously mixes poems like "Elevator Boy" and "Brass Spittoons," poems that made Hughes, as one reviewer at the time put it, an authentic "Proletarian Poet" (Larkin), with the vernacular, dance hall poems like "Saturday Night" and "The Cat and the Saxophone (2 a.m.)" and the equally vernacular, blues-based poems like "Lament over Love," "Po' Boy Blues," "Gal's Cry for a Dying Lover," "Bad Man," and "Hard Daddy." Though seemingly different, what unites these poems is that they all, as Margaret Larkin recognized in her 1927 review of Hughes's collection, "have their roots deep in the lives of workers" (84). Yet "Negro Servant" suggests an even more specific relation between the proletarian poems and the cabaret ones, as well as articulating the central strategy Hughes (and even McKay) would imagine service workers employing in order to manage the emotional estrangement of their labor. In contrast to his silence as the washwoman sings, Hughes describes a different song that service workers had taken and might take up. As in McKay's "Harlem Dancer," "Negro Servant" juxtaposes the emotional management of service with an imagined African primitivism. Instead of being "subdued, polite, / Kind, thoughtful to the faces that are white" (1–2), the poem celebrates tribal dances, drums, and veldt (grassland) at night. In contrast to the delicate care involved in catering to white faces, there are "songs that do not care!" (7). And while Africa, like its imagined watch fires, remains "forgotten" (6) and a long way away, there is in its place "Dark Harlem."

At six o'clock, seven, or eight,
You're through.
You've worked all day.
Dark Harlem waits for you
The bus, the sub—
Pay-nights a taxi
Through the park.
O drums of life in Harlem after dark!
O, dreams!

O, songs!
O, saxophones at night!
O, sweet relief from faces that are white!
(8–19)

Harlem after dark echoes the tribal dances, drums, and grasslands of Africa with its own drums, dreams, songs, and saxophones. In other words, Dark Harlem and cabaret life specifically offer a release from the emotional management of service labor; they provide, as the last line of the poem insists, "sweet relief from the faces that are white!" (19) and, implicitly, sweet relief from the falsely smiling faces that are required to serve those white faces. The poem, like the bus, subway, or taxi of lines 12 and 13, transports workers from service to saxophones, from emotional constraint to emotional release.

Thus, in addition to the list of strategies McKay credits African American workers with developing to meet the emotional estrangement of service labor—fantasies of revolution, "harlots, cards, and rum," leisure, and quitting—Hughes seems to add two more, Christianity and cabarets. (Shortly, I acknowledge the ways in which these strategies, particularly fantasies of revolution, may differ from each other.) Of the two, Christianity and cabarets, Hughes seems to have fewer qualms about endorsing jazz. As he writes in his celebrated manifesto "The Negro Artist and the Racial Mountain" (1926), for the "low-down folks, the so-called common elements," "jazz is their child" (92). As with children, Hughes means that the low-down folks had given birth to jazz but also that they receive something back from it; it gives them purpose and focus. They have invented it because they need it. Echoing some of his poems, Hughes confesses that

> jazz to me is one of the inherent expressions of Negro life in America; the eternal tom-tom beating in the Negro soul—the tom-tom of revolt against weariness in a white world, a world of subway trains, and work, work, work; the tom-tom of joy and laughter, and pain swallowed in a smile. (94–95)

Like the Negro who has "known rivers" and whose "soul has grown deep like the rivers," here, too, the Negro knows jazz—specifically, the "eternal . . . beating" not just of drums but of an African "tom-tom." As in "Negro Servant," the "drums of life in Harlem after dark" echo the "drums" of a "veldt at night." Just as in that poem, too, this "tom-tom beating in the Negro soul" sounds a "revolt against weariness in a white world" and a world of "work, work, work." The jazz tom-tom of "joy and laughter," too, provides relief from the racial mask- and service-work-inspired "pain swallowed in a smile." In short, if service "work, work, work" requires hiding pain behind a smile, requires suppressing and managing emotion in order to meet the expectations of white employers, then jazz rescues that pain, transforms it into "joy and laughter," and in so doing provides a cathartic release of emotions made all the more meaningful because it takes place on the right side of the racial mountain.

Nor is Hughes simply making this up; there is considerable historical evidence that jazz, cabarets, and dance halls played just this role in African American working-class life. In "'Work That Body': African-American Women, Work, and Leisure in the New South," the labor historian Tera W. Hunter examines how, in the late nineteenth and early twentieth centuries, African American domestic workers, who valued "autonomy and collective life and the creation of social spaces for respite and recreation" (154), sought to "offset . . . the rigors of wage labor in their own world of popular amusement" (159). Although her subject is Atlanta and not Harlem dance halls, her conclusions nevertheless match those of Hughes in a poem like "Negro Servant" or an essay like "The Negro Artist and the Racial Mountain"—that is, that dancing and music "diverted and drove away depression among a people whose everyday lives were filled with adversity" (163). Specifically, Hunter argues that black workers, in contrast to southern white elites and the black bourgeoisie, saw dancing "as a respite from the drudgery of toil and an important aspect of personal independence. Blacks could reclaim their bodies from appropriation as instruments of physical toil and redirect their energies toward other diversions" (165). In addition to reclaiming their appropriated bodies, I would add that dance halls allowed black workers to reclaim their appropriated emotions. In any case, "dancing enabled an escape from wage work" (167), and Hunter is surely right to observe that "in the world of urban poverty and segregation, where enjoyments were limited, the affirmation of life embodied in dancing captivated working-class women and men and offered moments of symbolic and physical restoration of their subjugated bodies for joy, pleasure, and self-delight" (166). "Cabaret, cabaret!" as one Hughes speaker exclaims in "Minnie Sings Her Blues" (1926), "That's where we go,— / Leaves de snow outside / An' our troubles at de door" (3–5).[19]

Within the last decade, many scholars and critics comprising the new jazz studies have for the most part followed Hughes's and Hunter's attitude toward music and the redemptive cultures of music. In one way or another, all these accounts take their cue from Paul Gilroy's claim in *The Black Atlantic* (1992) that "in the simplest possible terms, by posing the world as it is against the world as the racially subordinated would like it to be, this musical culture supplies a great deal of the courage required to go on living in the present" (36). Musical expression, and especially black musical expression, travels equally in what Gilroy calls a "politics of fulfillment" and a "politics of transgression" (37). That is, music may fulfill the "social and political promise that present society has left unaccomplished," but it may also facilitate "the emergence of qualitatively new desires, social relations, and modes of association" (37). Jazz and cabaret life, then, as an instance of black musical expression, are fundamentally utopian and constitute, as Gilroy puts it, "a distinctive counterculture of modernity" (36). "Its basic desire," he concludes, speaking of these black musical forms, "is to conjure up and enact the new modes of friendship, happiness, and solidarity that are consequent on the overcoming of the racial oppression on which modernity and its antinomy of rational, western progress as excessive barbarity relied" (38).

Whether citing Gilroy or not, many critics cast black musical traditions, including and especially jazz, in a similarly heroic mold. Some of their claims, however, have perhaps outpaced the evidence, as both Hughes and McKay themselves would recognize. To single out just one of these scholars, Shane Vogel has recently argued that the Harlem Renaissance era cabaret allowed "for a heterogeneous assortment of figures and subjective possibilities, especially as they consolidate disparate nightlife populations into their operation. After-hours sociability brackets the world 'out there' and creates a sense of an autonomous time and place where normal social configurations are undone or done differently" ("Closing Time" 402). Nightlife, thus, "twists and reverses—queers—the normalizing inscriptions of time and space" (406) and alters its "subjects' relations to dominant society" (406). In other words, when people patronize cabarets, they resist the various ways modernity shapes, trains, and normalizes its subjects, especially its racialized subjects. Cabaret performers enjoy similarly liberating conditions. "Such clubs," Vogel notes, "offered many black musicians a crucially supportive environment, both economically and socially" (407). And while one might think that in order to valorize cabarets Vogel must ignore the people who work there, here, too, cabarets offer up a distinctive counterculture of modernity, as Gilroy puts it. In addition to fostering "a range of sexual and racial subjectivities," cabarets and nightclubs "provided material and economic resources for those who rejected or were otherwise unable to function within the emergent middle-class regimes of employment" (406–7). For Vogel, service work does not entail any of the emotional costs depicted in Hughes's or McKay's poems but, instead, provides a reprieve from "middle-class regimes of employment," that is, presumably, white-collar jobs or service jobs working for those with white collars.

To be sure, it is not that any or all of these claims for cabarets or cabaret verse are by themselves wrong. They may well create or reflect distinct spaces, times, sexualities, and subjectivities. As "Negro Servant" suggests, jazz does, as Nicholas M. Evans has observed of Hughes's cabaret poems, provide "cultural therapy" (267) and, I would add, lessen the alienation and emotional estrangement of service labor.[20] Too often, however, as Vogel's rhapsody suggests, scholars have romanticized cabaret life and its jazz soundtrack. How, for example, do cabarets escape "regimes of employment," middle class or otherwise? Did cabarets function on a gift economy? Were tips outlawed? If how cabarets escaped regimes of employment is not entirely clear, the implication of believing they do is clear enough. To put it bluntly, whereas whites in the 1920s could take the A-train to Harlem in order to discover the supposedly primitive outposts of capitalist modernity, far too many recent critics take the train for more theoretically sophisticated if occasionally equally exaggerated reasons: queer, racially autonomous, and anticapitalist, jazz and cabarets challenge everything regrettable about modernity. Come for the hot jazz, stay for the counterhegemonic contestations of time, space, and power.

One does not have to invoke Theodor Adorno to voice some skepticism about these claims for jazz's basically utopian character.[21] At least three closely related problems—ones raised even in Hughes's and McKay's cabaret poems—should check any rush to embrace jazz or the cabaret as an untroubled counterculture of modernity. The first problem, and to be fair to him it is one Adorno would harp on, is that at the time Hughes is writing, the mid- to late 1920s, jazz was less "a distinctive counterculture of modernity," as Gilroy puts it, than the embodiment, symbol, and sound of machine-age modernity. As Ryan Jerving writes in "Early Jazz Literature (and Why You Didn't Know)," "Although jazz was sometimes figured in negative, critical relation to American modernity—as a primitive, saving remnant of precommercial values or, still more rarely, as a music actively resisting the imperatives of the developing culture industries—neither of those tropes was yet dominant. Rather, both defenders and attackers of jazz most often sounded it in affirmative relation to its time and place" (655). Far from being an exclusively Harlem Renaissance invention or art form, jazz in the 1920s functioned more as a quintessential product of the culture industry than as an instance of culture resisting industrial society.

To be sure, jazz could come to epitomize white, machine-age modernity only because it was actively separated from its historical and racial origins. In which case, as Jerving concludes, those who wished to put jazz "toward Harlem Renaissance ends . . . would have had to play jazz with or against the grain of, in Stuart Hall's phrase, 'all the grooves that [had] articulated it already'" (661). In a sense, Jerving describes what Hughes may seek to do in his jazz and cabaret poems: to reclaim the sound that was in vogue and rephrase it as a distinctly African American utopian beat. Even so, jazz and, least of all, cabarets could rarely bear these utopian burdens. Celebrants, contemporaneous and later, would have to struggle mightily to position jazz as somehow removed from and a critique of the economic realm. Part of that struggle involved forgetting that jazz and the cabaret were themselves an economic realm, a workplace, as many earlier Hughes poems showed, like any other (662). Hence the second problem in thinking of cabaret as a significant counterculture to modernity: people worked there, often miserably. Consider one of several Hughes poems that takes up this theme, "The New Cabaret Girl," which Hughes included in *Fine Clothes to the Jew.*

That little yaller gal
Wid blue-green eyes:
If her daddy ain't white
Would be a surprise.

She don't drink gin
An' she don't like corn.
I asked her one night
Where she was born.

An' she say, Honey,
I don't know
Where I come from
Or where I go.

That crazy little yaller gal
Wid blue-green eyes:
If her daddy ain't fay
Would be a surprise.

An' she set there a cryin'
In de cabaret

A lookin' sad
When she ought to play.

My God, I says,
You can't live that way!
Babe you can't
Live that way!

(1–24)

Essentially, the poem transplants the myth of the tragic mulatto from plantation to cabaret. The new cabaret girl's "daddy" is, according to the speaker, surely white, and as a result, as she puts it, "I don't know / Where I come from / Or where I go" (10–12). That is, her confusion about her origins—from where and whom she comes—seeps into a more general confusion, as though agency and the future ("where I go") depends on identity and the past ("Where I come from"). Judging from the lament at the end of the poem that one "can't / Live that way!" (22), the speaker seems to pity the new cabaret girl's conditions and share her bleak conclusions about their effects.[22]

By itself, this racially tragic condition would be enough to cast doubt on the supposedly utopian space of the cabaret. Far from transcending racial categories or strictures, the cabaret becomes the site where they are most enforced or, at least, most acute. Yet there is another way that one "can't / Live that way!," as the speaker tells the cabaret girl. Regardless of how pitiful or confused her origins, the new cabaret girl cannot "set there a cryin'" (17) when, as even the speaker knows, "she ought to play" (20). In other words, she is not just any girl but the new cabaret girl, and for cabarets to function as utopias they must not, just as she must not, display (let alone experience) any sadness. Indeed, what may make her "new" is that she has not learned that part of her job involves suppressing all emotions but those of "play" (20). In short, this "Babe" "can't / Live that way!" and neither can she make her living that way. She must learn, like McKay's Harlem dancer, to adopt a "falsely-smiling face," even if it means relegating her interior self and doubts to somewhere other than the "strange place" of the cabaret. Even if she learns this, though, and manages to live that way, one cannot live for long or well if one's livelihood depends on a sustained and estranging management and exploitation of one's own emotions. Thus these poems—McKay's "Harlem Dancer" and Hughes's "New Cabaret Girl"—assert that cabarets and dance halls were not beleaguered but hopeful utopias writ small but also ordinary places of employment, ones that frequently called on the same emotional-management skills that patrons, many of them themselves service workers, were desperately fleeing.

Finally, then, in addition to reminding readers that cabarets also functioned as emotionally alienating workplaces, many of Hughes's and McKay's poems (like "Brass Spittoons") also remind readers of the alienating day jobs worked by the people who visited cabarets at night. In doing so, these poems make cabarets seem more akin to religion—a painkiller for the working masses—than a utopian cure for the disease of modernity. In addition to "If We Must Die" and "A Capitalist at Dinner," the first batch of McKay poems printed in *The Liberator* in July 1919 contained "The Negro Dancers," a series of sonnets that outline the possibilities and limits of cabaret life. The opening sonnet describes "a basement den" peopled by "young dark-skinned women and men" who are "Drinking and smoking, merry," but also "vacant-eyed" (3–4). Their cheerful hollowness is matched by "A Negro band, that scarcely seems awake," which "drones out half-heartedly a lazy tune, / While quick and willing boys their orders take" (5–7). This sleepy, dormant scene is electrified, though, when "a happy, lilting note / Is struck" and "the walk and hop and trot begin" (9–10). The dancers, likened to "laughing figures," "spin" "around the room," "Dancing," as in other sympathetic accounts of the jazz scene, "their world of shadows to forget" (12–14).

In the second sonnet, the speaker gazes at the "lithe bodies gliding slowly by" (2), a vision—together with the "amorous . . . glances" (3) and "laughter gay" (5)—that, he claims, brings "a rush of rapture to my tired soul" (7). The scene has a similar effect, the speaker imagines, for the participants as well. "Dead to the earth / And her unkindly ways of toil and strife, / For them the dance is the true joy of life" (12–14). As in Hughes's "Negro Servant," the cabaret provides "sweet relief"—the sense of being rapt, carried away, perhaps to heaven—from work and, like that poem, exemplifies and connects dancers and observers alike to, as McKay puts it, "the deathless spirit of a race" (8) or, as Hughes would put it, "the eternal tom-tom beating in the Negro soul."

The final sonnet of the sequence, however, recalls "the world of shadows" that, in the first sonnet, the cabaret invites dancers to forget. In the course of exploring these shadows, the speaker loses patience with the dancers, eventually pitying their cheaply lit but ultimately benighted lot.

And yet they are the outcasts of the earth,
A race oppressed and scorned by ruling man;
How can they thus consent to joy and mirth

Who live beneath a world-eternal ban?
No faith is theirs, no shining ray of hope,
Except the martyr's faith, the hope that death
Some day will free them from their narrow scope
And once more merge them with the infinite breath.
But, oh! they dance with poetry in their eyes
Whose dreamy loveliness no sorrow dims,
And parted lips and eager, gleeful cries,
And perfect rhythm in their nimble limbs.
The gifts divine are theirs, music and laughter;
All other things, however great, come after.

(1–14)

In the octet, and in contrast to the "true joy of life" that is dancing, the speaker describes life for these "Negro Dancers" as, effectively, hell on earth. "Outcast" both from heaven and, as in McKay's poem of the same name, "the dim regions whence my father came" (1), this displaced "race" lives under the "world-eternal ban" (4) and is "oppressed and scorned by ruling man" (2). As with all fallen men, their only hope is death, which will "once more merge them with the infinite breath" (8). In the meantime, they have the rapture of "dance" (9) and "music and laughter" (13)—that is, God has endowed them with "gifts divine" to ease their oppression and, as in the second sonnet, the earth's "unkindly ways of toil and strife" (13). Jazz, and the cabaret scene more generally, McKay implies, provides a partial rapture, a temporary lifting of "the world-eternal ban" (4) that will only truly be lifted in death.

Yet, as the closing line of the poem suggests, these gifts are a pittance, merely walking-around money for an effectively purgatorial existence. "All other things," as the last line has it, "however great" those things may be—racial equality, economic security, unalienated labor—"come after" (14) death, after, not during, the cabaret. Accordingly, cabarets are less earthly utopias than, at best, down payments on and, at worst, a shabby imitation of heaven.

As I have argued throughout this chapter, Hughes's and McKay's service poems constitute an archive of feelings about service labor, including the strategies service workers deploy in order to combat its belittling or alienating effects. One of those strategies is leisure, particularly jazz and cabaret life. Yet reading McKay's and Hughes's service labor poetry—which is also, of course, to read poetry about service laborers and their cultures—brings to the front two propositions about jazz and cabaret that might otherwise hang in the background. First, these poems hold that cabarets are workplaces that extract decidedly alienating emotional labor from their workers. Second, assuming that one can overlook the labor that goes on there, these poems remind us that cabarets cannot function as utopias because they are would-be utopias that remain comparatively marginal to the decidedly dystopian worlds of labor and race that otherwise occupy people's lives. McKay's and Hughes's greatest contribution, then, may be to cast the cabaret scene as part of a larger racial and economic totality. Doing so makes it at once both easier and more difficult to view the cabaret, the dance hall, and their jazz soundtrack as a utopian time, space, and sound. It is easier because such liberated scenes, spaces, and subjectivities gain so much in contrast to the cramped and emotionally alienating labor that otherwise characterizes cabaret-goers' lives and more difficult because one realizes that such scenes and spaces take up a comparatively small part of workers' lives. As Onwuchekwa Jemie reminded readers of Hughes's jazz poetry, "after the clang and whir of the syncopation of the night quickly follows the silence wherein the burden of black reality resumes its soul-crushing weight" (416)—the weight of "slavery and poverty and frustrated dreams" (416). Or, as McKay puts it, "All other things, however great, come after" (14). For this reason, McKay's fantasies of revolution, even if at some level they remain merely fantasies, offer a much more pragmatic, and much less romantic, response to service capitalism.

To be sure, a marginal utopia built out of jazz and cabarets is better than no utopia at all, just as a counterculture is preferable to a hegemonic culture, and its existence, however qualified, does—and this is Gilroy's point—provide a model for remaking the dystopia of race and labor relations. Yet in celebrating the utopian possibilities of leisure, one may downplay the dystopian realities of race and, especially, labor. In glorifying splendid underdogs—and their splendid music—one risks, as Adorno famously quipped, glorifying the splendid system that made them so.

If critics have sometimes failed to recognize these smirches on the basically utopian character of jazz and cabarets, it may be because, like Hughes, they seek to recover a cultural practice that was previously and unjustly belittled. As Krin Gabbard writes, "[T]he institutionalization of jazz is consistent with current demystifications of the distinctions between high and low culture, with the growing trend toward multiculturalism in university curricula, and with the postmodernist cachet now enjoyed by marginal arts and artists" (1). In this last—the cachet of marginal arts and artists—one can recognize the outlines of a romantic anticapitalism that has often gripped modern poets and, occasionally, postmodern scholars of jazz as well. "The Romantic vision," as Michael Löwy and Robert Sayre observe, "is characterized by the painful and melancholic conviction that in modern reality something precious has been lost, at the level of both individuals and humanity at large; certain essential human values have been lost" (21). As McKay's and Hughes's service poems attest, one of the "essential human values" that has been lost in capitalist, racist modernity is autonomy, particularly emotional autonomy—the desire, unrecognized until lost, that one's emotions could function independently and without exploitation by others.

Because of this crisis, McKay, Hughes, and Hughes's later jazz-oriented critics have been tempted, as other romantic capitalists would, to idealize the past and the remnants of the past that survive into the present.[23] Where racist modernity alienates, Africa—and the echoes of Africa in jazz—integrates; where service labor divides, the cabaret makes whole. Yet, unlike many critics, McKay and, to a lesser but nontrivial extent, Hughes, tempered this romantic attitude toward cabaret with some skepticism. Whether the McKay of "The Negro Dancers" or the Hughes of many poems in *Fine Clothes to the Jew,* both poets recognize that the nightlife had to compete with—and could not finally compete with—the working day.[24]

To be sure, neither Hughes nor McKay, especially in the latter's later novel, *Home to Harlem* (1928), could entirely resist the siren song or the utopian stirrings of cabaret life.[25] Nor, in truth, should they have. However, perhaps because both Hughes and McKay had themselves been service workers—and came to partial fame as poets while serving others—they, and the poetry they wrote about service, seem more alive to its burdens and less vulnerable to the romantic belief that cabarets and jazz could provide anything but temporary, compromised, and incomplete relief from that labor.

CHAPTER 6

A Lost Art of Work: The Fate of the Craft Ideal in Carl Sandburg's *Chicago Poems*

Beginning with the turn of the century and reaching a peak in the years before World War I, journalists, businessmen, congressmen, labor leaders, and ordinary workers in the United States conducted an unprecedented debate about how and to what end men and women ought to work.[1] Most of that debate turned on how much control workers should or should not retain over their labor. On one side, efficiency experts like Frederick Winslow Taylor held that workers had altogether too much control over their work, so much so that they, as Taylor and other labor problem textbooks put it, hindered productivity and restricted output. As Taylor wrote in *The Principles of Scientific Management* (1911), "As was usual then [1878] and in fact is still usual in most of the shops in this country, the shop was really run by the workmen, and not by the bosses. The workmen together had carefully planned just how fast each job should be done, and they had set a pace for each machine throughout the shop, which was limited to one-third of a good day's work" (49). Taylor called this planned restriction of output "soldiering" and in front of a 1912 congressional committee appointed specifically to inquire into scientific management asserted "without fear of contradiction that this constitutes the greatest evil with which the working-people of both England and America are now afflicted" (14).[2]

For Taylor, the solution to this evil lay in the scientific management of labor, which entailed first discovering, through time and motion studies, the "one best way" to do a job and then redesigning the labor process so that each worker followed that one best way. Effectively, scientific management required, as Taylor admitted, transferring control of labor—how fast, how long, and in what way one worked—from workers, who had a tendency to soldier, to managers, who could engineer maximum production and extract a full day's work from each laborer. "As far as possible," Taylor had written in his earlier, more specialized volume *Shop Management* (1901), "the workmen should be entirely relieved of the work of planning," and "all possible brain work should be removed from the shop and centered in the planning or lay-out department" (98–99).[3]

On the other side of this debate, workers, unsurprisingly, resented being relieved of brain work and robbed of their control over the labor process. After Taylor and scientific management made the front pages in late 1910 and early 1911, organized labor went on the offensive. In a December 11, 1910, *New York Times* article, the former president of the United Mine Workers, John Mitchell, declared that workers subject to scientific management would go mad. For evidence, he cited Dr. William Mabon, superintendent of the Manhattan State Hospital for the Insane, who had written that "the brain cells that are not used in the piece of specialized work, which is most of those in the brain, finally go dead from lack of use, and then the worker is ready for the insane asylum" ("Mitchell against Brandeis Economy"). Even if specialized work did not "unbalance the minds of the worker," as Dr. Mabon asserted, workers and their advocates feared that scientific management nevertheless diminished the need for those minds, leaving workers as little more than mechanized puppets. James Duncan, vice president of the American Federation of Labor, wrote in 1911 in the *Journal of Accountancy*, "As a skilled workman I want no task nor task setter to harass me at my work. That . . . would reduce me to an automaton" (32). In 1912, a correspondent to the *American Machinist* wrote that scientific managers assumed "a monopoly of brains" and would schedule "every movement so that a man is simply one of the gears in the operation of the machine" (qtd. in Kanigel 444). Similarly, as Samuel Gompers, head of the American Federation of Labor, argued in 1911, the Taylor system makes "every man merely a cog or a nut or a pin in a big machine, fixed in the position of a hundredth or a thousandth part of the machine, with no need to employ more than a few mechanical motions nor any brain power except the little required in making those motions" (277). Even the congressional committee that invited Taylor to testify ultimately defended workers against scientific management. A workman, the committee concluded in its 1912 report, "would be less than a man if he did not resent the introduction of any system which deals with him in the same way as a beast of burden or an inanimate machine" ("Report on the Taylor and Other Systems of Shop Management" 540).[4]

For many reformers associated with the arts and crafts movement, however,

Taylor's critics had come at least a decade late to this debate about work under industrial capitalism. For these arts and crafts reformers, who achieved their greatest influence around the turn of the twentieth century, industrial capitalism—scientifically managed or not—had already turned workers into automatons and robbed them of what control they once had over their labor. "Work, especially in America," the furniture maker and crafts leader Gustav Stickley wrote in 1909 in the pages of *The Craftsman*, the leading arts and crafts journal in the country, "has come to mean the ignominious, arduous performance of duty, to be accomplished in a state of coma, to be finished swiftly, to be forgotten" ("The Truth about Work" 185). In 1902, in the same journal, the socialist A. M. Simons asked, "Is there any pleasure for the great producing masses in their work? To ask the question is to answer it. On every hand, performance of the essential labor of society is looked upon as an evil to be avoided, and few indeed who are actually concerned with it, ever think of looking there for something pleasurable, artistic, enjoyable. The production of 'goods' has become an evil" (37). Similarly, in his *Chapters in the History of the Arts and Crafts Movement* (1902), which introduced some of the key figures on the British arts and crafts scene (Thomas Carlyle, John Ruskin, William Morris, C. R. Ashbee) to an American audience, Oscar Lovell Triggs anticipated many of the critiques that would later be leveled at Taylor and scientific management. The "division of labor, especially in association with machinery and forced by competition," Triggs observed, by way of summarizing John Ruskin, "is a social wrong to the workman because it tends to degrade him to a mechanism, exercises but a single set of faculties, and dissociates him from the completed product, a knowledge of which alone makes his labor rational" (44–45).

Unlike later critics, who merely warned against the possibility that labor might be reduced to a cog, arts and crafts reformers offered a cure for a disease they assumed had already infected the patient. "The real labor problem," Triggs wrote, echoing countless others, "is not that of shorter hours or higher wages, but it is to change the character of work so that work will be its own reward" (48). At its best, the American arts and crafts movement sought to do just that, to change the character of work, to make it an art and its own reward. Reformers wrote articles, lectured, published journals, organized exhibitions, patronized existing craftsman, and started workshops and communities founded on arts and crafts principles. They failed to change the character of work, of course, but even so critics have not stopped debating why they failed or what their failure meant. In by far the most influential account of the movement, *No Place of Grace: Antimodernism and the Transformation of American Culture,*

1880–1920, T. J. Jackson Lears observes that American arts and crafts reformers confronted "the fragmenting impact of economic rationalization" and offered, however tenuously, "an alternative to alienated industrial labor" (93). Nevertheless, Lears charges, most American arts and crafts leaders eventually betrayed the anticapitalist principles they borrowed from the British movement, substituting "personal fulfillment" (80), "social engineering" (89), and "socialization" (83) for "social justice" (89). "Ambiguous from the outset," Lears argues, "their antimodern critique became progressively diluted within only a few years. Ultimately most applauded mechanization, the division of labor, the gap between urban work and suburban leisure—in short, the whole range of modern ills condemned by [John] Ruskin and [William] Morris" (83). "By World War I," he concludes, "the craft ideal had largely been reduced to a revivifying habit for the affluent" (65)—when, that is, it was not actively accommodating, even smoothing the way for, "the emerging corporate system" (79).

In this chapter, I track "the fate of the craft ideal," as Lears puts it, and the fate of these critical questions about work, through the poetry of Carl Sandburg.[5] Even more so than most of the poets in this book, Sandburg's emergence as a modern poet more or less coincides with his discovery of the poetic possibilities of the poor and working class. In 1912, Sandburg left his position as secretary to the Socialist mayor of Milwaukee, Emil Seidel, and moved to Chicago, where he began writing articles for various city newspapers, including the *Day Book*, the *Chicago Evening World,* and the journal *International Socialist Review* (Niven 234–35). Sandburg, his biographer Penelope Niven writes, "prowled the city in search of stories, telling them sometimes in prose, sometimes in poetry" (233). Unsurprisingly, given the left-leaning and tabloid papers he wrote for, Sandburg's journalism tended to muckrake in defense of the common man—the same mode that would occasionally surface in his first volume of poetry, *Chicago Poems* (1916).[6] "Hog Butcher for the World," Sandburg famously declares in the lead and title poem of that collection, describing the city as its labor and laborers writ large.

> *Tool Maker, Stacker of Wheat,*
> *Player with Railroads and the Nation's Freight Handler;*
> *Stormy, husky, brawling,*
> *City of the Big Shoulders. . . .*
>
> (1–4)

"Here was a directly phrased poetry of the contemporary world," David Perkins observes of *Chicago Poems.* "It gave sights and sounds. It showed people at work. It had something to say about the character and quality of their lives" (357).

Indeed, Sandburg's spinning of workers and the poor into defiantly modern poetry shocked his contemporary readers and critics. In 1914, after the poem appeared in Harriet Monroe's *Poetry,* an anonymous reviewer for *The Dial* complained of Sandburg's "Chicago," "It is not even doggerel, for doggerel at least admits the claims of rhythm, and this composition admits no aesthetic claim of any description, and acknowledges subordination to no aesthetic law" ("New Lamps for Old" 232). Then, getting personal, the reviewer attacked Sandburg's right to even compose poetry. Quoting from Harriet Monroe's introduction to Sandburg's poem, the reviewer writes, "We are told that the author 'left school at the age of thirteen, and worked in brickyards, railroads, Kansas wheat fields, etc.,' which we can well believe. That education might have made him a poet we will concede; that these unregulated word eruptions earn for him that title we can nowise allow" (232). "We are inclined to suggest," the reviewer concludes, "that this author would be more at home in brickyards than on the slopes of Parnassus" (233). Later, also writing in *The Dial,* William Aspenwall Bradley sketched Sandburg as the poetic equivalent of a bomb-throwing anarchist. The "bigness" of Chicago, Bradley claimed, was "inciting him . . . to a brutality and violence of expression about which there seems a good deal that is alien and artificial" (528).[7] While they now seem rather comically hysterical, these outraged reviews nevertheless suggest that while modern American poetry may have formed out of its uncertain encounter with the poor and working class, at the time that formation struck some, perhaps most readers of poetry as regrettable, even dangerous.

While more recent critics have sought to reconstruct the socialism informing these and other once controversial but now canonical early Sandburg poems, this chapter assumes another context for Sandburg's *Chicago Poems* (1916): the poet's timely and enthusiastic reading of the British critics of industrial capitalism, John Ruskin and William Morris, and to his participation in the turn-of-the-century American reform movement—the arts and crafts movement or "the craftsman ideal"—they inspired. Like Ruskin, Morris, and their American followers, Sandburg in his early poetry contrasts the degraded, disciplined work of industrial capitalism with what he and others imagined—perhaps naively—as the largely self-directed, self-expressive artisan and craft work of a preindustrial, precapitalist world. Moreover, like Ruskin, Morris, and some of their American followers, Sandburg would attempt to reconnect the divide between work and art, to write poetry that recognized work as an art, workers as artists, and artists as a sort of worker manqué.

Like others who participated in the arts and crafts movement, however, Sandburg also adapted—one might say distorted—Morris and Ruskin to his own political and poetic ends. As Lears and historians of the American movement have documented, many arts and crafts reformers appropriated trenchant critiques of industrial capitalism in order to elevate middle-class taste or, strangely enough, to justify the increasingly alienated conditions of industrial workers. Sandburg rarely shares in these grosser distortions of Ruskin and Morris, but the unlicensed poetic uses to which he puts those thinkers and reformers do reveal something about his (and others') evolving attitude toward industrial capitalism and its alienated workers. One of the tasks of this chapter, then, is to understand how Sandburg and his poetry enter into a dialogue with the arts and crafts movement, endorsing, challenging, questioning, and finally perhaps even rejecting its historical assumptions and contemporary relevance.

In what follows, I first document the ideas in Ruskin and Morris's indictment of industrial capitalism that would most influence their American readers, including the impressionable young Sandburg. In a second section, I track Sandburg's connections to the quasi-revolutionary program of the American arts and crafts movement that emerged from Ruskin's and Morris's writings and practices. I then offer readings of some of the poems Sandburg collected in *Chicago Poems* in order to mark the continuing influence of Ruskin, Morris, and the American arts and crafts movement on Sandburg's poetry long after he had supposedly left them behind. In addition to marking the influences, however, I also record the variations on Ruskin and Morris in those poems for what they might reveal about the fate of the arts and crafts movement and, more broadly, the fate of the question of how men and women ought to work, which, as the testimony of Taylor, Congress, and organized labor suggests, constituted one of the more pressing labor problems of this period. As one 1925 labor problem textbook observed of the first few decades of the twentieth century, "men and women became machine tenders" (Furniss and Guild 9), and the problem, for Sandburg as for others, was what, if anything, to do about this fact.

Finally, Sandburg's use and, as Lears might charge, misuse of arts and crafts principles provides an opportunity to reflect on the political possibilities (and constraints) of romantic anticapitalism. If romanticism, as Michael Löwy and Robert Sayre argue, "represents a critique of . . . modern capitalist civilization, in the names of values and ideals drawn from the past" (17), especially the medieval past (22), then arts and crafts, which idealized the medieval craftsman over against the alienated worker of modern industrial capitalism, offers a near-perfect example of romantic anticapitalism. It also offers a near-perfect example of why, as I have suggested throughout this book, romantic anticapitalism (and modern poets under its sway) could so often fail to respond adequately to the labor problem. As some reformers and writers sympathetic to labor recognized, given how radically and irrevocably industrial capitalism had altered existing modes of work and production, continued faith in the craftsman ideal could seem like backward-looking nostalgia. In which case, those who gave up on arts and crafts, or altered it almost beyond recognition, as Sandburg does, far from betraying revolutionary ideals or acceding to capitalist imperatives, instead may have recognized its limits, its basic irrelevance, to the most pressing labor problems. As a result, I treat Sandburg last in this book because he represents a poet whose antiromantic capitalism becomes slightly, albeit grudgingly less romantic, even as it manages to remain fundamentally anticapitalist and pro-labor. One might think that would be an easy enough task to accomplish, but for canonical modern poets, it proved surprisingly difficult.

While enrolled at Lombard College in Galesburg, Illinois, from 1898 to 1903, and for years after leaving the college, few people could claim as much influence over Carl Sandburg as his professor and later publisher, Philip Green Wright—the man Sandburg would later dub "The Illinois Prairie Leonardo" (*Ever the Winds of Chance* 26). Wright earned this praise in part for introducing the young Sandburg to socialism, though a distinctly non-Marxist version of socialism. As Sandburg observes in *Ever the Winds of Chance,* his uncompleted autobiography of his college years, Wright "couldn't go along with the main analysis of the capitalist system made by Karl Marx" (28). In place of Marx, as another Lombard alum and Wright devotee, John C. Weigel, recalled in an obituary for his former professor, "it was in his Sunday evening reading circle" that "students and faculty" might "appreciate for the first time perhaps the artistic longings of John Ruskin or the dreams of William Morris" (unpaginated). Sandburg also recalled attending those "lively free-for-all discussion[s] . . . in a big front room of the Wright house on Sunday nights in the winter months" and while there almost certainly shared Wright's appreciation for the longings and dreams of Ruskin and Morris. Indeed, Sandburg confessed that while at Lombard he was "lit up and somewhat intoxicated about Ruskin" and "for him something about 100 percent" (53).

While at Lombard College, Sandburg sought to intoxicate others with the spirit of Ruskin as well. His 1901 prize-winning undergraduate oration, "John

Ruskin: A Man of Ideals," suggests what the British art and social critic meant to his turn-of-the-century enthusiasts. Delivered to all of Lombard College's students and faculty and reproduced in that year's *Lombard Review*, Sandburg began his oration by reminding his audience, "In no other century were there ever such vast and important changes in science and industry as there was in the nineteenth century" (109). In addition to the exponential growth of locomotives and newspapers, Sandburg observed, the organization of economic production had changed as well. "In the eighteenth century almost everything was made by hand and with hand tools," Sandburg notes. "The workmen's house was generally his workshop" (109). "But all this was changed," he explains, "and the end of the nineteenth century saw scarcely a city without its long, high brick building, with its hundreds of rooms, hundreds of machines, and hundreds of men." These new factories and the material progress they represented, however, "satisfied only the wants of the body." Thankfully, though, "the age was not without strong earnest men who saw this, and across the hundred years of the century could be heard the voices of those crying for a higher progress" (109). For Sandburg, preeminent among these strong, earnest men was John Ruskin, who "compelled the English people to take a greater interest in art, nature, and the beautiful" and, perhaps more important, compelled them to realize that "factories crush the human body and darken the human soul" (110).

Not surprisingly, Sandburg's conclusions about factories resemble those drawn by Ruskin himself in "The Nature of the Gothic," chapter 6 of the second volume of his *Stones of Venice* (1853). There Ruskin details in a handful of pages what he believed industrial capitalism and its factories were doing to labor and thus the lives of the working class, grounding that analysis in a consideration of architecture through the ages. In "The Nature of the Gothic," Ruskin famously defends the "savageness of Gothic Architecture" (158) against the supposed fineness and grace of Grecian, Roman, and Renaissance architecture. He praises what he calls "the rude and wild" (155) work of Gothic architecture on the grounds that such architectural imperfections and excesses reveal the work of thoughtful, autonomous laborers—more thoughtful and autonomous, anyway, than the workers responsible for the rigidly executed and slavish symmetries of ancient and Renaissance architecture. "The Greek gave to the lower workman no subject which he could not perfectly execute," Ruskin claims. "The Assyrian gave him subjects which he could only execute imperfectly, but fixed a legal standard for his imperfection. The workman was, in both systems, a slave" (159). In contrast, Ruskin challenged his readers to gaze again

> upon the old cathedral front, where you have smiled so often at the fantastic ignorance of the old sculptors: examine once more those ugly goblins, and formless monsters, and stern statues, anatomiless and rigid; but do not mock at them, for they are the signs of the life and liberty of every workman who struck the stone; a freedom of thought, and rank in scale of being, such as no laws, no charters, no charities can secure; but which must be the first aim of all Europe at this day to regain for her children. (162–63)

For Ruskin, such Gothic architectural and sculptural excesses confirmed that "in the make and nature of every man, however rude or simple, whom we employ in manual labor, there is some power for better things: some tardy imagination, torpid capacity of emotions, tottering steps of thought," even though factory production had no use for such emotions and thoughts—in fact, actively worked against their expression (160). For Sandburg, then, Ruskin's significance lay in the fact that he made men (in Sandburg's words now) "see that the laborer is not a machine, but that he has a soul and that soul has a right to see and enjoy the clear sky, works of art, health, sanity, beauty" (110).

Ruskin concludes his chapter with a set of rules consumers might follow to ensure "a right understanding, on the part of all classes, of what kinds of labor are good for men" and what kinds likely to inspire "pleasure in the work by which they make their bread" (165). For his American interpreters, Ruskin's rules for consumption would prove both influential and, ultimately, impractical; in England, however, his trenchant critique and ineffectual solutions would later inspire another icon from Sandburg's Lombard College studies, William Morris, to yet further critiques of work under industrial capitalism and to socialism, the only practical solution Morris imagined for that barbarity. Like Ruskin, Morris, in a series of lectures given in the 1880s, objected to the gradual degradation of work and the enslavement of workers caused by the ascendancy of industrial capitalism, and like Ruskin, he looked backward to the Middle Ages for a mode of labor as yet uncorrupted by that mode of production. With the advent of the workshop system, Morris points out, the "division of labour in handiwork is carried to the highest point possible, and the unit of manufacture is no longer a man, but a group of men, each member of which is dependent on his fellows, and is utterly useless by himself" ("Art" 71). Industrial, machine-based modes of production, moreover, would soon render these divided and subdivided workers even more "useless." The machine system and the system of the factory, Morris argues, caused "the machine-like workmen of the workshop period [to be] supplanted by actual machines," and "when the process is complete," Morris half observed and half predicted, "the skilled workman will no longer exist, and his place will be filled by machines directed by a few highly trained and very intelligent experts, and tended by a multitude of people, men, women, and children, of whom neither skill nor intelligence is required" ("Art" 72). Whatever its advances over earlier modes of production, then, for Morris the machine system differed from the preindustrial craft system in that the former took from workers both their control over production and the fundamental basis for that control, a worker's skill and intelligence.

As he at times admitted, Morris claimed little that Ruskin had not implied in "The Nature of the Gothic." Morris did advance beyond Ruskin, however, by connecting (much more explicitly than Ruskin had) the degradation of labor under industrial capitalism with the degradation of art under that same system—a connection that would prove crucial to Sandburg's later artistic and poetic experiments. For Morris, art included more than the "Intellectual" or "cultivated" arts of painting, sculpture, architecture, music, and poetry; it also included what he variously called the "lesser," "Decorative," or "popular" arts—that is, "house-building, painting, joinery and carpentry, smiths' work, pottery and glass-making, weaving, and many others," or, more generally, "that side of art which is, or ought to be, done by the ordinary workman while he is about his ordinary work" ("Lesser" 102). For Morris, however, it is those lesser or popular arts that are imperiled and ultimately destroyed by the machine and factory systems of production. From a time when "all handicraftsmen were artists," Morris writes, society had advanced to a state where "the artist came out from the handicraftsmen, and left them without hope of elevation, while he himself was left without hope of intelligent, industrious sympathy" ("Lesser" 37). In other words, the extinction of these lesser arts led to the inevitable isolation of the greater ones, in turn depriving "greater" artists "of a sympathetic and appreciative audience" ("Art" 61). If industrial capitalism no longer required skilled or intelligent workers, it would no longer have a wide audience for skilled and intelligent art. "Art is man's expression of his joy in labour," Morris observes in his most famous aphorism, and absent that joyous labor, workmen cease to be artists and devolve instead into the deskilled, machinelike operatives who resent the cultivated arts and cultivated artists for abandoning them ("Art" 67). Morris shares their resentment. "I do not want art for a few," he asserts in his first lecture on the subject, "The Lesser Arts," "any more than education for a few, or freedom for a few" (54).

To be sure, one cannot read for long in either Ruskin or Morris without beginning to suspect that they invented as much as they described about the working conditions of medieval artisans. Indeed, it often appears that Morris, and even more so Ruskin, looked to the past not so much to understand it on its own terms as to justify their own critique of Victorian working conditions. As John Unrau damningly summarizes this tendency, Ruskin's study of the Gothic and its builders "reveals errors of historical fact, bias in presentation of supposedly scientific argument, suppression of a range of Ruskin's own aesthetic responses, an almost comical abandonment of common sense, and a rather vulgar condescension in attitude toward the 'workmen' (both medieval and Victorian) whom he is supposedly championing" (33). "Ruskin's conception of the artistic 'liberty of the labourer' in Gothic times is," as Unrau charges, "pure fantasy" (39). Not only did medieval codes of masonry condemn imperfections and excesses, which could be cause for dismissal and replacement, but master masons also frequently provided freemasons with drawings for buildings and sometimes even templates and cutouts for its details. Below the level of skilled masons, too, as Unrau observes, an army of "'roughmasons,' 'hardhewers,' and diggers and transporters of stone and mortar" toiled at unskilled, highly regulated work that nowhere approached creative or liberated labor. In short, Unrau writes, "[W]e can be sure that such men had no more opportunity for self-expression than an assembly line worker has today" (39–40).

Pure fantasy or not, many arts and crafts reformers in the United States accepted Ruskin, Morris, and their vision of medieval labor at face value. At its best, the movement they built borrowed Ruskin and Morris's critique of industrial, alienated labor and struggled to create an alternative, more humane system of labor and production. The movement did not take hold among industrial workers, who developed their own strategies for dealing with mechanization and industrialization, but, as Lears observes, instead "originated and flourished primarily under the educated bourgeoisie" who "began to see that labor in industrial America was being degraded as never before" (60). In response, Lears notes, many—as Ruskin and Morris had—became fascinated with the mythological figure of the premodern artisan, whose work was imagined to be "necessary and demanding," "rooted in genuine community," and "a model of hardness and wholeness" (60). As Lears notes of Ruskin and Morris, "the portrait was only partially accurate but it provided a sharp polemical focus" (76). However unmoored from facts, that is, this vision of the premodern artisan inspired a generation of reformers, who founded journals, collected and exhibited medieval and contemporary artisan furniture and crafts, and, more ambitiously, contributed to the foundation of several communes and workshops dedicated to re-creating the subsistence farming and autonomous, creative craft work of the medieval artisan.

In concert with his reading of Ruskin and Morris, the American arts and crafts movement would inspire in Sandburg his first passionate reaction against industrialization, urbanization, and modernization. As Sandburg acknowledged, gratefully, Philip Green Wright played an essential role in his thinking. In addition to introducing Sandburg to non-Marxist socialism, Wright also gave Sandburg a model for how to translate theory into action. Wright composed a sort of stiff, socialist-inspired poetry that borrowed heavily from Morris's own *Chants for Socialists* (1894). In the first decades of the twentieth century, too, Wright dreamed of bringing the arts and crafts movement to Galesburg, Illinois, including an unrealized "College for Adults" that would incorporate his already-working printing press, itself modeled on William Morris's Kelmscott Press (Niven 77).[8] Later Sandburg would try to further Wright's arts and crafts ambitions. After he left Lombard College in 1903, Sandburg tried to interest Wright in further "participation in the arts-craft movement" (qtd. in Crane 56), which, he wrote, was "an almost holy word" (58) to those who understood its significance. In another 1904 letter, Sandburg proposed that he, Wright, and John Sjodin, Sandburg's boyhood friend, whom he called "an active Socialist, a very earnest 'red,'" collaborate on "a publication which should be bold, reckless, joyous, gleeful, yet sometimes sad and austere and mocking, in dealing with socialism, 'New Thought,' sexology, and themes on which I have decided convictions" (*Letters* 24). Sandburg had also

> thought, too, that this publication might in some way be allied to an institution in which useful articles were made, and so made that in the process, the sense of beauty would be gratified, or the emotions of love and reverence moved. I would expect too, that such a movement would be hailed as an imitation, and ridiculed like any imitation. But in time, there would appear on its products, manual, artistic, and literary, the impress of the individuals connected with it. (24)

These letters and schemes readily suggest the influence of Ruskin, Morris, and the craftsman ideal on Sandburg: his concern that only "useful articles" be made and made in such a way as to gratify the sense of beauty; his intertwining of manual, artistic, and literary products; and his hope that such products would reveal the impress of the individual who made them.

Sandburg's fear that such a movement "would be hailed as an imitation," however, reveals a more immediate source for his musings. "If it was to be only an imitation of Kelmscott or Roycroft ideas," Sandburg writes later in the letter, "it would not die (having never lived), it would merely cease, as scores have done" (*Letters* 24). "Kelmscott" refers to the press William Morris started in the early 1890s; "Roycroft ideas," however, names one of the more public ventures of the arts and crafts movement in the late nineteenth and early twentieth centuries, one that Sandburg viewed with admiration and at remarkably close quarters. Those "Roycroft ideas" belonged chiefly to Elbert Hubbard, who, as T. J. Jackson Lears remarks, was "the most visible and eccentric craft leader in America" (68). Hubbard had made a fortune selling soap through innovations in mass-marketing techniques such as "fancy packaging, direct mail sales, premiums, and clubbing," but in 1893 he sold his interest in the Larkin Soap Company and toured England, visiting William Morris's Kelmscott Community and returning as a self-styled American counterpart to Morris (Boris 146). In 1896, he started the Roycroft Press in East Aurora, New York, and later expanded the enterprise into the Roycroft Community, which included cabinetmaking, a bindery, a farm, a bank, a blacksmith, cabinet shops, and a Roycroft Inn "to accommodate [the] throng of curious visitors" (147). "To the outside world," Eileen Boris observes, "East Aurora appeared a big commune and happy family" (148), and Hubbard, adopting the title "Fra Elbertus," appeared to be (according to one member of the British arts and crafts elite) "as picturesque as Ruskin" (146).

Future generations have drawn decidedly less worshipful conclusions about Hubbard. Instead of picturesque, they tend to describe him as a fraud, an opportunist, or, as Eileen Boris does, a manipulator of "anti-establishment symbols" (146). Sandburg, too, would eventually join in the reevaluation but only after a long period of mutual and influential admiration. In the interim, Sandburg published reverential prose sketches of Hubbard in early Chicago socialist journals, and in 1907 Hubbard invited Sandburg to lecture at Roycroft to the national audience of socialists and arts and crafts reformers whom Hubbard annually summoned to East Aurora (Niven 122–23). Sandburg delivered his oration on Whitman, saucily titled "An American Vagabond," and a week later his omnibus oration, "The Three Blunders of Civilization" (122–23). Partly as a result of those successful lectures, in 1909 Hubbard's weekly *The Fra* published Sandburg's "The Road and the End," a Whitmanesque invocation of the open road and unfettered individualism that Sandburg later included in *Chicago Poems*. Back in Chicago, too, Sandburg's literary career more or less progressed through channels made by his connections to figures and publications within the arts and crafts world.[9]

Far from abandoning them overnight, such schemes and influences would cast a shadow over the poems Sandburg was composing in the 1910s and would later gather together to form *Chicago Poems.*

Although Sandburg eventually supported U.S. involvement in World War I, the "War Poems" section of *Chicago Poems* reflects his original, fervent stance against the war. Most of the poems in that section, however, also reflect Sandburg's thinking about Ruskin and Morris. Indeed, these poems often use Ruskin, Morris, and ideas and language derived from them to articulate Sandburg's antiwar sentiments. "Salvage," for example, is an apostrophe to Morris himself and the only poem in *Chicago Poems* to name either Ruskin or Morris directly. In the poem, Sandburg summons the memory of Morris in order to condemn the tragic and unnecessary destruction caused by the war.

Guns on the battle lines have pounded now a year between Brussels and Paris.
And, William Morris, when I read your old chapter on the great arches and naves and little whimsical corners of the Churches of Northern France—Brr-rr!
I'm glad you're a dead man, William Morris, I'm glad you're down in the damp and mouldy, only a memory instead of a living man—I'm glad you're gone.
You never lied to us, William Morris, you loved the shape of those stones piled and carved for you to dream over and wonder because the workmen got joy of life into them,
Workmen in aprons singing while they hammered, and praying, putting their songs and prayers into the walls and roofs, the bastions and cornerstones and gargoyles—all their children and kisses of women and wheat and roses growing.
I say, William Morris, I'm glad you're gone, I'm glad you're a dead man.
Guns on the battle lines have pounded a year now between Brussels and Paris.

(1–7)

The central conceit of "Salvage" emerges in the contrast Sandburg draws between the creative hammering of the fifteenth-century workmen and the destructive "pounding" of twentieth-century guns.[10] As Sandburg recalls, Morris loved "the shape of those stones piled and carved" and "the walls and roofs, the bastions and cornerstones and gargoyles" of "the Churches of Northern France" since they materially embody the workmen's romanticized though nevertheless joyous life of aprons, hammers, children, women, wheat, and roses. In contrast, "Guns on the battle lines have pounded a year now," destroying those same churches that workmen once "got joy of life into." Given these scenes of thoughtless and, for Morris, irrevocable destruction, the only comfort to be "salvaged" from the battles in northern France is that the man who would have been most affected by this awesome destruction has mercifully died before being forced to witness it.

"Salvage" thus shows Sandburg using Morris to frame his opposition to the war. He does so by thinking architecturally—that is, by noting the historical irony that the churches Morris praises are precisely those destroyed by modern war. In other poems in Sandburg's 1916 collection, however, he does not use Ruskin and Morris to make sense of a needlessly destructive war but instead to describe and appreciate contemporary scenes of production (and distribution) where art is supposedly achieved in and through labor. In the short poem "Fish Crier," for example, conventionally degraded labor is elevated to the status of an art form.

> *I know a Jew fish crier down on Maxwell Street with a*
> *voice like a north wind blowing over corn stubble in January.*
> *He dangles herring before prospective customers*
> *evincing a joy identical with that of Pavlova dancing.*
> *His face is that of a man terribly glad to be selling fish, terribly glad that God*
> *made fish, and customers to whom he may call his wares from a pushcart.*
> (1–3)

With a "voice like a north wind" that blows over his prospective customers, the fish crier assumes an authority and influence out of proportion to his humble calling. Moreover, dangling herring before those same customers, he evinces "a joy identical with that of Pavlova dancing." The Pavlova here is Anna Pavlova, one of the great ballerinas of the early twentieth century and perhaps the greatest popularizer of that art. Unlike other dancers, Pavlova supposedly traded technical proficiency for a more inventive, more inspired style, which many of her admirers believed revealed a fervent, total devotion to the art. On the surface, of course, fish crying would seem to have little in common with ballet. And while fish crying is not a craft per se and not likely to produce popular art in the same way that, say, masonry might, or high art in the way that ballet might, Sandburg's fish crier can nevertheless experience a joy "identical with that of Pavlova dancing" since both commit body and soul to their art—that is, if art is, as William Morris claimed, nothing but "man's expression of his [or her] joy in labour." Pavlova may dangle her own body as her form of labor while the fish crier dangles herring, but both are nevertheless capable of "thrilling" or "blowing over" their audiences and both achieve the status of art through the joyous expression of their laboring bodies. Moreover, the fish crier's "gladness" in selling fish, his gladness in fish as a concept, and his gladness in customers who might desire fish all evoke the "pleasure" that Ruskin and Morris argued should characterize all work.

Sandburg complicates this picture, however, by describing the fish crier in somewhat displaced terms—a displacement that hints at his later departures from some arts and crafts tenets. In the second line, the fish crier is "evincing" his joy, suggesting that such joy might be as much an outward, superficial show as it is the expression of a sincere internal state. Similarly, in the third line of the poem, Sandburg does not say that the fish crier *is* "terribly glad to be selling fish" or "terribly glad that God made fish" but rather that "his face" is that of a man terribly glad about fish, again introducing a note of performance that perhaps belies the fish crier's actual, internal feelings about his labor. In other words, it could all just be an act to sell more fish. Of course, both of these readings are lent support by the troubling adjective "terribly," which at the least qualifies and perhaps even undermines the fish crier's supposed "gladness."

Granting these complications, though, Sandburg seems equally committed in the poem to collapsing the distance between what Morris would call the "intellectual" or "cultivated" art of ballet and the popular, degraded, low, would-be art of fishmongering. A similar, perhaps less ambivalent devotion to pleasure in labor informs another *Chicago Poem,* "Fellow Citizens," which more or less restates the rules that Ruskin prescribes in "The Nature of the Gothic" in order to determine "what kinds of labor are good for men" (*Stones* 165).[11] Like "Fish Crier," "Fellow Citizens" suggests how Sandburg would translate Ruskin and Morris into contemporary Chicago and the contemporary arts and crafts scene. Sandburg begins the poem by surveying some of Chicago's more prosperous and purportedly happy citizens.

I drank musty ale at the Illinois Athletic Club with the millionaire
manufacturer of Green River butter one night

And his face had the shining light of an old-time Quaker, he spoke of a beautiful daughter, and I knew he had a peace and a happiness up his sleeve somewhere.
Then I heard Jim Kirch make a speech to the Advertising Association on the trade resources of South America.
And the way he lighted a three-for-a-nickel stogie and cocked it at an angle regardless of the manners of our best people,
I knew he had a clutch on real happiness even though some of the reporters on his newspaper say he is the living double of Jack London's Sea Wolf.
In the mayor's office the mayor himself told me he was happy though it is a hard job to satisfy all the office-seekers and eat all the dinners he is asked to eat.

(1–6)

Each of the three men Sandburg describes derives some measure of happiness from his life and work. The millionaire manufacturer has a "peace and a happiness up his sleeve" from his prosperous and handsome family, while Jim Kirch extracts happiness from tweaking social mores or by helping others extract resources from South America. The mayor derives considerably less happiness from his labor—the job of satisfying job seekers and the toil of eating so many dinners—but he is happy all the same. In contrast to these figures, the second half of the poem describes a fourth man, whose happiness impresses the speaker more than that of any of his other fellow citizens.

Down in Gilpin Place, near Hull House, was a man with his jaw wrapped for a bad toothache,
And he had it all over the butter millionaire, Jim Kirch, and the mayor when it came to happiness.
He is a maker of accordions and guitars and not only makes them from start to finish, but plays them after he makes them.
And he had a guitar of mahogany with a walnut bottom he offered for seven dollars and a half if I wanted it,
And another just like it, only smaller, for six dollars, though he never mentioned the price till I asked him,
And he stated the price in a sorry way, as though the music and the make of an instrument count for a million times more than the price in money.
I thought he had a real soul and knew a lot about God.
There was a light in his eyes of one who has conquered sorrow in so far as

sorrow is conquerable or worth conquering.
Anyway he is the only Chicago citizen I was jealous of that day.
He played a dance they play in some parts of Italy when the harvest of grapes
is over and the wine presses are ready for work.

(7–16)

This last scene from "Fellow Citizens" occurs "near Hull House," placing it geographically close to one of the earliest and most inspired sites of the American arts and crafts movement. Like Sandburg, Hull House's cofounders, Jane Addams and Ellen Gates Starr, early on read and admired John Ruskin, so much so that Ruskin and William Morris would profoundly influence their settlement project on Chicago's West Side. Addams later reported in her autobiography, *Twenty Years at Hull House* (1910), that residents even considered decorating the interior of their workshop with a mural of William Morris even though "beyond the Socialists, few of the neighbors had heard of [him]" (227). For her part, Starr believed in Morris and the arts and crafts movement so much that she abandoned her position as a lecturer at Hull House in 1897 and apprenticed herself to one of William Morris's associates, the London bookbinder T. J. Cobden-Sanderson. Several years later she returned to Hull House convinced, along with Morris (in fact, speaking his language), that "only by re-creation of the source of art can it be restored as a living force" and that such re-creation would come only through "the freeing of the art power of the whole nation and race by enabling them to work in gladness and not woe" (165). Under Starr's influence, Hull House rejected mere lectures on the arts and instead opened a bookbindery, an art gallery, and a studio, which, Addams notes, "merged into the crafts and well within the first decade a shop was opened at Hull-House under the direction of several residents who were also members of the Chicago Arts and Crafts Society" (215). The shop further evolved into the Hull House Labor Museum, which Addams hoped would "build a bridge between European and American experiences in such wise as to give them both meaning and a sense of relation" (139). For Addams, sounding a little bit but not altogether quite like Morris, the Labor Museum would demonstrate that "culture is an understanding of the long established occupations and thoughts of men, of the arts which have solaced their toil" (141).

I will have more to say about the form the arts and crafts movement took at Hull House, but now it is enough to note that Sandburg's "maker of accordions and guitars" in "Fellow Citizens" could well be an exhibit at the Hull House Labor Museum. Despite his toothache, the maker of guitars and accordions inspires the poet's envy because of his greater claims to happiness, which spring from the preserved, preindustrial conditions of his labor. Unlike the butter millionaire, Jim Kirch, or the mayor, the "maker of accordions and guitars" is the only citizen to derive happiness exclusively from his labor and for all the reasons Ruskin and Morris argued workers should derive pleasure from work. He produces beautiful things, as Sandburg dreamed of producing in his early arts and crafts schemes. Unlike workers subject to the division of labor, too, the maker of accordions and guitars "makes them from start to finish," exercising complete autonomy over production and complete control over the finished product of his labor. The craftsman would also prefer to remain free of the constraints of the market, stating "the price in a sorry way, as though the music and the make of an instrument count for a million times more than the price in money." Moreover, Sandburg believes the man has "a real soul," largely because he believes he can see its expression—its impress—in the objects the craftsman makes. Finally, the craftsman is a type of Morris's popular artist in a double sense: he produces art in the course of his labor, and he creates a more traditionally recognized art when he plays "a dance they play in some parts of Italy when the harvest of grapes is over and the wine presses are ready for work." Even that dance, celebrating the harvest of grapes, invokes an integration of art and work absent among his fellow citizens.

All this pleasurable labor compares rather badly, of course, with the labor of the butter millionaire, Jim Kirch, the mayor, and, curiously enough, the speaker of the poem himself. Art expressed through work, Sandburg implies, is better (and leads to more happiness) than art qua art, even poems. One could ascribe such envy to the somewhat common desire among intellectuals to do something with their hands, but Sandburg also invites readers to recognize the equality and mutuality (or potential equality and mutuality) of head and hand work, thereby reversing the traditional hierarchy between those two modes of labor. Drawing on arts and crafts critiques, "Fellow Citizens" articulates the conditions that make it possible for workers to do something with their hands that is also doing something with their heads, which is also (to borrow from Ruskin) to do something with their souls. Those conditions might remain quite rare—one accordion and guitar maker in a city of fellow citizens. But that they exist at all suggests—at a time when Taylor and other efficiency engineers sought to remake the labor process in order to seize whatever control workers retained over their labor—another, more humane answer to the question of how men and women ought to work. If they wish to be happy, the poem implies, people ought to work like the accordion and guitar maker.

In addition to occurring near Hull House, "Fellow Citizens" also shares some of Hull House's evolving attitudes toward arts and crafts principles; both poem and settlement house, that is, give voice to and yet manage to alter arts and crafts ideals as Ruskin and Morris originally imagined them. In an instructive passage from *Twenty Years at Hull House,* for example, Jane Addams discusses her reasons for founding the craft shop, explicitly comparing such crafts to the mechanical sort of labor most of the workers in her neighborhood would have done. "Wrapping bars of soap in pieces of paper," she observes,

> might at least give the pleasure of accuracy and repetition if it could be done at a normal pace, but when paid for by the piece, speed becomes the sole requirement and the last suggestion of human interest is taken away. In contrast to this the Hull House shop affords many examples of the restorative power in the exercise of a genuine craft. (215)

It is hard to know what Ruskin or Morris would have made of this passage. However much they may have inspired Addams and the educational program at Hull House, her reflections on the Hull House version of arts and crafts also suggest the ways that she, Hull House, and some elements of the American arts and crafts movement would depart from the British critics and their adamant critique of alienated industrial labor. Neither Ruskin nor Morris, for example, ever imagined that pleasure could be found in "accuracy and repetition." They generally damned accuracy and, especially, repetition; Ruskin called it slavery. Moreover, Ruskin and Morris wanted to make all work a genuine craft rather than (as Addams here describes its potential benefits) making genuine craft work a "restorative" for alienated industrial work. Addams, the historian Eileen Boris writes, believed that "handicraft activities could . . . combat industrial alienation, both by humanizing industry and by integrating the worker into industrial society" (132). "Rather than trying to eliminate division of labor and mechanization," Boris continues, "she strove to compensate for their deadening of spirit" (79). Indeed, a year earlier, in *The Spirit of Youth and the City Streets* (1909), Addams rejected Ruskin's and Morris's hopes for remaking factory labor, accepting, as Boris put it, "the inevitability of mass production" and settling instead "to educate factory hands to a self-conscious role in the industrial process."

> If a child goes into a sewing factory with a knowledge of the work she is doing in relation to the finished product; if she is informed concerning the material she is manipulating and the processes to which it is subjected; if she under-

> stands the design she is elaborating in its historic relation to art and decoration, her daily life is lifted from drudgery to one of self-conscious activity, and her pleasure and intelligence is registered in her product. (122)

For Addams, as this sentence reveals, workers would no longer learn and practice a craft; instead, they would learn a craft in their free time and draw comfort from it as they practiced a degraded, divided version of it while at work. "A man who makes, year after year, but one small wheel in a modern watch factory," Addams argues, "may, if his education has properly prepared him, have a fuller life than did the old watchmaker who made a watch from beginning to end" (122). For Addams and other arts and crafts reformers who had similar designs, education and manual training would pacify—rather than eliminate—the fragmenting and alienating effects of the division of labor and industrial modes of production. As Lears says of Oscar Lovell Triggs, Addams was thus guilty of preaching "socialization, not revolution" (81).

Based on "Fellow Citizens," it is hard to imagine that Sandburg ever believed that the maker of accordions and guitars could derive just as much happiness from a guitar and accordion factory as he could from making them from start to finish and playing them afterward. In other words, while Sandburg may not have always preached revolution, he does not seem to have preached socialization either—and "Fellow Citizens" suggests that he has a deeper appreciation for the special conditions of the guitar and accordion maker's mode of production than Addams or the reformers at Hull House did. Nor, of course, did Sandburg ever think very much of factory work, even if its workers could manage to learn about their work's "historic relation to art and decoration." As one of Sandburg's personae puts it in "Mill-Doors," for example, factories "tap your wrists, / In the dark, in the silence, day by day, / And all the blood of you drop by drop" (6–8).

Despite Sandburg's conclusions about bloodsucking factory work, "Fellow Citizens" and "Fish Crier" nevertheless reflect a belief—shared with Addams and other prominent arts and crafts reformers in the United States—that one could reproduce joy in labor without necessarily eliminating alienated labor itself. Both "Fish Crier" and "Fellow Citizens" in fact have very little to say about alienated labor at all, except quite indirectly. Fish crying, for example, does not take place in a factory, nor is it a craft or a lesser art degraded by mechanical production. It is not even an act of production, but of distribution, which may explain its qualified ("terribly") vision of fish crying "gladness" when no such qualification attaches to the maker of accordions and guitars. Moreover, the fish crier does not state the price in a sorry way, as the accordion and guitar maker does, but stakes his claim to artfulness on shouting the price of his art in a joyous way. He thus does not practice his art free of the constraints of the market, as the maker of accordions and guitars desires, but as a function and expression of the market. Despite these variations on Ruskin and Morris, the fish crier, Sandburg seems to invite readers to believe, nevertheless expresses and experiences just as much joy in his labor and creates just as much art as the maker of accordions and guitars.

"Fellow Citizens" continues these minor but telling variations. In that poem, Sandburg does not contrast the integrated, autonomous work of the maker of accordions and guitars with the divided, alienated work of butter workers, for example, but with capitalists, politicians, and managers. In other words, the poem only indirectly—and barely that—compares the maker of accordions and guitars with a worker in a factory. The point is not that Sandburg must do these things, or that he uses Ruskin and Morris or crafts as a way to socialize alienated industrial workers, but that he struggles to translate Ruskin and Morris into a specific American setting, and he takes considerable license in that translation. In "Fish Crier" and "Fellow Citizens," those licenses seem harmless enough: seeing joy and art in forms of labor where Ruskin and Morris could not imagine it existing or contrasting workers with the economical and political elite rather than other alienated workers. Yet when Sandburg returns to thinking architecturally, this time not of Gothic churches but of their twentieth-century equivalents, skyscrapers, his adaptation of Ruskin and Morris to an American context raises even more questions about his evolving attitude toward the craftsman ideal and its applicability to the alienated labor and laborers of modern industrial capitalism.

In "Skyscraper," the final poem in the "Chicago" section of *Chicago Poems,* Sandburg joins other modernist poets in scrutinizing what John Timberman Newcomb calls "the central visible symbol of capitalist modernity" (97). Unlike the majority of those poets, however, but very much like Ruskin and Morris before him, Sandburg looks to these great buildings for what they reveal about the work and workers involved in their construction and their day-to-day operation. In "Salvage," Sandburg believes Morris "loved the shape of those stones piled and carved for [him] to dream over and wonder because the workmen got joy of life into them." In "Skyscraper," too, Sandburg eventually loves the shape of skyscrapers because it allows him to dream and wonder over the workers who built and work in them and, ultimately, get their joy of life into them. The problem, however, is that Sandburg sees no qualitative difference between Gothic cathedrals and modern skyscrapers—despite the radical difference (or imagined radical difference) in modes of construction and continuing modes of labor that separate the two buildings. Consider the first two stanzas of the poem.

By day the skyscraper looms in the smoke and sun and has a soul.
Prairie and valley, streets of the city, pour people into it and they mingle
among its twenty floors and are poured out again back to the streets,
prairies and valleys.
It is men and women, boys and girls so poured in and out all day that give
the building a soul of dreams and thoughts and memories.
(Dumped in the sea or fixed in a desert, who would care for the building or
speak its name or ask a policeman the way to it?)

Elevators slide on their cables and tubes catch letters and parcels and iron pipes
carry gas and water in and sewage out.
Wires climb with secrets, carry light and carry words, and tell terrors and
profits and loves—curses of men grappling plans of business and
questions of women in plots of love.

(1–6)

Both stanzas attempt to rescue the enormous structure of the skyscraper from its seemingly imperious indifference to humanity. While the skyscraper "looms in the smoke and sun," like some barely visible God, it nevertheless has—and Sandburg's diction recalls Ruskin—"a soul." Its soul does not derive from anything material but, rather, from the fact that it is a construction (like the republic in Lincoln's "Gettysburg Address") of the people, by the people, and for the people.[12] "It is men and women," Sandburg insists, "boys and girls so poured in and out all day that give the building a soul of dreams and thoughts and memories." Similarly, Sandburg imitates the convention of reciting the new forms of technology that make skyscrapers possible, yet he does so to remind readers of the humanity—the secrets, words, terrors, profits, loves, in short, the souls—such forms of technology actually serve (Newcomb 98). The skyscraper thus becomes its own entity, its own community, as full of love, ambition, terror, and tragedy as Sherwood Anderson's contemporary fictional community, Winesburg, Ohio. Just as Sandburg imagines William Morris gazing on Gothic churches in northern France and seeing "the songs and prayers [in] the walls and roofs, the bastions and cornerstones and gargoyles," so Sandburg himself gazes on this seemingly inhuman skyscraper and sees "a soul of dreams and thoughts and memories."

Yet note what has happened in Sandburg's translation of Gothic church into modern skyscraper: whereas for Ruskin the pieces and parts of the Gothic churches themselves embody the material evidence of workers' dreams and souls, for Sandburg the dreams and souls of the workers emerge in spite of the inhuman and monolithic skyscraper. Whereas workers supposedly got their joy of life into Gothic churches, into their walls, roofs, bastions, cornerstones, and misshapen gargoyles, the skyscraper itself has no joy of life or soul in its outward, visible form; rather, such joy and soul appear only as the result of the humans for whom it was built and who plot and work and love in it. That is all well and good, although it would be the equivalent of Ruskin's claiming a Gothic cathedral had a soul because of the parishioners and clergy who plot, work, and pray in it. But that is not how a building gains a soul.

Sandburg does indirectly acknowledge this difference in the origins of the skyscraper's "soul" in the stanzas that follow, which linger even more deeply over the construction of the building and ultimately resort to a revealing use of personification.

Hour by hour the caissons reach down to the rock of the earth and hold the building to a turning planet.
Hour by hour the girders play as ribs and reach out and hold together the stone walls and floor.
Hour by hour the hand of the mason and the stuff of the mortar clinch the pieces and parts to the shape an architect voted.
Hour by hour the sun and the rain, the air and the rust, and the press of time running into centuries, play on the building inside and out and use it.

Men who sunk the pilings and mixed the mortar are laid in graves where the wind whistles a wild song without words,
And so are men who strung the wires and fixed the pipes and tubes and those who saw it rise floor by floor.
Souls of them all are here, even the hod carrier begging at back doors hundreds of miles away and the bricklayer who went to state's prison for shooting another man while drunk.
(One man fell from a girder and broke his neck at the end of a straight plunge—he is here—his soul has gone into the stones of the building.)

(7–14)

In these lines, Sandburg personifies the skyscraper: its caissons reach down and hold, its girders "play," and the stuff of its mortars "joins" the mason's hand in "clinching" the pieces and parts together. It is a powerful image, but it also reveals that the inhuman skyscraper must be transformed—anthropomorphized—into the hand and soul of a workman reaching, playing, grabbing, and clinching. Such personification is telling. Ruskin and Morris claimed to perceive the hand and soul of the workman in the pieces and parts of Gothic cathedrals—obviating the need for a poet to bring such workers or their constructions to life. The modern skyscraper, however, has no outward pieces and parts that will communicate that soul. Instead, Sandburg must remind readers of its life and soul, and of the workers who give it that life and soul. Such personification is necessary since the pieces and parts of the skyscraper reveal only the "hand of the mason," not his "soul" or "joy." His hand is just another raw material, the equivalent of "the stuff of the mortar."

So while the mason and other workers have in fact built the skyscraper, they have not made it in the sense that medieval workers made Gothic cathedrals or the maker of accordions and guitars makes his accordions and guitars—that is, from start to finish, as a work of art, as pleasure, and getting their joy of life into it. Yet for Sandburg the skyscraper has a soul nonetheless. In "Salvage," Sandburg believes Morris appreciated Gothic cathedrals since workers actively "got joy of life into them." For the man who fell from a girder and broke his neck, however, "his soul has gone into stones of the building," a phrase that echoes Ruskin's *Stones of Venice* but nevertheless portrays the transfer of soul into building as a passive, almost residual exchange—as much the effect of workers' being (or dying) as their doing or making. The difference is slight but, ultimately, quite meaningful. Workers may have built the skyscraper, and, as the second stanza implies, even died in its building, but they had little say in its design—even though Sandburg attempts to give that authority over design the aura of democracy by describing it as an architect's "vote." But it is doubtful whether the architect ever submitted the design of the building to a workers' quorum. His, and that of whoever paid him to design the building, were the only votes cast. The worker's soul has therefore not really designed or built anything. And while one may see the mason's hand—that is, his labor—in the skyscraper, just as one can see the labor of the hod carrier, the bricklayer, the electrician, and the pipe fitter, the soul, strictly speaking, belongs almost exclusively to the architect. In other words, the mason has himself become a tool, shaping his hand—and, presumably, his soul—to the shape an architect "voted." The charge that Ruskin levels at Greek and Assyrian workman, then, applies equally well to the builders of skyscrapers: he "was, in both systems, a slave," if by slave one means (with Ruskin) the worker who could not freely express his soul in his work but instead followed the design of others. The soul that Sandburg claims workers put into the skyscraper, then, is really just their labor. For Morris and Ruskin, though, soul was not just labor—it was what workers expressed through labor when they retained control over the design and execution of that labor.

Curiously enough, when Sandburg reworks Ruskin and Morris to celebrate the construction of contemporary skyscrapers, he has not departed from the Chicago arts and crafts scene so much as aligned himself with one of its most famous proponents—and, not coincidentally, one of its most famous architects. In 1901, Frank Lloyd Wright delivered a talk provocatively titled "The Art and Craft of the Machine" to the Chicago Arts and Crafts Society, on which he also served as a member of the Board of Trustees. In this frequently incoherent speech, Wright nevertheless clearly expresses his belief (heresy to the arts and crafts crowd) that "in the Machine lies the only future of art and craft" (55). In the course of the talk, it emerges that Wright agrees in the main with reformers like William Morris and John Ruskin since "luxury" and "greed" had made the machine into "a terrible engine of enslavement," "deluging the civilized world with a murderous ubiquity, which plainly enough was the damnation of their art and craft" (56). For all his agreement with Ruskin and Morris, though, and despite all his damnations of the machine, Wright is out to prove Ruskin and Morris irrelevant. "The Art of old," Wright argues, "idealized a Structural Necessity . . . and accomplished it through man's joy in the labor of his hands" (62). The machine, however, has rendered such structural necessities and joyous labor "obsolete and unnatural" (63). The machine, Wright argues, "will surely and swiftly, by its own momentum, undo the mischief it has made" (56) and "the new art" (59) will emerge from the machine, "the destroyer of . . . present ideals and tendencies, [but also] their salvation in disguise" (68).

For Wright, therefore, an Arts and Crafts Society ought to abandon its commitment to handcrafts and its aversion to the industrial machines that destroy those crafts. Instead, it should attempt to influence manufacturers in the artful production of goods. Its members should make "excursions to factories" and study "the machine in process." "[N]ot in the spirit of the idea that these things are all gone wrong," Wright maintains, but "looking for that in them which would most nearly approximate the handcraft ideal; not looking into them with even the thought of handcraft, but getting a scientific ground-plan of the process in mind, if possible, with a view to its natural bent and possibilities" (68–69). Whereas an artist's tools were once a hammer and a gouge, "to-day [they] are processes and machines" (69), and once an artist has mastered these "processes and machines," he can realize the full potential of machines, thus "mastering the drudgery of earth that the plastic art may live; that the margin of leisure and strength by which man's life upon the earth can be made beautiful, may immeasurably widen." Thus empowered, the artist, with the aid of the machine, could "emancipate human expression!" (59–60).

In this new, emancipating art, Wright implies, workers, just as they do in "Skyscraper," would play a vital though diminished role. Workers would enlist in the artist's and manufacturer's vision—"the shape an architect voted," in Sandburg's terms—which would (in Wright's terms) "alleviate their insensate numbness" and provide "real help in adjusting the *Man* to a true sense of his importance as a factor in society, though he does tend a machine" (70, emphasis Wright). This language of "adjusting" and "factors," though, tips Wright's hand. Wright shares much with Jane Addams, who argued that knowledge of the original, integrated craft would give comfort to workers performing a degraded, divided version of it. Wright argues something quite similar: even though they only tended machines and would no longer express their own artistic visions in their labor, workers would nevertheless draw comfort from their knowledge of and participation in the greater artistic and emancipating vision they helped effect. "The artist of today," Wright concludes, "is the leader of an orchestra, where he once was a star performer," which is well and good for the artist, but under that arrangement, workers would no longer express their souls but rather the souls of their conductors—that is, architects and engineers (69). They would cease to be artists themselves and instead become artists' aids. They would, to continue Wright's metaphor, play second fiddle to the architects and design engineers who would call the tunes and conduct the orchestra. Art, then, would no longer be man's expression of his joy in labor. At that point, art would be an artist's—or an architect's—joy expressed through other workers' labor. At best, workers would be instruments in the creation of a sort of collective art; at worst, they would be the hired help. Either way, the instinct for craftsmanship and artistic expression would trickle upward to engineers, architects, and designers, the new artists of the machine age.

Although nearly fifteen years separate Wright's talk from Sandburg's published poem, Sandburg nevertheless seems to translate Wright's arts and crafts of the machine age into poetry. For Wright, "the tall modern office building is the machine pure and simple" (60), and his talk ends with a vision of the city as an organic body, the skyscraper as the trembling response to its pulse, and the machine as "the texture of the tissue of this great thing" (73). The machine, then, like the skyscraper, Wright concludes, "is the thing into which the forces of Art are to breathe the thrill of ideality! A SOUL!" (73). In "Skyscraper," Sandburg, too, breathes a soul into the "pure and simple" expression of the machine, the skyscraper, and praises the architect as a democratic visionary. Moreover, the scenes of labor Sandburg goes on to describe underscore the vital but nevertheless instrumental function of workers to the art of the skyscraper.

On the office doors from tier to tier—hundreds of names and each name standing for a face written across with a dead child, a passionate lover, a driving ambition for a million dollar business or a lobster's ease of life.

Behind the signs on the doors they work and the walls tell nothing from room to room.
Ten dollar-a-week stenographers take letters from corporation officers, lawyers, efficiency engineers, and tons of letters go bundled from the building to all ends of the earth.
Smiles and tears of each office girl go into the soul of the building just the same as the master-men who rule the building.

(15–18)

The "walls" masons have built "may tell nothing," unlike the walls of the medieval churches, which told quite a bit to Ruskin and Morris, but, Sandburg assures readers, each worker, regardless of his or her status or outward anonymity, nevertheless contributes to the soul of the building. And whereas before the mason got joy of life into the walls and churches he built, the new workers of monopoly capital—office girls and bricklayers, hod carriers and, remarkably, even efficiency engineers—will now breathe a soul into their skyscrapers by means of their passive contributions to the whole. Indeed, one's soul—and one's art—is expressed in smiles and tears, through ambitions and daydreams, not walls or gargoyles, not works of art. Moreover, the expression of that soul no longer even belongs to workers: it goes toward the soul of the building. To update Morris yet one more time, then, for Sandburg, very much following Wright, art in "Skyscraper" is now but man's (or woman's) expression of joy (or sorrow) in his participation in the soul, profit, and paperwork of the skyscraper and the machine age modern corporation. "Skyscraper" thus follows Wright in no longer looking into factories or skyscrapers "with even the thought of handcraft." Or, rather, Sandburg no longer looks to those places for evidence of joy or art in labor or handcraft but instead for the component, productive, even alienated labor that constitutes (or nevertheless should constitute) the new forms of joy and the new expressions of the human, laboring soul under advancing industrial capitalism.

In the course of the "Chicago" section of *Chicago Poems,* then, Sandburg begins as a poet who seemingly appreciates, however qualified and complicated that appreciation, the value not just of labor but of pleasurable labor, art as man's expression of his joy in labor, and indirectly the role of industrial capitalism in degrading that pleasurable, artistic labor. He ends, however, as the poet of "Skyscraper," which trades that vision of pleasurable, joyful labor for one that can surround the new, modern working class of masons, stenographers, and night watchmen with as much dignity and artistry as their mediaeval counterparts, whether they merited it or not. As a result, Sandburg focuses less on a critique of alienated labor or a celebration of pleasurable labor and more on the productive, collective possibilities of the machine and its symbolic expression, the skyscraper. One can see Sandburg the devotee of Frank Lloyd Wright here but also Sandburg the socialist. Like Lewis Hine's later portraits of workers raising the Empire State Building, Sandburg's poem can humanize skyscrapers by representing the workers who built them and work in them, thereby undermining the tendency to see skyscrapers as finished, abstracted commodities and thus to give credit where credit is due—that is, to workers. In other words, "Skyscraper" offers a labor theory of skyscrapers, and thus a labor theory of value. As such, it suggests that the ultimate responsibility of society is to the well-being of the laborers who provide value and souls rather than to the owners of skyscrapers or to the companies that occupy them. People over profits, as the old socialist saying goes.

But the Sandburg of "Skyscraper" also avoids considering anything about the quality or kind of labor in his labor theory of value, or else he obscures the differences in quality and kind beneath so much talk of "the soul." Twentieth-century masons, not to mention twentieth-century stenographers, do not get the same joy of life in what they build as Ruskin imagined fifteenth-century masons did; there is no "invention" or "creation" (in the artistic sense of the terms), only skill, only, in both cases, one literally, dictation. Yet the skyscraper nevertheless supposedly reflects the "soul" of that twentieth-century mason and stenographer. To point out this discrepancy is not to slight the labor, the skill, the craft, perhaps not even the art of workers who take pride in the skyscrapers they helped build or in the work that daily goes on there, rightly so, but it is to point out that Sandburg borrows the language of Ruskin and Morris to describe a mode of production (and reproduction) very much different from the one Ruskin and Morris believed ought to exist if that language was to be justified.

Indeed, Sandburg has so far departed from Ruskin and Morris that even efficiency engineers manage to sneak into the poem and, for that matter, the soul of the building. Their presence seems especially strange since, as organized labor had charged, efficiency engineers had done more than most to turn workers into automatons and, thus, to make pleasurable, soulful labor an impossibility. But when pleasurable, soulful labor is not what counts, then even efficiency engineers can pitch in. True, at first glance the efficiency engineers in the poem seem merely to assist in Sandburg's penchant for social leveling: the "Ten dollar-a-week stenographers" who "take letters" from "the master-men who rule the building," including efficiency engineers, nevertheless contribute "just the same" as those master-men to "the soul of the building"; their smiles and tears matter just as much as those of their supposed betters, even those who might scientifically manage their labor. Even so, those betters, including efficiency engineers, do in fact contribute to the soul of the building. As the earlier line has it, the names on office doors stand "for a face written across with a dead child, / a passionate lover, a driving ambition"—that is, behind the nominal surfaces of the tall office building lies the emotional life of workers, including efficiency engineers. They, too, their tears and smiles, contribute to the soul of the office building just the same as the tears and smiles of office girls. With the exception of organized labor, few people claimed that efficiency engineers lacked souls—or, for that matter, the sorrow, passion, or ambition that constitute souls and thus the soul of the building. Nevertheless, Sandburg has provocatively transformed efficiency engineers from shapers of labor to laborers "just the same," soulful ones no less. I'm glad you're a dead man, William Morris, one almost mutters on reading this.

Yet here, too, Sandburg, in his democratic embrace of efficiency engineers, does not so much depart from as align himself with the leading edge of arts and crafts discourse. As Lears points out, in 1911 no less a figure than Gustav Stickley published an editorial in *The Craftsman* that praised Frederick Winslow Taylor and other "efficiency engineers" for their efforts to eliminate "waste of human effort" ("Waste" 343). With the zeal of a convert, Stickley argues that "the 'efficiency engineer' has demonstrated that a workman can double and treble his output, shorten his hours of work, and increase his income—to say nothing of swelling the profits of his employer—by simply eliminating superfluous motions" (343). Stickley goes on to recount one of Taylor's favorite examples of scientific management, "a factory where girls were employed to inspect for the flaws [in] the little steel balls used in bicycle bearings" (345). Repeating Taylor's claims, Stickley writes that in addition to the other welcome results (higher wages, a shorter working day, cooperation between employer and employee), "the application of 'efficiency' methods enabled thirty-five girls to do the work formerly done by one hundred and twenty" (345). In turn, Stickley dismisses claims by Samuel Gompers and other representatives of organized labor that scientific management "tends to transform every factory into an industrial speedway" (344), arguing instead that organized labor opposed scientific management because it "is more likely to force them to change their attitude towards this question of efficiency, to recognize the wastefulness of their present theories of 'making work,' and of letting the least efficient element in their membership set the standard for a day's work" (344). As in Wright's speech and, to some degree, Sandburg's poem, for Stickley the new artists of the machine age are those, architects and engineers, who can manipulate processes and machines, master the drudgery of earth. Nowhere in the article, though, does Stickley mention pleasurable labor or work as an art. Ruskin and Morris, to whom Stickley had previously devoted whole issues of his journal, are conspicuous in their absence.

From Lears's perspective, it is a regrettable—yet clarifying—performance. "Stickley's embrace of Taylorism was," he writes, "only an exaggerated version of the entire movement's fate" (91). "Influenced by a developing corporate liberal ideology," Lears argues, craft leaders "sought to heal the wounds in the modern psyche not through a reassertion of autonomous will but through the smooth adjustment to the 'inevitable' process of rationalization" (89). As Wright's speech anticipated and Stickley's article confirmed, "Morris's hatred of civilization became transformed beyond recognition" (89).

The question, then, is whether Sandburg's transformation of Ruskin and Morris, his men of ideals, into the soul of the skyscraper counts as "transformed beyond recognition," whether, that is, when Sandburg includes efficiency engineers in his list of those who contribute to the soul of a building, for example, or when he expands the category of soulful labor to include, effectively, all labor, he leaves himself open to the charge Lears levels against the arts and crafts reformers who "betrayed Morris's vision while pretending to refine it" (89). And while Sandburg may not deserve that judgment, his airy pronouncements of workers' souls informing the soul of the skyscraper do at least seem to make him guilty of the slightly less damning charge Lears elsewhere makes against craft leaders, that of "blunt[ing] the polemical edge Morris had given to the figure of the artisan" (91).

But the mistake in this discussion may be to assume that such transformations, betrayals, and blunting are something one could be guilty of or should feel guilty about. In other words, even if Sandburg's adaptations are "transformations beyond recognition," those transformations may not be as regrettable as Lears thinks. To be sure, there is much that is worth preserving in Ruskin and Morris, but their vision had its limits, too. For one, they seem incapable of recognizing what Mike Rose has called the mind at work: the myriad of decisions and practices—mathematical, spatial, psychological, even aesthetic—that characterize all but the most routine and alienated labor. Rose, for example, devotes an entire chapter to the art and craft of waiting tables, which is not the first form of work either Ruskin or Morris would have looked to for evidence of artistic or soulful labor, but that does not necessarily mean it does not go on there all the same. Moreover, by focusing almost exclusively on the expression of an individual's soul in and through labor, Ruskin and Morris risk neglecting the expressive possibilities of collective and cooperative labor.

Still, Sandburg's and others' transformations of Ruskin and Morris does matter, although not necessarily because, as Lears would have it, they betray or blunt Morris's vision. Rather, Sandburg's and other craft leaders' transformations of Ruskin and Morris may instead matter because they represent the moment not when reformers lost their courage or betrayed their ideals but when industrialization and mechanization became an accomplished, permanent, and irrevocable fact of modernity. Accordingly, somewhere between Wright's speech and Sandburg's "Skyscraper," the question for reformers, revolutionaries, and working-class-sympathetic poets would no longer be (as it had been for Morris, Ruskin, and their American early adopters) whether production would be based on the division of labor and the tending of machines but, rather, the slightly less inspiring questions of how labor was to be divided, how best to reconcile workers to the alienation inherent in the tending of machines, and, for the socialists anyway, how to take control over production so as to reduce the working hours of the day and improve the material conditions of workers. Fewer people asked, and perhaps had less and less to gain by asking, whether work could be something one might want to do, could be made not just meaningful or just but also joyful.[13]

Indeed, by the time Sandburg published *Chicago Poems* in 1916, and perhaps even earlier, this question—of the possibilities for joyful labor—could (and did) seem naive. And how could it not when the likelihood of anything more than a boutique handicraft economy seemed more remote than ever? By World War I, for example, nearly a third of all wage earners employed in the manufacturing sector worked in factories employing more than five hundred people (Chenery 154). Nor were the majority of these factories simply scaled-up workshops manufacturing goods previously made by craftsmen. As early as 1900, the largest manufacturing plants in the United States produced steel, locomotives, meat, agricultural machinery, pipe, electrical machinery, ships, textiles, railroad cars, sewing machines, carpets, electrical equipment, glass, railroad cars, cotton, watches, silk, wire, oil, chemicals, plumbing supplies, saws, belts and hoses, cash registers, guns and ammunition, and cables and springs (Nelson, *Managers and Workers* 7–8). With one or two exceptions, few of these industries had a previous life as crafts, and even fewer (textiles, carpets, glass, perhaps guns) had ever been or could possibly be an art as Ruskin or Morris defined it. In short, as a 1925 labor textbook put it, "Crafts have been devoured by the machine" (Furniss and Guild 14), not in the sense that machines now did work once done by craftsman but, rather, in the sense that machines had remade the U.S. economy, ingested and processed and transformed the preindustrial economy and its modes of labor.[14]

Witnessing this new order of industrial capitalism, even labor reformers like William Ludlow Chenery concluded, as he put it in his 1922 volume *Industry and Human Welfare,* "It is improbable that the kind of pleasure in work of which William Morris was the prophet can ever be restored in factories where men and women spend their days and nights in the continual repetition of a single set of operations" (152). As such, Chenery continued,

> some trade union leaders and manufacturers . . . now regard the matter without misgivings. They assert that repetitious work can never be rendered truly interesting. Happiness, accordingly, must be found outside of work. Consequently, they contend that hours should be shortened so that leisure may exist, and that wages should be raised so that leisure can be enjoyed. That idea is in itself a child of the machine age. So far as men can now see there is in truth no prospect of a change of repetitious labor. (152)

If Chenery was correct about the bleak prospects for changing industrial modes of labor, then as the twentieth century progressed a revival of handicrafts could seem increasingly unlikely or even, as the socialist A. M. Simons wrote as early as 1902, "ludicrous" (39). Attacking those who "play at production in private workshops" (40), Simons wrote that "Seeing no way to correlate the gigantic industrial forces of to-day, and to use them for their purposes, they look backward to a simpler and inferior social stage, and become reactionary" (40). "Even Morris," Simon adds, "was not wholly free from this defect" (40).

To this more pessimistic way of thinking, then, Sandburg and other craft leaders are not leading but lagging indicators. Their betrayal of Morris's vision did not advance so much as it did reflect the intensification of industrial capitalism and alienation. The real question for some craft leaders, therefore, and craft-conscious poets like Sandburg, seems not to have been *whether* to cut bait on Morris and Ruskin's inspiring yet superannuated vision but *when*. Some, to switch metaphors, gave up the ghost earlier than others. Some, including socialists like Simons, remained ambivalent from the start.

Simons's charge that arts and crafts true believers were reactionaries in radical clothing raises one of the enduring paradoxes of romantic anticapitalism. Put briefly, the paradox would go something like this: those, including the poets represented in this book, who hated capitalism the most, and who longed more than others for a return to a precapitalist past, frequently did the least to alter it or, in their total opposition to capitalist modernity, remained indifferent toward efforts to amend it. Because of this paradox, Michael Löwy and Robert Sayre draw a useful distinction between romantic anticapitalism and what they call a modernizing anticapitalism, which is "an approach that criticizes the present" not based on past values but "in the name of certain modern values—utilitarian rationalism, efficiency, scientific and technological progress—while calling on modernity to surpass itself, to accomplish its own evolution, instead of returning to the sources, reimmersing itself in lost values" (28). That division between romantic and modernizing anticapitalism makes itself especially clear in whether one believes that Sandburg and other craft leaders "betrayed" Morris's vision. For the romantic anticapitalists, Ruskin and Morris's critique of industrial forms of labor—and even the tepid American reform movements brewed from that critique—raised fundamental questions about the form and content of labor that critics, reformers, and poets in the intervening years have less and less often asked. That silence has produced a lost art of work, a lost sense of work as an art, workers as artists, and, perhaps equally dispiriting, a lost sense of artists as workers who might repair the divide among intellectuals, artists, and workers. These notions once inspired productive, radical work, and they may do so again, but they tend to get lost in Sandburg's poetry, as they are mostly lost in the present moment. If so, according to this way of thinking, one would do well to rescue them from "the enormous condescension of posterity," as E. P. Thompson described the fate of the "lost causes of the people of the industrial revolution" (13).[15] In poems like "Fish Crier" and "Fellow Citizens," Sandburg seems to do just that—to rescue a vision of work as art, however qualified, when industrial capitalism threatened to make it invisible and forgotten. Other poems, however, like "Skyscraper," show Sandburg, perhaps acting under the pressure of an industrial capitalism that had arrived to stay, transforming that art of work into something more pragmatic and realistic but also less productive and radical than it was—and less productive and radical than it might have been. "This was a key moment in the reformation of capitalist cultural hegemony," Lears writes, articulating the romantic anticapitalist position, when "humanist reformers, even the perceptive Jane Addams, began unwittingly to accommodate themselves to the corporate system of organized capital" (80).

For modernizing anticapitalists like A. M. Simons and, perhaps, Carl Sandburg, though, socialists and reformers had no choice but to remake—if not leave behind altogether—Morris's vision. Even if modernity had not rendered it at best marginal and at worst irrelevant to the mainstream of economic life, it was not clear that a return to past values, even ones as irreproachable as joy in labor, would actually leave the world or even workers better off. Now is not the time to stage a debate about whether failures in production or distribution best account for the existence of poverty and inequality, except to say that compelling arguments exist on both sides. If so, then efforts to increase productivity, even Taylor's, can be made to seem not just necessary but praiseworthy.[16] From this modernizing anticapitalist perspective, those who clung to Morris's vision could seem, as Simons charged, reactionary, unconnected to the "industrial forces of to-day" (40). By contrast, then, Simons, Addams, Stickley and Sandburg look less like betrayers of Morris's vision or unwitting accommodators of corporate capital than they do like reluctant modernists desperate to salvage something from Morris's vision. When their efforts look awkward, as they inevitably do, or they seem to betray that vision, that may owe not to their own personal or political failings but to the irrelevance of Morris (and Ruskin) to modern industrial capitalism.

CONCLUSION

Distinctions with and without a Difference

This book begins with William Carlos Williams, and it may clarify the discussion to end with him as well. In 1935, Williams published *An Early Martyr and Other Poems,* which includes a poem, titled "Proletarian Portrait," with a revealing publication history. The short poem describes "A big young bareheaded woman / in an apron . . . standing / on the street" (1–4) with "Her shoe in her hand" (7). It concludes:

> *Looking*
> *intently into it*
>
> *She pulls out the paper insole*
> *to find the nail*
>
> *That has been hurting her*
> (7–11)

Prior to including it in *An Early Martyr and Other Poems,* Williams had published the poem twice before. It first appeared in Beatrix Reynolds and James Gabelle's 1934 volume *Galaxy: An Anthology,* under the title "Study for a Figure representing Modern Culture." Shortly thereafter, Williams showed the poem to Ezra Pound. In a March 1935 letter to the exiled poet, Williams thanks him "for the proper criticism of the gal holding a shoe in her hand looking for the nail in it" (166). Pound's letter, including his "proper criticism" of the poem, does not survive, but in a conversation with John C. Thirwall in the late 1950s, Williams recalled Pound's criticism. "Ezra Pound wrote that he didn't like this because of the proletarian tone," Williams told Thirwall. "He thought it was obvious and so what? 'She might have done as well in Russia as in Passaic'" (*Collected Poems* 540). Williams must have been stung by Pound's criticism, for when the poem next appeared, in the April–June 1935 edition of *Direction,* he had changed the title to "Proletarian Portrait," perhaps on the principle that if you draw attention to a potential fault with a poem it ceases to be a fault and instead becomes a provocation.

I would like to spend a moment with both titles, however, and the poem itself, in part because they resonate with the arguments I have offered thus far but mostly because they advance the history beyond the date—roughly 1930—at which I stop. To put it simply, Williams's original title ("Study for a Figure representing Modern Culture") shows where modern poetry and the labor problem had been; the other, later title ("Proletarian Portrait") shows where it would go.

Throughout this book, I have argued that what would become canonical modern American poetry emerges in no small part out of modern American poets' uncertain encounter with the poor and working class. Modern American poetry looks the way it does, and arrives when it does, because poets began to write about the labor problem and those who lived that problem, albeit in ways, as I have also argued, that tended to evade the exigency of those problems. Williams's poem, under its original title, "Study for a Figure representing Modern Culture," makes the point. Even without benefit of the later title, one could gather from her physique and dress that the "figure" here, the "gal holding a shoe," as Williams put it, is a worker. For Williams, then, this figure, a worker, represents "Modern Culture."[1] Not every modern poem is about workers, of course, but enough are to justify an extrapolation from Williams's poem. For poetry to be modern, it must represent figures, like this worker, who themselves represent modern culture. In short, workers represent modern culture, and modern poetry is represented by workers.

Yet Williams's second, revised title, "Proletarian Portrait," together with the content of the poem, distinguishes it from the earlier labor problem poems that he and other modern poets wrote. Consider what this figure representing modern culture is doing: she is looking for a nail in her shoe, and by finding it the "big young bareheaded woman" is identifying what "has been hurting her." Read allegorically, as Pound must have read it, the poem does have a rather obvious proletarian tone. In the context of the Great Depression, in the midst of one of the greatest strike waves in U.S. history—autoworkers in Toledo, rubber workers in Akron, longshoremen in San Francisco, teamsters in Minneapolis, and textile workers along the East Coast all struck in 1934—the young worker seems to represent more than modern culture, and more than just herself. At some level, she stands in for all workers, who will find—if they had not already found—what had been hurting them, whether nails or capitalism, and, presumably, remove it. Hence Pound's complaint that, as Williams remembered it, "She might have done as well in Russia as in Passaic." Pound implies that Williams's representation of Passaic workers—that is, the big, young, bareheaded woman from the poem—is influenced by his knowledge of Russian ones. Poked and prodded by capitalism, Passaic workers—or so Pound charges Williams with believing—might one day follow their fellow Russians' example in finding their problems and solving them. Even if Williams did not intend quite such a proletarian poem, in the 1930s, primed by experiments in proletarian literature, readers like Pound would inevitably see it that way.

In addition to showing where it had been, then, Williams's poem, together with its new title, suggests where modern American poetry and the labor problem would go. At first glance, the poem demonstrates that the labor problem—although the term slowly drops out of usage—would continue to manifest itself in modern poetry and the work of modern poets well past the founding and formative decades of the 1910s and 1920s. As with the earlier moment of 1913, the depression years, particularly 1934, seem to have compelled poets to once again—assuming they ever stopped—take up laborers and, however obliquely, their labor problems. And, indeed, each of the poets I discuss in this book would, in one form or another, continue their uncertain encounter with workers and the poor. Moreover, as my chapters on Williams and to some extent Eliot suggest, their later encounters with this problem would depend a great deal on their prior forays.

At the same time, however, 1934 differed dramatically from, say, 1913, not just because of the Great Depression but, as Pound's criticism and Williams's revised title imply, because of communism, the specter that had haunted Europe and, after 1917 but especially after 1934, now haunted the rest of the industrialized countries, including the United States. With a simple change in title, Williams hints at a whole new political and literary moment. The study of a "figure" representing modern culture becomes, instead, a portrait of a "proletarian": Marx's term for those "who live only so long as they find work" (479) and who, as the *Manifesto of the Communist Party* puts it, would be the inevitable "grave-diggers" (483) of capitalism and the bourgeoisie. To be sure, in the 1910s and 1920s modern poets and culture had plenty of radical political formations to get spooked by—socialism, anarchism, and, after 1917, as the postwar red scare attests, a disorganized but nevertheless embryonic communism. None of these, however, could match the pressure of communism in the 1930s nor encapsulate, as the promise or perils of communism did, the question of modern industrial capitalism and its labor problems. Beginning in the 1930s, then, as Williams's new title suggests, communism would change how laborers and labor problems make their way into modern American poetry. Increasingly, modern poets' encounter with the labor problem would take place in the context of debates about capitalism, communism, and, slightly later, fascism. For some poets, these debates would lead them to continue their escapades in romantic anticapitalism, while for others they inspired their most radical departures from it.

Williams offers a case in point. A poem like "The Yachts," also from *An Early Martyr,* allegorizes the infernal relationship between rich and poor in depression era America. The opening eight stanzas of the poem admiringly portray the America's Cup yacht races Williams had seen off Newport, Rhode Island, in the summer of 1935. In Dante-like *terza rima,* absent the *rima,* Williams describes the yachts, "mothlike in mists, scintillant in the minute / brilliance of cloudless days, with broad bellying sails," gliding "to the wind tossing green water / from their sharp prows" (6–9). The yachts, Williams elaborates, "appear youthful, rare / as the light of a happy eye, live with the grace / of all that in the mind is fleckless, free, and naturally to be desired" (15–18). In the closing three stanzas of the poem, however, the sea, through which the yachts imperiously and gracefully "slip through," is revealed to be composed of bodies.

Arms with hands grasping seek to clutch at the prows.
Bodies thrown recklessly in the way are cut aside,
It is a sea of faces about them in agony, in despair

until the horror of the race dawns staggering the mind,
the whole sea become an entanglement of watery bodies
lost to the world bearing what they cannot hold. Broken,

beaten, desolate, reaching from the dead to be taken up
they cry out, failing, failing! their cries rising
in waves still as the skillful yachts pass over.

(25–33)

The poem, Paul Mariani writes, articulates "the ambivalence [Williams] had felt watching all that aristocratic skill while knowing that it was a nation of poor people who in reality supported this small privileged class" (370). In his own words, Williams described the poem as "a false situation which the yachts typify with the beauty of their movements while the real situation (of the poor) is desperate while 'the skillful yachts pass over'" (*Collected Poems* 541). The poem, like "Proletarian Portrait," reveals how much Williams's aesthetics and politics had perhaps changed as a result of the Great Depression. Instead of glossing over the suffering of the poor or finding beauty in their poverty, as he had in his earlier counterpastoral poems, in "The Yachts" Williams opposes the suffering of the poor with the beauty of the yachts. Moreover, he seems to recognize not only that the poor suffer but, crucially, that their suffering is caused or ignored (or both) by the rich. Unlike in those earlier poems, here the rich have nothing to learn from the poor except that they are, at some level, responsible for their poverty. Unlike those earlier poems, too, it is not the poor that "stagger the mind" or "astonish . . . beyond words" but "the horror of the race," the pursuit of leisure underwritten by human suffering. A reader, Williams implies, no longer needs to come into contact with the poor, as he had earlier prescribed, but, rather, into contact with the "real situation (of the poor)," their desperation, which is in part an effect of the rich.

Yet poems like "Proletarian Portrait" and "The Yachts" can also mislead or, rather, misrepresent Williams's politics in the 1930s. "I am not a Marxian," Williams explained to Babette Deutsch in 1949, a statement that did not result, as so many other renunciations of the time did, from McCarthy era pressure to disavow one's earlier radicalism.[2] In fact, Williams was never a conventional Marxist, nor, despite publishing in Communist-affiliated journals like *New Masses* or championing openly Communist poets like H. H. Lewis, did Williams ever join the party or even think of himself as a Communist. Moreover, despite poems like "Proletarian Portrait" and "The Yachts," Williams's anticapitalism remained essentially romantic even after the onset of the Great Depression, as his dalliances with Major C. H. Douglas's social credit theories, his continued investment in the arts and their capacity for renewing, redeeming vision, and some of the other poems in *An Early Martyr* all attest.

Similar explorations could be made into the later politics and poetics of the other poets taken up in this book. Each, as I have suggested, continued to use poetry to confront labor problems, and most—but not all—continued to use poetry to articulate romantic solutions to those problems. T. S. Eliot, for example, took up the plight of the unemployed in his *Choruses from the Rock* (1934).

His solution, in that poem and other writings from the period, entailed a return to Christianity, a turning back of the clock on capitalist modernity. Edna St. Vincent Millay's 1937 verse drama *Conversation at Midnight* features, among other interlocutors, a young Communist, Carl, who often gets the better of his fellow conversationalists, this despite the fact that Millay left no doubt that "Communism is repugnant to me" (qtd. in Milford 387). Following the publication of *Harlem Shadows* in 1922, Claude McKay began to write more prose than poetry. The poetry that he did compose from 1925 until his death in 1948, however, documents his break with the Communist Party and oftentimes casts a retrospective glance at his earlier, radical self, all the while remaining conscious of the suffering and inequalities visited on black workers because of their race and class. Early in the 1930s, Langston Hughes took a sharp turn to the political Left and, over the course of that decade, produced one of the most compelling bodies of radical poetry ever written by an American. While *Chicago Poems*, in my reading, showed Carl Sandburg moving away from the romantic anticapitalism of the arts and crafts movement, his subsequent works, especially *The People, Yes* (1936), and his increasingly homespun persona, show him drifting toward a rather naive celebration of the folk. Other poets, too, for whom the labor problem only occasionally surfaces in their early poetry—I am thinking of Wallace Stevens—would, under the pressure of the Great Depression, begin to address it far more seriously than they had before. All of which is to say that as modern American poetry entered its establishment phase, poets continued to confront the labor problem in their own, oftentimes eccentric ways. Critics and biographers have recovered part of this history, but, as even this brief survey indicates, much remains that has gone untold or unexamined.

Leaving that book to another day, and in all likelihood another scholar, I would like to offer a final word on modern American poetry and its encounter with the labor problem in the period (1909–27) covered by this book, first by making some distinctions and then by largely dissolving those distinctions.

In chapter 6, I outline two possible ways to read Carl Sandburg's attitude toward and use of arts and crafts principles. On the one hand, some might charge that Sandburg's unwarranted application of these values—his loose talk of souls of buildings instead of souls of workers, his celebration of architects and efficiency engineers—constitutes a betrayal of them, a giving in to modern industrial capitalism. By contrast, others would argue that Sandburg's adaptations of these arts and crafts principles should not be read as evidence of personal or political venality but, rather, as a belated recognition that arts and crafts may have been unsuited to a rapidly evolving industrial capitalism and the reforms it most required. I believe the latter account gets it right. Nevertheless, much the same debate might be had of all the varieties of romantic anticapitalism that modern poets summoned in order to make sense of and perhaps solve the labor problem. Whether Williams's need to admire the authentic poor and not reform them out of existence, Eliot's allegiance to nonrational states of consciousness, Millay's fascination with bohemian, voluntary poverty, or Hughes and McKay's occasional faith that jazz and the remnants of Africa could redeem modern workers' emotional alienation—what each has in common with the other is how radically they seem to depart from conventional solutions to the labor problem or, more broadly, the industrial forces of modernity. As I note in chapter 1, the solution to the labor problem was (and remains) the comparatively basic task of redistributing power and wealth. Moreover, reformers and labor economists at the time offered any number of realistic proposals through which that redistribution might occur. For many and different reasons, however, those solutions seem not to have interested modern poets; rather, they opted for occasionally more radical and always more romantic attitudes toward capitalism and its labor problem.

True, one must acknowledge distinctions among these poets. One could, in fact, rather easily distribute these and other modern poets along a sort of romantic anticapitalist continuum, their place determined by how much their nostalgia for the past or hatred of the present brings them closer to or farther from a realistic account of the labor problem. As I write in chapter 6, Sandburg comes last in the book because his poetry foregrounds the inexorable facts of industrial capitalism: its economies of scale, its division of labor, its innate tendency to alienate workers from their work. Moreover, his poetry acknowledges that these facts perhaps mark the inevitable defeat of romantic anticapitalist visions like the craftsman ideal. Similarly, and while the same cannot always be said of their critics, Langston Hughes and Claude McKay occasionally recognize the limits of romantic anticapitalism, whether it takes the form of dreams of the glory that was Africa or dreams of the glory of what—jazz—survives of Africa.

By contrast, and occupying the other end of the spectrum, Eliot's romantic anticapitalism seems to relieve him altogether from the crisis of the labor problem. For Eliot, the poor and working class exist almost exclusively to distinguish the poet's tortured but complex consciousness from what he takes to be their automatic, occasionally even subhuman one. These figures allow him to object to and distance himself from the rationalization and mechanization of everyday life under capitalism. For Eliot, however, the poverty or suffering of the poor as such does not much matter. The same is true, to some extent, for William Carlos Williams and Edna St. Vincent Millay, who would fall somewhere in the middle of this romantic anticapitalist spectrum. Both resent capitalist modernity, both recognize the significance of poverty, but neither can articulate any special ethical urgency about the poor and working poor or imagine any kind of political alliance with them.

Despite these very real differences in the degree of their romanticism, however, few poets during the early decades of the twentieth century—Claude McKay perhaps comes the closest—seem capable of undertaking a sustained, nonromantic critique of capitalism.

However, that tendency toward romantic—rather than, say, modernizing—anticapitalism is, perhaps, what makes these poets attractive to later critics and readers. "Without utopias of this type," Löwy and Sayre conclude of the tradition of romantic anticapitalism, "the social imaginary would be limited to the narrow horizon of what really exists, and human life would be an oversize reproduction of sameness" (254). "Without nostalgia for the past," they elaborate, "there can be no dream of an authentic future" (255). Modern poets, as I have argued throughout this book, did not lack for nostalgia for the past or hatred of the present—in both resides their dream of an authentic future. And while I have my doubts about utopias or the uses of nostalgia, and could not distinguish an authentic from an inauthentic future, one can perhaps more easily respect modern poets' desire to be out of touch with, to be at odds with, the many things—alienation, hyperrationality, mechanization, commodification, meaningless work, emotionally alienating work, or soulless work—they found regrettable about modernity. Ironically, the response Frank Lentricchia imagines genteel poets made to the charge that they were out of touch with modernity—"they intended to be out of touch; it was the nature and function of poetry to be out of touch" (xi–xii)—applies equally well to the modern poets who followed. Like their genteel predecessors, modern poets and their romantic anticapitalist politics intended to be out of touch with capitalism and modernity, including the prosaic yet profound efforts to change them for the better. Only by being out of touch could one imagine truly transcending—rather than merely reforming—modern industrial capitalism.

Unlike their genteel predecessors, though, who also sought to be out of touch, modern poets could not pretend that capitalism and modernity did not exist; their status as modern poets depended on their being in touch with the workers and the poor of modern capitalism. So they acknowledged the labor problem (poverty, strikes, slums, immigration, alienation) and those it affected—indeed, let it inspire some of their most compelling poems—and then pursued out-of-touch solutions to it.

Notes

CHAPTER 1

1. A quick, admittedly partial survey may nevertheless illuminate the extent of this turbulence. In November 1909, some twenty thousand mostly female workers struck the shirtwaist manufacturers in and around Manhattan. The strike quickly turned violent. Pickcters assaulted strikebreakers, and police—both city and those hired by the manufacturers—attacked and arrested picketers. In July of 1910, the mostly male cloak and suit makers followed suit. As in the 1909 strike, as Graham Adams notes, "both adversaries"—strikers and manufacturers—"employed belligerent methods" (114), including, unlike in 1909, workers storming factories and destroying property. In addition to the 1909 IWW-led strike at the Pressed Steel Car Company in McKees Rock, Pennsylvania, in which dozens of workers were injured and a dozen killed, in December of that year, a strike among streetcar workers in Philadelphia quickly turned into a citywide general strike, one marred by rioting, violence, and death (Dubofsky 114–21; Adams 181–88). A few months later, in February 1910, workers struck the Bethlehem Steel Company in Bethlehem, Pennsylvania. In the course of that strike, police shot and killed one striking worker and wounded another (Adams 189–92). Throughout the latter half of 1911 and into 1912, the "timber wars" between sawmill workers and lumber barons raged in eastern Texas and western Louisiana, culminating on July 7, 1912, with a riot between workers and hired gunmen that left four dead and forty wounded (Dubofsky 121–27).

2. Of course, modern American poets were not the first group of American writers to address work and poverty. Nicholas Coles and Janet Zandy's *American Working-Class Literature: An Anthology* (2007) collects five centuries' worth of writing about work, workers, and working-class rebellion. Less well documented, though perhaps just as compelling, is American writing about poverty. Indeed, back when surveys of American literature began with the Puritans, a case could be made that, with John Winthrop's "A Model of Christian Charity" (1630), writing in North America begins with the dual questions of poverty and inequality. The 1850s, too, witnessed renewed literary interest in poverty, particularly among writers (Thoreau, Melville, Hawthorne) who would go on to form the canon of American literature. Rebecca Harding Davis's "Life in the Iron Mills" (1861) marks the beginning of realist and naturalist writing about poverty, which culminates in the turn of the century writing about poverty in Jacob Riis, Stephen Crane, Edith Wharton, Theodore Dreiser, Jack London, and, to a certain extent, W. E. B. Du Bois. (See Gavin Jones's *American Hungers: The Problem of Poverty in U.S. Literature* [2007].) My claim, then, is not that modern American poets are the first or only writers to address problems of work or poverty but, rather, that their desire to address these problems makes possible—and urgent—whole new kinds of poetry.

3. "For the seven years following 1915," the labor historian David Montgomery writes, "the ratio of strikers to all industrial and service employees remained constantly on a par with the more famous strike years of 1934 and 1937" (95). "Tight labor markets, an improving economy, and the consequent rise in union militancy," Joseph A. McCartin observes, "combined to unleash a mammoth strike wave" (39). The year 1919 seemed especially harrowing. It was, as Regin Schmidt writes, "one of those dramatic years, like 1968, filled with unrest, protest, and a clashing of social and political forces, when, for a short moment, the future of the nation seemed to hang in the balance" (24). In January of that year, Seattle workers participated in a citywide general strike. After Seattle, the situation grew even more desperate. By August of 1919, 400,000 coal miners, 120,000 textile workers, 50,000 garment workers, and 300,000 steel workers had all gone out on strike. All told, by the end of 1919, nearly one 1 of every 5 workers—millions of them—had participated in a strike (Gerstle 229). All these strikes played out, of course, against the backdrop of the Bolshevik Revolution in Russia in 1917, where there but for the grace of the newly formed Federal Bureau of Investigation it appeared the United States was heading, especially once the bombs started going off. In April 1919, two mail bombs exploded at the office of the mayor of Seattle and the home of a U.S. senator. In the coming days, another thirty-four bombs were discovered, either at post offices (where they lingered because of, of all things, insufficient postage) or already headed to their targets, capitalists such as John D. Rockefeller, J. P. Morgan, and other, as one pamphlet found with a bomb called them, "class enemies" (Gerstle 229). In June of 1919, bombs exploded in eight cities, and the next year, 1920, witnessed the deadliest terror attack in U.S. history. At midday on September 16, a horse-drawn carriage loaded with dynamite and window sash weights parked across the street from the Wall Street headquarters of J. P. Morgan. The bomb killed 38 people and injured some 400 others. (On the Wall Street bombing, see Beverly Gage's recent *The Day Wall Street Exploded: A Story of America in Its First Age of Terror* [2009].)

4. In addition to a host of articles and book chapters, cited in the chapters that follow, there are several book-length exceptions to this rule, including David Frail's *The Early Politics and Poetics of William Carlos Williams* (1987) and Paul R. Cappucci's *William Carlos Williams' Poetic Response to the 1913 Paterson Strike* (2000). Each book includes extended treatments of these poets' responses to the labor problem, although none calls it by that name. Moreover, Phillip R. Yannella's *The Other Carl Sandburg* (1996) documents the poet's socialist years and influences, while Alan Filreis's *Modernism from Left to Right* (1994), though bounded by the decade of the 1930s, takes up Wallace Stevens and his encounter with the depression era political and literary Left. Another obvious exception to this literary history has been the research of Cary Nelson and those inspired by his work. (In particular, see Nelson's *Repression and Recovery* [1992] and *Revolutionary Memory* [2002].) More often than not, however, this work is devoted to recovering forgotten poets or offering criticism about recovered poets.

5. Regarding the question of causality, the evidence suggests that the labor problem was a necessary but not sufficient cause for the emergence of modern American poetry. As my citations to it suggest, the labor problem—and references to it—began as early as the 1870s, while modern American poetry developed later, beginning in, say, 1909. Clearly, some other social, cultural, and, mainly, artistic elements had to be in place—

and were not prior to 1909—for modern American poetry to develop the way it did. By itself, then, the labor problem would not have made modern American poetry (it was not sufficient); nevertheless, modern American poets became modern, I argue, by writing about the labor problem and those who lived it (it was necessary).

6. A note on usage may be needed here. *Labor problem* is an arguably biased term with which to describe the conflict between labor and capital that played out during these decades. That is, it describes a problem besetting the nation as a whole, including, or so the term implies, the public good and, thus, the public more generally. To the degree that laborers caused the labor problem, then, the term risked aligning the public with capital and against laborers. It took for granted, one could infer, that labor and the public were mutually exclusive categories. One could have as easily and perhaps more accurately referred, for example, to the "capitalist problem." Workers, moreover, rarely used the term to describe their own suffering or grievances. That said, those who used the term *labor problem* did not unthinkingly take capital's side in its fight against labor. Rather, in addition to the public good, they seem to have been equally interested in the welfare of workers, which, they held, would ultimately determine the number and severity of disruptive labor problems.

7. While acknowledging that "there is nothing fundamentally objectionable about the employment of women" (146), that "it is futile to insist that 'woman's place is in the home'" (147), and that "the problem is not to prevent the employment of women" (147), Watkins—and other labor problem reformers—nevertheless did fear that women, like children, "may enter into competition with men and so depress wage scales and conditions of work" (146–47). Moreover, because "the future welfare of the race is so peculiarly dependent upon the health of women," the obvious solution to the problem of women in industry was "to eliminate the necessity of employing mothers whose services in the home may be far more valuable to society" (147). One solution to the problem of women in industry, then, Equal Pay for Equal Work, which, as Watkins notes, "in recent years there has been much agitation of," was frequently pursued less for the protection of women from discrimination and more for the protection of men from being displaced from industry.

8. Some industries were especially deadly. Between 1907 and 1920, for example, some twenty-five hundred coal miners were killed annually (192). Worse still employers did not always fully compensate their injured or ill workers, even after the passage of workmen's compensation laws in the first decades of the twentieth century.

9. Because of "the complexity of modern industrial life"—world instead of local or domestic markets, seasonal industries, more rapid business cycles—production could rarely match demand for very long, frequently outstripping it. Thus, Watkins argued, and unlike in earlier economic stages, factories often closed, albeit temporarily, and workers suffered from regular periods of unemployment (209). "The frequency with which acute unemployment has occurred," as Watkins put it, "and the increasing number of individuals who have become victims of seasonal fluctuations in employment, have given unemployment a place among the major problems of our industrial system" (209)—not least because it was "probably the greatest single factor in breeding social unrest" (213). "An industrial system that fails to guarantee regularity of employment," Watkins warned, "will be indicted by the masses who suffer degeneration of the standard of life" (213). If

so, the U.S. industrial system faced serious threats, as unemployment and underemployment were widespread. "Wage-earners in the principal manufacturing and mining industries in the United States," Watkins observed, "lose on an average from one-fifth to one-fourth of the working time during normal years, and in highly organized trades and industries, during periods of greatest industrial activity, from 7 to 20 per cent of all the members of unions are unemployed during the year" (215). The seasonal nature of some forms of labor periodically made the problem particularly acute. "In the winter months of any year," Watkins writes, "the army of unemployed in our great cities numbers several hundred thousand, while in periods of industrial depression several million workers are unemployed" (215). It was in the minds of these workers, willing but unable to work, that "revolutionary philosophy finds fertile soil" (213).

10. In 1913, for example, the number was 1,197,892. "Thus, at the present time," Watkins noted in 1922, "almost thirty million people in the United States, or approximately 28 per cent of the total white population, are either foreign-born or born of foreign parentage" (265). The changing demographics of immigration were particularly sharp in cities. In most American cities with populations of 100,000 or more, "foreign-born whites constituted from 20 per cent to 40 per cent of the total" (285). In the city of New York, roughly one out of every three people was foreign born (285).

11. Among the psychological causes was, although Watkins does not call it by this name, alienation. As my final chapter shows, Carl Sandburg was especially interested in this problem. "Work becomes drudgery," as Watkins described it, "for the great mass of industrial workers whose native impulses and aspirations are stifled by the oppressive monotony of machinery. Men become mere automatons, just cogs in the complex mechanism of industry" (309).

12. On industrial democracy, see two volumes in particular: Nelson Lichtenstein and Howell John Harris's collection *Industrial Democracy in America: The Ambiguous Promise* (1996) and Joseph McCartin's *Labor's Great War: The Struggle for Democracy and the Origins of Modern American Labor Relations, 1912–1921* (1997).

13. Low wages had direct effects on other measures of quality of life—not least basic matters like life and death. Whether measured by morbidity or infant mortality rates, Watkins and other reformers concluded, low wages inevitably led to a shortened life. The very poorest workers died at a rate "three and one-half times that of the well-to-do," and the infant mortality rate, while one in sixteen for the wealthiest families, soared to one in six for the poorest. Besides outright death, too, as a 1918 report from the U.S. Children's Bureau showed, roughly "one-third of all American school children of pre-school and school age are said to be malnourished" (64). "As we ascend the social scale," Watkins observed, "the span of life lengthens and the death rate diminishes gradually" (63). Worse still, these "necessitous conditions," as Watkins described them, coincided in the late nineteenth and early twentieth centuries with the amassing of great fortunes and deep inequality. An 1896 study showed, for example, that "seven-eighths of the families in this country held but one-eighth of the national wealth, while 1 per cent of the families held more of the nation's wealth than the remaining 99 per cent" (58–59). This "tendency of wealth to concentrate in relatively few hands," Watkins wrote, "and the existence of a number of what may legitimately be termed 'excessive incomes' are facts that have a significant effect upon the growth of social unrest among the masses" (67). "Such

inequalities," he observed, "explain to a great extent the present world protest of the working classes" (57).

14. By relating worker unrest to low or nonexistent wages—in other words, poverty—reformers unmade the usual division between workers and the poor. With the exception of paupers, a supposedly special category unto themselves, the poor were workers and vice versa. Hence, in the chapters that follow, I follow reformers and poets themselves in treating labor and poverty as, if not quite interchangeable problems, nevertheless deeply connected ones, two sides of the coin of low wages.

15. Van Dyke's own poetry, alas, adheres to these guidelines. For what the genteel poets had to say about labor, see his "Work."

16. While it is not clear that radical and socialist poets of the late nineteenth and early twentieth centuries belong to the genteel tradition proper, many of these left-wing poets did address the labor problem head on. For a survey of radical poetry during this period, see Paul Buhle's essay "Poetry (English Language) 1870–1930" in the *Encyclopedia of the American Left*. With good cause, Buhle cites Marcus Graham and Ralph Cheyney's 1929 volume *An Anthology of Revolutionary Poetry*, which is an astonishingly various collection of radical poets and poetry about the labor problem. In particular, though, one should mention two poets, Charlotte Perkins Gilman and Edwin Markham. Gilman's *In This Our World* (1914) contained many poems of social protest, which, as Buhle notes, would be "used popularly by soapbox speakers for almost two generations" (582). In the 1893 edition (published under the name Charlotte Perkins Stetson), see the poems included under the heading "Our Human Kind," which included works like "The Poor Ye Have Always with You" and "Mr. Rockafeller's Prayer" [*sic*]. In the 1914 edition, see the section titled "The March," which includes such poems as "The Wolf at the Door" and "To Labor." More famously, Edwin Markham's frequently reprinted poem "The Man with the Hoe" (1899) sympathized with the farmer, "the slave to the wheel of labor," and raged at the "masters, lords and rulers in all lands" whom Markham charges with having made and kept this "thing"—that is, the farmer—in abject, ignorant bondage. After the success of "The Man with the Hoe," Markham offered a companion poem, "The Man under the Stone," which cast the workingman as a doomed Sisyphus. Both Gilman and Markham are represented in the "Man's Brotherhood" section of Wallace and Francis Rice's *The Humbler Poets: A Collection of Newspaper and Periodical Verse, 1885 to 1910* (1911), which is another good source for poetry about labor and poverty from this period. And while these poets and poems are perhaps exceptions to the rule of genteel poetry—or do not even share a category with the genteel—they do suggest that the turn-of-the-century poetry scene was less monolithic and rarified than an exclusive focus on Van Dyke and his crowd would imply or than the modernists imagined it to be.

17. One may see this possibility for identification between artists and workers in Pound's comparison of magazines, which offered the only real market for poetry in the United States, to factories. In 1913, Pound wrote that "the system of magazine publication is at bottom opposed to the aims of the serious artist" ("Patria Mia" 110). "The whole matter," he continued, warming to his subject, "is that the editor wants what fits the scheme of his number. As the factory owner wants one man to make screws and one man to make wheels and each man in his employ to do some one mechanical thing that he can do almost without the expenditure of thought, so the magazine producer wants

one man to provide one element, let us say one sort of story and another articles on Italian cities and above all, nothing personal" (111). As Williams suggests, one can imagine modern poets identifying with their equally specialized and equally instrumental others, factory workers. In practice, of course, Pound's comparison tended in the opposite direction: not sympathy or identity with factory workers but outrage that creative artists, who deserved better, should share their conditions.

18. For Brooks's conclusions about Hughes, which would have enormous influence for the formation of the modern American poetry canon, see the chapter "Metaphysical Poetry and the Propaganda Art" in his *Modern Poetry and the Tradition* (1939).

19. Witness a recent sentence from a Caleb Crain review of Morris Dickstein's *Dancing in the Dark: A Cultural History of the Great Depression* (2009). "In the first decades of the twentieth century," Crain writes, "modernists like Joyce and Eliot had fractured and elaborated literary form, but the human misery of the thirties challenged American writers to return their attention to content" (93). While modernists like Joyce and Eliot certainly disrupted literary form, Crain implies that "content" and "human misery" remained the peculiar interest of 1930s writers. As I argue throughout what follows, this particularly ingrained piece of conventional literary historical wisdom simply does not hold up to scrutiny. Modernist writers did not sacrifice attention to content for attention to form. In addition to being dead wrong about the first decades of the twentieth century, commonplaces like the one expressed by Crain also mislead readers about the 1930s. As scholars like Alan Wald have pointed out, an exclusive focus on the 1930s cuts off the vibrant and in many ways continuous exchange writers had with radical politics in the middle decades of the twentieth century. See Wald's *Exiles from a Future Time: The Forging of the Mid–Twentieth Century U.S. Literary Left* (2001), as well as *Trinity of Passion: The Literary Left and the Antifascist Crusade* (2007).

20. Even for Langston Hughes and Claude McKay, the arguable exceptions to this history, the case is not so clear. Although they were originally recovered for their racial politics, lately scholars have been interested in these poets' connection to radical politics—or, rather, the relation between race and radical politics in their poetry and thinking. But scholarship on these poets' racial and radical politics oftentimes glosses over the many poems they wrote about labor and the labor process more generally. On Hughes and his radical politics, see relevant chapters from Robert Schulmann's *The Power of Political Art* (2000), Anthony Dawahare's *Nationalism, Marxism, and African-American Literature between the Wars* (2007), and Jonathan Scott's *Socialist Joy in the Writing of Langston Hughes* (2006). On McKay, see Tyrone Tillery's *Claude McKay: A Black Poet's Struggle for Identity* (1992) and chapters from William J. Maxwell's *New Negro, Old Left* (1999).

21. Of only the most recent publications, consider Eric Shocket's *Vanishing Moments: Class and American Literature* (2006), Gavin Jones's *American Hungers: The Problem of Poverty in U.S. Literature, 1840–1945* (2007), Patrick Chura's *Vital Contact: Downclassing Journeys in American Literature from Herman Melville to Richard Wright* (2005), Peter Conn's *The American 1930s: A Literary History* (2009), or Morris Dickstein's *Dancing in the Dark*. With the exception of Schocket, who devotes an uneven chapter to T. S. Eliot, and Dickstein, who briefly considers William Carlos Williams, Robert Frost, and Wallace Stevens, all form their arguments around readings of prose works. One recent exception

to this rule is John Lowney's *History, Memory, and the Literary Left: Modern American Poetry, 1935–1968* (2006), but it remains an exception. As James Smethurst recently pointed out in his review of Lowney's book, even "in the comparative boom of scholarship on the American artistic Left of the 1930s and 1940s over the last fifteen or twenty years . . . poetry has received short shrift" (787).

22. Indeed, Whitman would not be out of place in this book. He seems, for example, to have preferred celebrating labor and laborers to acknowledging labor problems or the iniquities of capitalism, and when he did acknowledge these problems, his solutions take decidedly romantic forms. In particular, recent critics have charged Whitman with idealizing an artisan republican utopia at just the moment when industrial capitalism was destroying that artisan economy. Moreover, Whitman seems to have resented capitalism less than many critics originally, and rather hopefully, thought. On Whitman's inability (or unwillingness) to confront capitalism and its effects for his ideal artisan republic, see M. Wynn Thomas's *The Lunar Light of Whitman's Poetry* (1987) and Jason Stacy's more recent *Walt Whitman's Multitudes* (2008). On Whitman's ambivalent embrace of the market and its democratic, self-fashioning possibilities, see Andrew Lawson's *Walt Whitman and the Class Struggle* (2006), particularly the first chapter, "Sex, Class, and Commerce." For a contrary perspective, on Whitman's radical, working-class sympathies, see Betsy Erkkila's *Whitman the Political Poet* (1989).

CHAPTER 2

1. Most discussions of late-nineteenth- and early-twentieth-century poverty concern the urban poor. Yet at least one contemporaneous observer, Edward T. Devine, claimed in his 1909 work *Misery and Its Causes* that "poverty was more prevalent in the countryside than in the cities" (18).

2. All etymologies derive from *Webster's New World College Dictionary.*

3. Grandgent, it should be noted, was quoting from Frederic Harrison's *The Cult of the Foul* (1912). Even in a volume like *The Lyric Year,* though, one could see this cult creeping onto the poetry scene. Despite the overwhelming presence of poems like Cawein's "The Voice of April," the anthology also included Louis Untermeyer's Shakespearean protest poem, "Caliban in the Coal Mines," and the editors awarded first prize to Orrick Johns's epic immigrants-observed poem "Second Avenue," which begins "In gutter and on sidewalk swells / The strange, the alien Disarray, / Flung from the Continental hells, / from Eastern dark to Western day" (1–4).

4. Sergio Rizzo makes a related point about "The Red Wheelbarrow" and Williams's erasure of the African American farmer who inspired the poem.

5. I cite Edward T. Devine's *Misery and Its Causes* (1909) above, but more relevant to Williams may be Henry Herbert Goddard's 1912 book *The Kallikak Family: A Study in the Heredity of Feeble-Mindedness.* Godard, a prominent psychologist and eugenicist, supposedly traced the origins of one of his "feeble-minded" patients, Deborah Kallikak, to a single dalliance between her great-great-great-grandfather, Martin Kallikak, and a feebleminded barmaid. According to Godard, their offspring—and subsequent offspring—lived lives of poverty, insanity, and feeblemindedness in southern, rural New Jersey.

6. The city of Passaic, as Weaver also notes, had a number of dubious distinctions: a higher percentage of foreign-born inhabitants than any other American city and the highest infant mortality rate in all of New Jersey. In large measure, these, and the native-born rural poor, were Williams's patients.

7. As in many of T. S. Eliot's poems, more often than not the workers and poor whom poets tend to encounter (or must encounter) are women. "K. McB." may suggest why. In an era when most middle-class and wealthier homes had servants, and those servants were almost always women, it is perhaps not surprising that better-off poets like Williams (and Eliot) frequently chose to write about those figures of the working class and poor with whom they were most familiar. More generally, women workers or women living in poverty were perceived to be less militant, less of a labor problem, especially when it came to violence, and therefore possibly a safer bet for modern poets to make of them what they would.

8. In 1910, for example, the city of New York proposed to build a public pool at the north end of Central Park. That plan was scuttled, however, because of opposition from a group of wealthy New Yorkers calling themselves the Central Park Preservation Committee (Wiltse 67–75). The *New York Times*, echoing the concerns of then mayor William Gaynor, wrote that "if it [the swimming pool] becomes popular and is used by all classes it will become foul in a very short time" ("Gaynor"). The next day, the editors noted that the plan for a swimming pool was "not likely to be carried out for a number of reasons," including the fact that "the proposed wading and swimming pools would become disease breeders" ("Protecting"). As Jeff Wiltse observes, the *Times* was not alone in its fears. A majority of middle-class Americans "perceived immigrants, laborers, and blacks as equally dirty and prone to carry communicable diseases. As a result, they avoided swimming in the same pool with the working classes no matter their race or ethnicity" (76). They also avoided reading about them—except in the pages of contemporaneous social science, which made "exposing rural degeneracy" an honorable academic pursuit (Danbom 31). In short, well-to-do readers liked their poor degenerate and far away.

9. Williams could gain access to the lives of the poor, but he could not always gain access to their thoughts or feelings. Indeed, he did not have to do so if his goal remained putting readers into contact with the poor and working class. Physical, proximate contact served that function as well as any more intersubjective contact. That is not always a regrettable limitation, either, given the awkward results that sometimes happened when Williams (or many other writers) tried to reproduce lower-class consciousness. With very few exceptions, then, Williams remains deliberately "outside" the heads of his poor and working-class subjects, adopting instead the persona and stance of the outside observer, the recording consciousness—indeed, the visiting doctor. As a result, as Williams's career progresses, he writes many fewer poems like "Sicilian Emigrant's Song" (1913), a dialect poem that purports to reproduce the thoughts and feelings of a Sicilian emigrant arriving at Ellis Island.

10. To give Frail his due, he does recognize what Williams is about in this poem. "In 'Sick African,' then," he writes, "Williams refuses to make commentary or allegory about 'the woman question,' race, or economic class. . . . Instead, he presents a concrete moment in a particular couple's life, the significance of which Williams refuses to comment

on. It becomes a political poem, or rather a comment on a political poetry, through Williams's gesture of submitting it to *The Masses*" (105).

11. "To Elsie," from several years later, may be the most famous exception to this rule, although its encounter with the rural and degenerate poor is equally transformative.

12. Indeed, Williams so feared appearing even remotely political that he pulled—after some prodding from his publisher—the subtitle of *Al Que Quiere!*, which was to have been *The Pleasures of Democracy* (Mariani 144–45). That decision is regrettable since the subtitle would have revealed much about the volume of poetry. In the 1910s and 1920s, to describe a poet or poetry as "democratic" meant that they or it looked to the common man as a source of poetry and therefore treated the hod carrier, bricklayer, or colored day worker with as much dignity and solemnity as would otherwise be reserved for the more exalted and more traditional subjects—both topics and people—of poetry. To describe the "Pleasures of Democracy," then, would signal the moral ambiguities Williams brought to his poetry of the poor and working class, just as in "Pastoral" he describes the color of light in which the poor and their ramshackle housing appears as that which "pleases him best" (18). Nevertheless, Williams opted not to give this signal and withdrew the subtitle.

13. For many Williams critics—so many, in fact, as to appear quite strange—it is just this refusal to write as a political poet that wins their praise. Indeed, if any critical consensus existed about Williams, it would be this one. As early in the William Carlos Williams revival as 1968, James Guimond set the tone, writing that "because he presented [his environment] so objectively, Williams' poems of the 1930's never seem proletarian—even when they are constructed of proletarian materials. His poems have none of the dutiful dreariness or preachy indignation characteristic of so much proletarian writing" (133). In 1978, Robert von Hallberg echoed Guimond in praising Williams for rising "above partisanship" and wishing to "rather preserve than serve" (148). Von Hallberg distinguished between the poet of description and the poet of explanation, and Williams—blessedly—belonged to the former. "The descriptive poet," von Hallberg wrote, "is restrained by his task. He is the scribe for his subject; his office is to copy rather than transform, and his writing embodies an implicit reverence for his subject" (132). That, clearly, was good. "The explanatory poet, however," von Hallberg continues, "is obligated more to his audience than to his subject. He *must* transform his subject, make it plain, lay it out flat for all to see" (132). And that, just as clearly, was bad. But Guimond and von Hallburg were not alone in praising this quality in Williams. Here is Paul Cappucci on Williams's *Life along the Passaic River*, his 1938 collection of short stories: "He portrays the lower-class people living around the river, but he refrains from attaching an overt political commentary or moral message to his story" (113). Or, as Williams's biographer, Paul Mariani, wrote of his stories in *Blast*, they "revealed more eloquently than any propaganda could what the economic situation in America had done to thousands of lower-class American families, and how those families had somehow managed to survive" (345). Or Cappucci again: "Williams thus represents the poor without preaching to his readers" (130); "He simply represents her as he sees her and thus avoids any social sermons that she may deliver to his readers" (132).

14. "May it not be," Williams asks in "The Neglected Artist," "that the world of art

does offer an asylum, a working place for the reestablishment of order?" "We should begin," he concludes in that essay, "by seeing the arts in the large as a world which may be a haven for us—not just as a picture or two, a concert or two, but a great, continuous tradition, a contemporary world from which we may draw power and enlightenment in a very special manner today" (91). Or, as Williams also wrote in "The Neglected Artist," dropping the pretense of having an artist speak for him:

> The whole Renaissance was a rule of so many tyrants. It was they who hired the masters to work for them. The great artists of the time did not stop to attack such men. They were their friends. They made masterpieces. And in their work lies a depth of understanding which must ultimately do away with all tyrants and cruelty, all violence of which art is the antithesis. (83)

In the long run we will all be dead, as John Maynard Keynes pointed out, but for Williams "the long run" is exactly the period of time necessary for art to accomplish its political effects. "He had only to paint," as Williams has his artist say, and the same could be said for the poet—he had only to see. "For Williams," as Bram Dijkstra explains, "the identification of a poem as a composition of sharply, visually, delineated objects and events was a sufficient justification of its existence, as it is commonly accepted to be in painting" (5). That belief held true even when the objects to be delineated were workers or the poor.

15. As it happens, and perhaps unsurprisingly, others, even contemporaries of Williams, criticized the poet on similar grounds. In a 1934 essay in *Dynamo: The Journal of Revolutionary Poetry,* the poet Sol Funaroff (writing under the pseudonym Charles Henry Newman) wrote of the Objectivists, a group that occassionally included William Carlos Williams, "Actually, the Objectivist has no objective, has no sense of direction in the sense of movement towards a goal. His aim is really the aim of the camera, its lens focused upon an object, to snap a lifeless photograph. It is the act of the recorder and not the creator, the man of purpose" (94). Likewise, and of Williams specifically, Funaroff offered this observation: "He sees details of poverty but he does not recognize or relate to its cause" (26–29). Funaroff is a Communist, and, to his mind, the "cause" of poverty is capitalism; essentially, then, Funaroff is taking Williams to task for not being a Communist. Nevertheless, Funaroff is onto something quite damning about Williams's poetry of the poor. Williams sees the details of poverty, and demands that we see them too, but he gives no indication whatsoever that he or his readers should change anything about the poor except their attitudes toward them.

16. As with "To Elsie," exceptions abound—especially in the 1930s when Williams took a slight turn to the political left. Poems like "Proletarian Portrait" and "The Yachts" at times rise (or sink, according to your perspective) to the level of advocacy. See my remarks on Williams in the conclusion.

CHAPTER 3

1. "Sprouting" is the word Eliot decided on when the poem appeared in *Prufrock and Other Observations;* when the poem appeared in *Poetry,* housemaids were instead "Hanging despondently at area gates," rather more like the clothes they laundered.

2. As evidence of this growing awareness, it is perhaps worth quoting Eliot's thoughts about Baudelaire. In a talk given in 1950, Eliot declared,

> I think that from Baudelaire I learned first, a precedent for poetic possibilities, never developed by any poet writing in my own language, of the more sordid aspects of the modern metropolis, of the possibility of fusion between the sordidly realistic and the phantasmagoric, the juxtaposition of the matter-of-fact and the fantastic. From him, as from Laforgue, I learned that the sort of material that I had, the sort of experience that an adolescence had had, in an industrial city in America, could be the material for poetry; and that the source of new poetry might be found in what had been regarded hitherto as the impossible, the sterile, the intractably unpoetic. That, in fact, the business of the poet was to make poetry out of the unexplored resources of the unpoetical; that the poet, in fact, was committed by his profession to turn the unpoetical into poetry. ("What Dante Means to Me" 126)

3. "Here it lies," the authors of the guidebook intoned, "crowded in between and around two great universities: a city of workers, most of whose thousands never even dreamed of going to college, many of whom never even contemplated high school; yet a city no less real than its intellectual other self, with no less lusty a heritage and no less potent and problematic a future" (191).

4. Eric Sigg's chapter "Divisions and Precisions: Ambivalence and Ambiguity" from his *The American T. S. Eliot* (1989) is a valuable exception to this rule. Some of my conclusions about the "Preludes" match his.

5. Gordon continues, "Another sister, Marian, had studied at Miss Folson's school for social service in Boston. Of his Boston cousins, Martha was to be a physician—she later specialized in child care and public health—and her sister Abigail was going into education—her school in Roxbury was to be the precursor of all programmes for special needs" (46).

6. Hunter's conclusions about tramps, a species of pauper, are relevant here as well. Like the "helpless fields" of Eliot's "Second Caprice," which are "sinister, sterile and blind," tramps, Hunter writes, "possess no foresight" even as they are "rarely retrospective" (129). Moreover, like the automatic dwellers of the slums in Eliot's poems, especially those of "Rhapsody on a Windy Night," which I take up later, tramps are robbed of "systematic memory" (129) and thus live, as Gavin Jones puts it, in "a perpetual present" (94).

7. Cambridge, as Samuel Atkins Eliot observed, was home to "a score or more vigorous philanthropic agencies" (124), and "it would be difficult," he continued, "to discover any physical, moral, or spiritual need that is unsupplied by one or another of these channels of a generous community spirit" (125).

8. Fetishism, as Eric Schocket notes of similar poems from the period, is Eliot's "key figural form" (158), and fragmentation, as Manju Jain writes, "is a negation of individual identity" (65).

9. From a Bergsonian perspective, it should be noted, "images" may not connote unreality; rather, for Bergson, all memories, all perceptions, are images, and, as in imagist poetry, may therefore have more and not less effect on those who perceive them.

10. As Russell summarizes it, "Intellect is the power of seeing things separate from

one another, and matter is that which is separated into distinct things" (*History* 794). But in reality, as Russell notes, for Bergson "there are no separate solid things, only an endless stream of becoming" (794).

11. Concerning "external perception," Bergson writes, "there is only a difference of degree, not of kind, between the so-called perceptive faculties of the brain and the reflex functions of the spinal cord" (*Matter and Memory* 299).

12. For a poet like Eliot who supposedly held the romantics in low regard, he adopts a number of their tropes, including, in these poems, what Löwy and Sayre call "the Romantic fascination with night" (32) and the "favorable evaluation of madness" (41), both signs of the "individual's ultimate break with socially instituted reason" (41).

13. Although it is a fairly common trope, references to oysters and oyster restaurants appear throughout *New York by Gas-Light,* perhaps nowhere so memorably as at the outset of the book, where, as Foster describes it, "The oyster-cellars, with their bright lamps casting broad gleams of red-light across the street, are now in full tide, and every instant sees them swallow up at one entrance a party of rowdy and half-drunken young men, on their way to the theater, the gambling-house, the bowling-saloon, or the brothel—or most to all in turn—while another is vomited up the other stairway, having already had their fill of oysters and bad brandy" (8–9). Oysters are also served in the "one-night cheap hotels," what Foster calls the hotels where "so long as you conduct yourself quietly and don't dispute the bill, you may do any and everything you please—stay as long as you like, go when it suits you, at any hour of the night or day, and no questions asked nor observations made" (40).

14. To be sure, by the end of the poem, Prufrock draws on other cultural resources—mermaids and crabs—to combat his ennui. Such a substitution, however, also confirms the mythical (and escapist) function of slum culture at the outset of the poem. This interplay between class and myth suggests that another model for Eliot's urban primitivism might be the nascent field of anthropology. As Marianna Torgovnick observes of primitivist discourses more generally, "Frequently, the working class or other subordinate segments of the population become associated or identified with primitives. . . . These Others are processed, like primitives, through a variety of tropes which see them as a threatening horde, a faceless mass, promiscuous, breeding, inferior" (18). "To study the primitive," then, "is thus to enter an exotic world which is also a familiar world. . . . Primitives are our untamed selves, our id forces—libidinal, irrational, violent, dangerous" (8).

15. For Eliot to describe these "sexual attacks"—the impasse between practicality and impulse—as "nervous" recalls one of the central cultural maladies of modernist antimodernism. In *American Nervousness,* Charles Beard argued that an overcivilized and overfrenetic modern world had given rise to a morbid self-consciousness and a paralysis of will. "Tortured by indecision and doubt," T. J. Jackson Lears observes, Beard's "neurasthenic seemed a pathetic descendent of the iron-willed Americans who had cleared forests, drained swamps, and subdued a continent" (50). Moreover, Beard and others influenced by him concluded that the indecisive and paralyzed modern subject needed to escape an enervating modernity for the supposed primitivism of what one 1894 editor called the "Oriental people, the inhabitants of the tropics, and colored peoples generally" (qtd. in Lears 52). To that list of the supposedly relaxed and reposed, Eliot adds the poor and working class.

16. Eliot borrowed Sweeney's name from a Saint Louis doctor (F. L. Sweany) who, like the influential American "nerve" specialist Charles Beard, treated (according to Sweany's advertisement) "MEN WHO ARE WASTING AWAY" and an urban bourgeoisie suffering from "Nervous Debility" (Crawford 28). Moreover, Eliot supposedly based Sweeney's manliness and sexuality on a Boston bartender (according to Vivian Eliot) and (according to Conrad Aiken) an Irishman, Steve O'Donnel, from whom Eliot took boxing lessons as an undergraduate at Harvard in an effort not to waste away (*Waste Land* 125; *T. S. Eliot: A Symposium* 21).

17. Compare a poem like "Aunt Helen" with the following stanzas from "Sweeney Erect," which takes place in a whorehouse with an epileptic prostitute on the bed and Sweeney poised to shave some of that infamous hirsuteness.

Sweeney addressed full length to shave
Broadbottomed, pink from nape to base,
Knows the female temperament
And wipes the suds around his face.

(The lengthened shadow of a man
Is history, said Emerson
Who had not seen the silhouette
Of Sweeney straddled in the sun.)
(25–32)

While the quatrains do lend the poem a lighter, satiric touch, the poem seems more repulsed than liberated by Sweeney's physicality. Sweeney is animal and degenerate—not playful and appetitive. Moreover, had Emerson seen the shadow this representative man casts while having sex, Eliot implies in "Sweeney Erect," he would have drawn much less sanguine conclusions about history or looked for alternate ways to explain its progress, since few would want a history driven with straddled Sweeney at the wheel.

18. This number indicates page rather than line number, since lineation for the draft version of *The Waste Land* would only confuse.

19. All these episodes combine to confirm what Kenneth Asher points out in *T. S. Eliot and Ideology* (1998): "The curse of *The Waste Land* is brought about by an amorphous—hence unhealthy—sexuality" (43). "In the case of Sweeney," Asher continues, "we can plainly see . . . that at some level [Eliot's] insistence on classical order is motivated by his loathing of the sexual impulse" (41). The poem as a whole, then, Asher argues, demonstrates the need for "ritualistic regulation of impulse," which "for Eliot, as for Freud . . . , at its most basic, is sexual" (43). "The difference is," Asher concludes, "that according to Eliot it is the *failure* to restrain this energy that has caused the discontent of modern civilization" (43). What Asher underestimates, however, is that for the Eliot of *The Waste Land,* sexual impulse and energy are not generalized and generally disruptive but usually either originate in or are expressed by Sweeney and the working class more generally. The curse of *The Waste Land,* then, is not just sexuality but, more often than not, working-class sexuality.

CHAPTER 4

1. See also Reed's account of the arrest in his "War in Paterson."

2. The Rockefeller bombing is perhaps the least well known of these events. Because of his role in the Ludlow massacre of 1914, John D. Rockefeller Jr. became something of a pariah in New York City, at least in radical leftist circles. Protesters stood vigil outside his East Side mansion, and when Rockefeller and his family fled the city for their country estate they were followed by still more protesters. Worse yet, Alexander Berkman, whose 1892 attempt to assassinate Henry Clay Frick had failed, began plotting yet another attack, in the course of which a bomb being assembled in a tenement building accidentally discharged, killing three of the plotters and a young woman. The bombing alienated many would-be political allies. See Christine Stansell's account of the events in *American Moderns* (111–17).

3. *A Few Figs from Thistles* has a fairly convoluted publication history. A much smaller, limited first edition, published by Frank Shay, appeared in 1920 and in subsequent years. In 1922, Harper and Brothers published an expanded edition.

4. For example, John Reed's *The Day in Bohemia* (1913), discussed shortly, refers to both Puccini's *La Bohème* and Murger's *Scènes de la Vie de Bohème.*

5. In the summer of 1912, Millay's sister Norma took a job as a waitress at the local hotel, the Whitehall Inn. At a staff party that she attended with her sister, Millay recited "Renascence," her long, precocious poem about death and transcendence that would place third in a popular poetry contest and effectively launch her career. "Stunned," as Millay's biographer, Nancy Milford put it, "by this provincial girl's assured performance" (69), Dow, along with her wealthy friends in New York, paid Millay's way through Vassar.

6. See Debra Fried, "Andromeda Unbound: Gender and Genre in Millay's Sonnets."

7. "Midnight Oil," equally pithy, offers a similar sentiment: "Cut if you will, with Sleep's dull knife, / Each day to half its length, my friend,— / The years that Time takes off *my* life, / He'll take from the other end!" The poem, to reduce it to a cliché, celebrates living fast and dying young. On doing things one might regret but cannot quite bring oneself to regret, see also "The Penitent."

8. Even before the city of Manhattan made the Staten Island Ferry free in 1997, it had always been a bargain. At the time Millay wrote "Recuerdo," it had become an even better bargain. In 1917, Staten Island's then state senator George Cromwell sponsored a bill, which ultimately passed, that lowered the fare on the Staten Island Ferry from five cents to two. The *New York Times* complained, calling it "a boon" to those who lived on Staten Island and to the "excursionists" who packed the ferries during the summer months for a trip to its hills and beaches ("Staten Island Ferry" 12).

9. "Bohemia," as Elizabeth Wilson defines it, "is the name for the attempt by nineteenth and twentieth century artists, writers, intellectuals and radicals to create an alternative world within Western society (and possibly elsewhere). Despite the exaggerated individualism of its citizens, bohemia was a collective enterprise; the bohemians created and participated in a social milieu created *against* the dominant culture, as the artist made a startling transformation from paid ideologue to violent critic of society in the unfamiliar world of 'modernity'" (2–3). "Components of the myth," she adds, "are

transgression, excess, sexual outrage, eccentric behavior, outrageous appearance, nostalgia and poverty—although wealth could contribute to the legend provided the bohemian treated it with contempt, flinging money around instead of investing it with bourgeois caution" (3).

10. LaFargue would have liked slightly more, although he would have been disappointed in the modesty of their demands, workers who made I. G. Blanchard's song-poem "Eight Hours," with its refrain of "Eight hours for work, eight hours for sleep, eight hours for what we will," one of (if not *the*) most popular labor songs of the nineteenth century.

11. Within the past two decades, critics have occasionally challenged Veblen's work. For feminist critiques, see Kathleen Donohue's "What Gender Is the Consumer?" and Rachel Bowlby's "Sad Hearts and Supermarkets"; for a more general critique, see T. J. Jackson Lears's "Beyond Veblen." Despite these critiques, recent work in positive psychology and neuroscience has confirmed many of Veblen's basic insights. See Robert H. Frank's *Luxury Fever* (1999) and Peter C. Whybrow's *American Mania* (2006).

12. Veblen's famous, almost certainly apocryphal example is "a certain King of France" who, "in the absence of the functionary whose job it was to shift his master's seat . . . sat uncomplaining before the fire and suffered his royal person to be roasted" (43). "In doing so," Veblen notes, "he saved his Most Christian Majesty from menial contamination" (43). Less implausibly, Veblen examines how this "tabu on labour" manifests itself in clothing. "It goes without saying," he notes, "that no apparel can be considered elegant, even decent, if it shows the effect of manual labor on the part of the wearer, in the way of soil or wear" (170).

13. "In the early 1920's," Ware wrote, "the Village was the Latin Quarter of New York" (95). It was "America's bohemia, where flourished free love, unconventional dress, erratic work—if any—indifference to physical surroundings, all-night parties, crowding, sleeping where one happened to be, walking the streets in pajamas, girls on the street smoking, plenty of drink, living from moment to moment, with sometimes a pass at creative work but often not even that" (95). At the same time, though, as Ware notes, "Greenwich Village was . . . the home of . . . a large body of Italian immigrants" (5).

14. The word makes its way into English via French, where it is derived either from the Arabic *baghiy*, meaning "whore" or "prostitute," or from a French idiom (*bagasse*), "army baggage"—that is, "camp follower"—perhaps like the American word *hooker*, which is mistakenly thought to derive from the prostitutes that followed the Union General Joseph Hooker and his troops from camp to camp during the Civil War.

15. The question of the "king's" ethnic identity, whether he is "white" or Italian, must remain unsolved. On the one hand, he speaks Italian, or, at least, enough Italian to understand quaint Italian quips, and is at ease with the Italian street urchins, ordering them about and laying his hand on their heads. On the other hand, it is not clear why an Italian would refer to another Italian as "Little dirty Latin child," unless it is in imitation of the romanticizing (and fastidious) tendencies of bohemian Villagers. In any case, as Ware's book documents and Reed's poem suggests, cross-ethnic relationships remained rare, even unthinkable.

16. Although his bohemian status is not quite as secure as Millay's, Randolph

Bourne's famous essay "Trans-National America" (1916) nevertheless suggests that Villagers could not just tolerate but also champion immigrant culture.

CHAPTER 5

1. In his 1914 poem "The Congo: A Study of the Negro Race," which would remain a crowd-pleaser at his readings until his death in 1931, Lindsay channeled African and African American primitivism to construct a rhythmically beguiling portrait of black urban life.

2. "The blues, spirituals, shouts, and work poems of my second book," Hughes reports in *The Big Sea,* "were written while I was dragging bags of wet wash laundry about or toting trays of dirty dishes to the dumb-waiter of the Wardman Park Hotel in Washington" (271–72).

3. To be sure, African American critics and intellectuals had slightly different—and more defensible—reasons for their objections to "low-rate" poetry than did genteel critics. In particular, as Hughes notes in his autobiography, *The Big Sea,* "The Negro critics and intellectuals were very sensitive about their race in books. (And still are.) In anything that white people were likely to read, they wanted to put their best foot forward, their politely polished and cultured foot—and only that foot" (204). Because of racist depictions of African Americans in most fiction, movies, and plays, Hughes explains, "[W]hen Negroes wrote books they wanted them to be books in which only good Negroes, clean and cultured and not-funny Negroes, beautiful and nice and upper class were presented. Jessie Fauset's novels they loved, because they were always about the educated Negro—but my poems, or Claude McKay's *Home to Harlem* they did not like, sincere though they may be" (204).

4. In addition to Claude McKay the railroad steward and Langston Hughes the busboy, as Sidney Bremer observes, Countee Cullen waited tables in Atlantic City while Zora Neale Hurston was, at various times in her life, a maid, manicurist, secretary, and chauffeur (138). "Barred from industries reserved for white or male workers," African American women, in particular, as Tera W. Hunter observes, "were primarily confined to domestic work from adolescence until disability or death" (155). Men, too, while enjoying more opportunities than women, were also channeled into service work. As Catherine Cocks writes, "In the years just after the Civil War, black men seem to have dominated high-class personal service jobs. Even before emancipation, black servants in the North may have signaled a family's—and presumably a hotel's—claim to high social status by analogy to the 'aristocratic' planter families of the South" (89).

5. See the chapter "Kitchen Mechanics and Parlor Nationalists: Andy Razaf, Black Bolshevism, and Harlem's Renaissance" in William J. Maxwell's *New Negro, Old Left.*

6. On Hughes in particular, see "Defining the Blues" in Steven Tracy's *Langston Hughes and the Blues* (1988). More generally, and to cite only the most recent volumes, on the blues and literature, see Adam Gussow's *Seems Like Murder Here: Southern Violence and the Blues Tradition* (2002), A. Yemisi Jimoh's *Spiritual, Blue, and Jazz People in African-American Literature: Living in Paradox* (2002), Barbara A. Baker's *The Blues Aesthetics and the Making of African-American Identity in the Literature of the South* (2003), Tony Bolden's *Afro Blue: Improvisations in African American Poetry and Culture*

(2004), and Graham Lock and David Murray's edited collection *Thriving on a Rift: Blues Music in African-American Literature and Film* (2009). On jazz and literature, see Nicholas M. Evans's *Writing Jazz: Race, Nationalism, and Modern Culture in the 1920s* (2000), Kristen K. Henson's *Beyond the Sound Barrier: The Jazz Controversy in Twentieth Century American Literature* (2003), T. J. Anderson's *Notes to Make the Sounds Come Right: Four Innovators of Jazz Poetry* (2004), Jürgen E. Grandt's *Kinds of Blue: The Jazz Aesthetic in African-American Fiction* (2005), David Yaffe's *Fascinating Rhythm: Reading Jazz in American Writing* (2005), Michael Borshuk's *Swinging the Vernacular: Jazz and African-American Modernist Literature* (2006), Paul McCann's *Race, Music, and National Identity: Images of Jazz in American Fiction, 1920–1960* (2008), and Shane Vogel's *The Scene of Harlem Cabaret: Race, Sexuality, Performance* (2009). Certainly, an interest in jazz or the blues as a defining matrix did not preclude an interest in labor or class. Indeed, Baker located the origins of the blues in what he called an "economics of slavery" and in a "desperate class" of people who "worked the agricultural rows, searing furnaces, rolling levees, bustling roundhouses, and piney-woods logging camps of America" (3). Earlier, he wrote, "As a force, the blues matrix defines itself as a network mediating poverty and abundance in much the same manner that it reconciles durative and kinetic" (8). With the exception of Nicholas M. Evans, however, critics after Baker have in general not tended to follow these leads. Moreover, the working belief that blues and jazz constitute African American literature's lingua franca may also account for the comparative dearth of scholarship on McKay, whose sonnets—about service or not—only rarely, though revealingly, forge any connection to the blues, jazz, or vernacular traditions. As a result of this critical tradition, McKay's poetry has occasionally been downgraded. Nathan Huggins remarked in *Harlem Renaissance* (1971) that "formal matters as well as personal attitudes inhibited McKay from transforming the bitterness and disillusionment—which no doubt many Negroes felt—into memorable or powerful art" (220) largely because his sonnets "are strangled by arbitrary restraints of form which McKay could not master" (220). This disappointment with McKay's formal poetry—together with the disciplinewide predilection for narrative over poetry—may also account, in addition to fondness for the vernacular, for the preponderance of interest in McKay's vernacular-based fiction (*Home to Harlem, Banjo*) and the comparative dearth of scholarship on his poetry.

7. Curiously, the poem offers a crude version of the Hegelian master-slave dialectic. In Hegel's schema the master asserts his temporary triumph over the slave because in his or her struggle for recognition the slave fears death more than the master does, and because of this fear consents to slavery. As Hegel makes clear, however, this dialectic is soon sublated: the master, increasingly dependent on the slave, grows vulnerable to the slave's growing independence, itself achieved through labor. In McKay's version, the servant (a word derived from *servus,* "slave, serf") reasserts his (and ultimately their, the collective) position in relation to capitalists and masters by no longer fearing their own collective death, indeed by offering it up. That vision of collective death reveals the dependence of masters on slaves and capitalists on servants.

8. As Daniel M. Gross argues in *The Secret History of Emotions* (2006), "Reading Aristotle, or for that matter most canonized literature up to the nineteenth-century social realism of Emile Zola and Charles Dickens, might give one the impression that people

from a lowly station have no emotions at all, let alone the emotions of social responsibility, such as magnanimity or angry indignation" (4). Gross surely exaggerates, but his point remains all the same.

9. For a very brief discussion of work songs, see Edward Hirsch's chapter "Re: Form" in his collection, *How to Read a Poem* (1999).

10. The speaker's invocation of "A woman to sleep with" may refer to prostitution, the other form of service work that many women undertook, often out of a desire to escape other, less remunerative service work. Among other Harlem Renaissance prostitution poems, including the title poem of McKay's *Harlem Shadows*, see Hughes's poem "Ruby Brown," which has its protagonist turning to prostitution after rejecting "the money from a white woman's kitchen" (14).

11. That is not to say, however, that emotion plays no role in production. One might cite many examples, but Stanley Aronowitz's study of worker absenteeism at a Lordstown, Ohio, General Motors factory suggests that how workers feel about their work very much affects the output of that work. See *False Promises* (1973). Studs Terkel's *Working: People Talk about What They Do All Day and How It Makes Them Feel* (1974) is also relevant here.

12. Since Hochschild's study, the sociological literature of service work has grown. One work, Robin Leidner's *Fast Food, Fast Talk: Service Work and the Routinization of Everyday Life* (1993) deserves special mention, as does the collection *Working in the Service Society* (1996), edited by Cameron Lynne Macdonald and Carmen Sirianni. It should be noted that few researchers have attempted to verify empirically Hochschild's claims about the psychological costs of emotional labor, and those who have done so have not always confirmed its observations. For a study that both supports and refutes key elements of Hochschild's thesis, see Amy S. Wharton's "Service with a Smile: Understanding the Consequences of Emotional Labor," although Wharton's analysis does not take race into account, which, as the McKay and Hughes poems suggest, profoundly affects the emotional effects of service. On race and service, especially as this relation applies to women workers, see Evelyn Nakano Glenn's "From Servitude to Service Work: Historical Continuities in the Racial Division of Paid Reproductive Labor" and Judith Rollins's "Invisibility, Consciousness of the Other, and *Ressentiment* among Black Domestic Workers."

13. Countee Cullen's "Atlantic City Waiter" (1925) turns on just this divide between alienated service labor and African authenticity. In that poem, the waiter cannot, despite his halfhearted efforts, hide the pride in his African origins nor his past (and thus present) stature behind the smiling, obeisant face required to serve white diners.

14. See Andrew K. Sandoval-Strausz's recent *Hotel: An American History* (2007), as well as Catherine Cocks's *Doing the Town: The Rise of Urban Tourism in the United States, 1850–1915* (2001), especially her third chapter, "At Home in the City: First Class Urban Hotels, 1850–1915."

15. As Aristotle observes, forgetting (or never knowing) someone's name can function as a form of contempt. The general placeholder "boy," while infantilizing, is also full of contempt.

16. Dawahare claims that Hughes and other Harlem Renaissance writers were both pushed and pulled toward the "cultural nationalism of the post-war period" ("Langston

Hughes" 26). They were pulled by the largely "nationalist discourses of the period," those which connected cultural and linguistic autonomy to political and national autonomy. "If the self-determination of 'nations,'" Dawahare writes, echoing this line of thinking, "was good for European peoples, then it was good for those of African descent" (24). Thus, if African Americans could be shown to have developed a distinct culture, they could make a claim to autonomy at best and equality at worst. "For Hughes, and many other writers in and around the Harlem Renaissance," Dawahare writes, "'race' must be the foundation of a national art" (26). Hughes, like many Harlem Renaissance writers, embraced "black nationalism and Pan Africanism out of a desire to resist the avalanche of white racism in America and to create a distinctly black culture that fairly represented and honored black life" (25). It was a "dream of equality achieved through cultural production" (27), or, as David Levering Lewis put it, "civil rights by copyright" (xxviii). In contrast, Hughes and other Harlem Renaissance writers were pushed toward black cultural nationalism or, so Dawahare claims, by the Red Scare, which, by "destroying organized labor and left-wing organizations," drove "a wedge of nationalism through the labor movement" (23) and black intellectuals and activists. One can trace this history in the fate of A. Philip Randolph's *The Messenger,* a radical, socialist newspaper that in the course of the 1920s—especially after its editors were charged under the Espionage Act—softened its radical politics. In addition to Dawahare, see Theodore Kornweibel's *"Seeing Red": Federal Campaigns against Black Militancy, 1919–1925* (1999).

17. As Anthony Dawahare argues, "In general, Hughes's subjects are politically incapacitated by a weariness of social oppression, which is not to say that they do not find forms of personal joy, relief, and resistance in cultural activities such as music, dance, and song. In various ways, Hughes seems to insist in [*sic*] a kind of *carpe diem* for the black oppressed" (26).

18. As Stephen Tracy observes, "Clearly, Hughes did not exalt spirituals and gospel music because of any fervent belief in Christianity" (103). Indeed, Hughes's description of the washwoman's gospel is a rather perfect gloss on Marx's notion that religion is the opiate—a painkiller—of the masses.

19. As Nicholas M. Evans points out, even this poem cannot construct the cabaret as a place that can permanently or reliably keep trouble at the door. "Cabaret nightlife is invaded," he notes, "indirectly, by the demands and repercussions of urban life; jazz therapy proves insufficient to assuage Minnie's worries about impending isolation" (270). Minnie, as the title of the poem has it, already has the blues; she sings them in (and in spite of) the cabaret.

20. By using his phrase "cultural therapy," I risk misrepresenting Evans's argument, which is actually closer to my own. Evans perceives a major aesthetic and political shift between the Hughes of *The Weary Blues* and *Fine Clothes to the Jew.* In the former, Evans argues, Hughes "saw jazz as valuably primitive, as defining a black racial/cultural essence, and as embodying a hybrid America" (205). By the time of *Fine Clothes to the Jew,* however, Hughes locates "the significance of African-American expressive culture in the context of racial and socioeconomic oppression" (242). "Rather than imagining jazz as part of a timeless, transcendent racial essence and community," Evans argues, the Hughes of *Fine Clothes to the Jew* "places the music in dialogue with the social problems of 1920s Harlem" (242). Specifically, Evans credits Hughes with disrupting "the notion

that a black world of coherent identity is distinct from and helps to counter the effects of a white world of socioeconomic labor. Part of the disruption involves the speakers' recognition that cabarets are, after all, commercial venues. Thus, the effects of labor and commerce invade the joy of cabaret nightlife, and the speakers openly acknowledge that joy's status as tenuous and largely imaginary" (264). Thus for Hughes and those he writes about, the cultural therapy of jazz and cabaret had its limits.

21. Although it helps. In his 1967 essay, "Perennial Fashion—Jazz," Adorno takes on those whom he calls the "jazz ideologists" (124). Here is a representative sentence: "Anyone who allows the growing respectability of mass culture"—which, for Adorno, includes and encompasses jazz—"to seduce him into equating a popular song with modern art because of a few false notes squeaked by a clarinet; anyone who mistakes a triad studded with 'dirty notes' for atonality, has already capitulated to barbarism" (127). Of jazz listeners, and dancers, Adorno offers this: "They call themselves 'jitter bugs,' bugs which carry out reflex movements, performers of their own ecstasy. Merely to be carried away by anything at all, to have something of their own, compensates for their impoverished and barren existence" (128). Adorno's objection to jazz, in addition to its complicity with the culture industry, was also formal—or, rather, he saw the culture industry affecting jazz even at the level of composition and form. See Robert W. Witkin's "Why Did Adorno 'Hate' Jazz?" To be sure, Adorno attacks the commercialized, mass culture version of jazz proffered by the likes of Paul Whiteman and other popularizers. How much his critique applies to the more local, more authentic version of jazz that Hughes, McKay, and more critics have in mind remains open for debate.

22. Another Hughes poem from *Fine Clothes to the Jew,* "Closing Time," echoes this theme of the cabaret as a space that not only cannot mitigate workers' misery and suicidal fantasies but may cause them as well.

23. One is left to wonder, in addition to its obvious romantic anticapitalist appeal, what emotions jazz—and the occasionally purple prose of jazz writing—inspires and fulfills in its critics. Here, too, Gabbard is useful. "Like almost everyone else," he writes, "disciples of jazz respond to the sensual, libidinous dimensions of their music. If jazz has few conventionally sacred dimensions, it may have an even greater agonistic appeal as its advocates resist the class and racial prejudices of society at large that regularly stigmatize their work. With jazz in particular, strong emotional attachments of youth can persist throughout the devotee's life, especially when that attachment signifies a crucial developmental moment such as the willful rejection of bourgeois values" (18). Gabbard is discussing "traditional," belles-lettres jazz writing, but his diagnosis perhaps applies to more recent critics as well.

24. Within years of writing "Negro Servant," for example, Hughes would take a long hiatus from writing about jazz. As Ryan Jerving notes, "As if to acknowledge the difficulty of rearticulating a white-identified—or at least nation- and commerce-identified—jazz to specifically New Negro or extracommercial ends, Hughes largely stopped writing jazz poems after the 1920s" (664). He continues, "When Hughes turned to music for most of the 1930s and 1940s, he turned to forms far less unambiguous in their racial or anticommercial identification—martial music, revolutionary anthems, blues, chants, ballads, toasts, work songs—in order to undergird poems that were increasingly explicit in their race conscious, proletarian, or anticolonial stances" (664).

Similarly, Nicholas M. Evans observes that "writers like Hughes often became less concerned with people's cultural negotiation of living and working conditions than with the direct, material improvement of those conditions" (274).

25. In *Race, Music, and National Identity,* Paul McCann argues that for the McKay of *Home to Harlem,* "jazz is a music of rebellion against the hypocrisy of an oppressive society and challenges the assimilationist values of his Harlem Renaissance peers" (56).

CHAPTER 6

1. As Robert Kanigel has summarized some of those questions, "Was work simply an exchange of labor and skill in return for pay? Was it best written off as a necessary evil, the other fourteen or sixteen hours of the day left for the real business of living? Or did it encompass a spiritual and moral dimension? Did the worker's own experience . . . count in the reckoning? Or ought workers simply to obey orders? How hard and fast should we work? Who is to say, and to what end? How was one to use time? In whose control was work to reside? Did the owner of a company have license to do as he wished, or did he bear a responsibility to his workers and the community?" (462).

2. The evil of soldiering afflicted workers—and not just owners of factories—because, as Taylor told the committee, "any men who deliberately restrict output in any industry are robbing the people . . . of the wealth that justly belongs to them" (19). That is, by producing less, workers ensured that the poor and other workers had less to consume.

3. In addition to increasing productivity and liberating output, scientific management, Taylor promised, would also solve the labor problem. "The great revolution that takes place in the mental attitude of the two parties under scientific management," Taylor told the congressional committee, "is that both sides take their eyes off of the division of the surplus as the all-important matter, and together turn their attention toward increasing the size of the surplus until this surplus becomes so large that it is unnecessary to quarrel over how it shall be divided" (29–30). "Those who are working under scientific management," Taylor concluded, "have come to look upon their employers as their best friends instead of their enemies" (32–33).

4. For more on the competing claims of scientific management and organized labor—and an attempt to determine the merits of each—see Robert Franklin Hoxie's report to the Commission on Industrial Relations, *Scientific Management and Labor* (1916).

5. This chapter originally appeared as an article in *American Literature.* In revising it for this book, I have, as will be evident to anyone familiar with the original, revisited some of the conclusions I draw in that article.

6. One article in particular, "Looking 'em Over," published in the *International Socialist Review* in September 1915, reveals Sandburg's interest in Frederick Winslow Taylor and debates about efficiency. On the morning of July 24, 1915, the steamship *Eastland* sunk while still tied to a dock on the Chicago River. Aboard the *Eastland* that morning were several thousand employees of the Western Electric Company who had been enlisted to attend a company picnic. When the *Eastland* sank, "over 1,000 men, women, and children," Sandburg reports, "trapped like rats in a cellar, [were] drowned" (132).

Sandburg used the disaster to attack "American efficiency" and William C. Redfield, then head of the Department of Commerce, which oversaw steamboat inspection in the country. Redfield was, Sandburg writes, "since the death of Frederick C. Taylor [*sic*] . . . the most widely quoted authority on efficiency" (133). He also, Sandburg charges, ignored multiple warnings about the safety of various Chicago steamships because he naively trusted the owners of the ships when they told him that "everything was all right with the inspection service and there was no danger" (133). "So he," Sandburg writes, "like a faithful bureaucrat, considering himself responsible only to business, lifted no finger to change the inspection service" (133). "Fathead Redfield sat in his easy chair in Washington," Sandburg writes, in high dudgeon, "chatted with business men on the beauties of efficiency, his ears deaf . . . to every plea for more human safety and more social efficiency on the lake steamships" (134). His kind of efficiency, Sandburg asserts, "is a business efficiency not a social efficiency," and "that is one prime explanation of why the *Eastland* became a coffin boat from which truckloads of dead working people were hauled away one Saturday" (134). Of efficiency more generally, Sandburg writes that the "gospel of efficiency is worth taking and using—if you want to make profits and if, first of all, the consideration is how much money you are going to squeeze out of the business even if you must squeeze out life, blood and manhood of working-men in the profit-making operation involved" (133).

7. For Bradley, Sandburg was "merely a clever reporter, with a bias for social criticism" and a "rather gross, simple-minded, sentimental, sensual man among men, going with the scarcely qualified gusto through the grimy business of modern life, which, mystical mobocrat, he at once assails and glorifies" (528–29). Surprisingly, even Sandburg's contemporary poet, correspondent, and friend, Amy Lowell, also found "a good deal" that was alien and artificial about Sandburg, especially alien. Her evaluation of *Chicago Poems* in *Tendencies in Modern American Poetry* (1917) is remarkable both for what it reveals about how contemporary critics responded to modern working-class poetry *and* because it speculates on the intellectual and political origins of Sandburg's early poetry—something this chapter will also go on to do. Inspired in turn by eugenics, social Darwinism, and a thinly veiled elitism, Lowell's review begins by lumping Sandburg into the "new America which I have called multi-racial" (201). Sandburg, Lowell continues, "springs from the strong immigrant class which comes yearly in boat-loads to our shores" (201). Echoing her contemporary nativists, Lowell does not hide her contempt or regret for these boatloads of aliens. "It is [Sandburg] and his ilk," she charges, "who are moving us away from our Anglo-Saxon inheritance. It is he and his ilk who bring us the points of view which are working so surely, if insidiously, upon the whole body of the people" (202). One of the most insidious and infectious points of view, for Lowell, is Sandburg's socialism, which, she concludes, mars his otherwise fine poetic sensibility since it is a theory "built upon false premises" (202). In his prejudice against the rich and unchecked sympathy for "the man in rags begging on the street-corner," Lowell writes, Sandburg and his poetry reveal their ignorance of what Lowell calls "natural law" (216). "Perhaps science was not one of the subjects in Mr. Sandburg's courses at Lombard College, for, to him, all cruelty is man-made, he has but to sweep away the man who made it, and behold, it is gone, all study of the lives of wild animals and fishes notwithstanding" (216).

8. For more on the relationship between Sandburg and Wright, see Joan St. C. Crane's *Carl Sandburg, Philip Green Wright, and the Asgard Press, 1900–1910* (1975).

9. In addition to prose sketches of Hubbard, Sandburg published his first poems in *To-Morrow,* a journal edited by Oscar Lovell Triggs, a professor of English at the University of Chicago. Triggs had earlier helped found the Chicago Arts and Crafts Society in 1897, the Industrial Art League in 1899, and the Morris Society in 1903 (Lears 67). After two visits to the offices of *To-Morrow* in 1905, Sandburg found "the same somber gladness" that he had found "at the Roycrofters and at the Asgard" (Crane 17). While at the University of Chicago, Triggs, as it happens, also taught Lilian Steichen, who would later marry Sandburg after taking her degree. Their love letters, later collected by their daughter Margaret in *The Poet and the Dream Girl* (1987), reveal a courtship oftentimes forged by their mutual interest in socialism and the work of Edward Carpenter, whose writings borrowed heavily from Ruskin and Morris. In her second letter to Sandburg, after learning of his interest in poetry, Steichen echoed Morris when she complained, "Art now-a-days (indeed ever since the decadence of communal folk-poetry) is by and for the privileged minority—it is a thing of Snobbery—a diversion of the leisure class. Give me something more inclusive, more universal! Something that is for the masses!" (10).

10. The "old chapter" Sandburg has in mind is probably Morris's 1889 lecture, "Gothic Architecture."

11. Those rules were:

> 1. Never encourage the manufacture of any article not absolutely necessary, in the production of which *Invention* has no share.
> 2. Never demand an exact finish for its own sake, but only for some practical or noble end.
> 3. Never encourage imitation or copying of any kind, except for the sake of preserving records of great works. (165–66)

12. In his 1905 article for *The Craftsman,* "The Architectural Discussion: Form and Function Artistically Considered," the architect (and Frank Lloyd Wright mentor) Louis H. Sullivan uses similarly Lincolnesque language to summarize the artistic possibilities of the skyscraper. Sullivan describes "a natural and satisfying art, an architecture that will soon become a fine art in the true, the best sense of the word, an art that will live because it will be of the people, for the people, and by the people" (458). Earlier in the essay, Sullivan, one of the first architects to realize the potential of steel-frame construction and, thus, one of the first architects of the skyscraper, poses a rhetorical question that Sandburg's poem seems to answer. "How shall we impart to this sterile pile, this crude, harsh, brutal agglomeration, this stark, staring exclamation of eternal strife, the graciousness of those higher forms of sensibility and culture that rest on the lower and fiercer passions? How shall we proclaim from the dizzy height of this strange, weird, modern housetop the peaceful evangel of sentiment, beauty, the cult of a higher life?" (454).

13. For recent and provocative considerations of these questions, see Russel Muirhead's *Just Work* (2004), Richard Sennett's *The Craftsman* (2008), Alain de Botton's *The Pleasures and Sorrows of Work* (2009), and Matthew B. Crawford's *Shop Class as Soulcraft: An Inquiry into the Value of Work* (2009).

14. One can see this not just in what the modern economy produced but how it produced it. Daniel Nelson observes in *Managers and Workers: Origins of the New Factory System in the United States, 1880–1920* (1995) that "the legacy of the handicraft shop had ceased to be an important force in shop management" (10). "A new order," he concludes, "different in its broad outlines, had emerged" (164).

15. "Our only criteria of judgment should not be whether or not a man's actions are justified in the light of subsequent evolution," Thompson writes, implicitly addressing skeptics like Simons. "After all, we are not at the end of social evolution" (13).

16. As Robert Kanigel puts it, "[O]nly the slightest shift in perspective . . . changes Taylor's hat from black to white" (17). Certainly Thorstein Veblen found Taylor's hat more white than black. In *The Instinct of Workmanship and the State of the Industrial Arts* (1914), Veblen associated scientific management with what he calls the instinct of workmanship, which he defines, variously, as "efficient use of the means at hand and adequate management of the resources available for the purposes of life" (31), and as "the contriving of ways and means to the end sought" (32). While acknowledging that "the limit of tolerance native to the race, physically and spiritually, is short of the unmitigated materialism and unremitting mechanical routine to which the machine terminology incontinently drives," Veblen, citing Taylor's rival Harrington Emerson and his work *Efficiency as a Basis for Operation and Wages* (1909), nevertheless argued that "efficiency conduces to the common good, and is also a meritorious and commendable trait in the person who"—and, as Veblen later makes clear, the society that—"exercises it" (349).

To be sure, later critics of Taylor and scientific management like Harry Braverman are certainly right to note that scientific management soon became (or had always been) as much or more about controlling workers as about achieving efficiencies. That is, Taylor, and even less so the owners and managers of factories who used scientific management to control workers, were no saints. Even so, one cannot dismiss Taylor or the urge for efficiency quite so quickly. Perhaps this ambivalence is best expressed by the economist Robert F. Hoxie, who in 1914, as part of the Commission on Industrial Relations, conducted hearings on scientific management. In his subsequent report to the commission, Hoxie summarized the competing claims scientific management and labor made on the nation. "On the one hand," he observed, scientific management could be defended on the grounds that "the right of investigation, perpetual desire and experiment to find new ways of doing things, knowledge, science, efficiency—all these—advance in the apparent nature of our world" (138). In addition to noting that these advances could act for good or ill, Hoxie on the other hand acknowledged that "neither organized nor unorganized labor finds in scientific management any adequate protection to its standards of living, any progressive means for industrial education, or any opportunity for industrial democracy by which labor might create for itself a progressively efficient share in efficient management" (138). The challenge, then as now, was how to balance efficiency with security or, if security loads the dice against the craftsman ideal, then say the desire for meaningful work.

CONCLUSION

1. *Culture* is a notoriously slippery word. I believe Williams uses it in the anthropological sense of the ideas or customs of a particular people or group of people in a particular period—a synonym, perhaps, for *modern civilization.*

2. These distinctions did not matter to various federal officials in the 1950s, who delayed and finally blocked Williams's appointment to a position with the Library of Congress because of his earlier political writings and associations. Williams, as Paul Mariani has written of the incident, "became a target of suspicion and the object of an official witch hunt, with his own FBI file and all" (592).

Works Cited

Unless otherwise noted, poems come from the following standard editions.

Eliot, T. S. *Collected Poems, 1909–1962*. San Diego: Harcourt Brace, 1963.
Hughes, Langston. *The Collected Poems of Langston Hughes*. Ed. Arnold Rampersad and David Roessel. New York: Vintage, 1995.
McKay, Claude. *Complete Poems*. Ed. William J. Maxwell. Urbana: U of Illinois P, 2004.
Millay, Edna St. Vincent. *Collected Poems*. New York: Perennial, 1981.
Sandburg, Carl. *Chicago Poems*. 1916. Urbana: U of Illinois P, 1992.
Williams, William Carlos. *The Collected Poems of William Carlos Williams*. Vol. 1, *1909–1939*. Ed. A. Walton Litz and Christopher MacGowan. New York: New Directions, 1986.

Ackerman, William A. "Notes on Railway Management." *North American Review* 137 (December 1884): 531–46.
Adams, Graham. *The Age of Industrial Violence, 1910–1915: The Activities and Findings of the United States Commission on Industrial Relations*. New York: Columbia UP, 1966.
Adams, Thomas Sewell, and Helen L. Sumner. *Labor Problems: A Text Book*. 8th ed. New York: Macmillan, 1914.
Addams, Jane. *The Spirit of Youth and the City Streets*. 1909. New York: Macmillan, 1921.
Addams, Jane. *Twenty Years at Hull House*. 1910. Urbana: U of Illinois P, 1990.
Adorno, Theodor. *Minima Moralia: Reflections on a Damaged Life*. 1974. Trans. E. F. N. Jephcott. New York: Verso, 2006.
Adorno, Theodor. "Perennial Fashion—Jazz." *Prisms*. 1967. Boston: MIT P, 1983. 119–32.
Ahearn, Barry. *William Carlos Williams and Alterity: The Early Poetry*. Cambridge: Cambridge UP, 1994.
Alcaues. *Greek Lyric I: Sappho and Alcaeus*. Trans. David A. Campbell. Cambridge: Harvard UP, 1990.
AN ANGLO-AMERICAN. *The Labor Problem in the United States: An Independent Contribution towards Its Resolution*. New York: Atheneum, 1878.
Anderson, T. J. *Notes to Make the Sounds Come Right: Four Innovators of Jazz Poetry*. Fayetteville: U of Arkansas P, 2004.
Aristotle. *On Rhetoric: A Theory of Civil Discourse*. Trans. George A. Kennedy. New York: Oxford UP, 1991.
Aristotle. *Politics*. Trans. Ernest Barker. Oxford: Oxford UP, 1998.
Aronowitz, Stanley. *False Promises: The Shaping of American Working Class Consciousness*. 1973. Durham, NC: Duke UP, 1992.

Asher, Kenneth. *T. S. Eliot and Ideology.* Cambridge: Cambridge UP, 1998.

Atkins, Elizabeth. *Edna St. Vincent Millay and Her Times.* Chicago: U of Chicago P, 1936.

Baker, Barbara A. *The Blues Aesthetics and the Making of African-American Identity in the Literature of the South.* New York: Peter Lang, 2003.

Baker, Houston, Jr. *Blues, Ideology, and Afro-American Literature.* Chicago: U of Chicago P, 1997.

Beard, Charles. *American Nervousness, Its Causes and Consequences.* New York: G. P. Putnam's Sons, 1881.

Bergson, Henri. *Creative Evolution.* 1907. Trans. Arthur Mitchell. New York: Henry Holt, 1911.

Bergson, Henri. *Laughter: An Essay on the Comic.* 1911. Trans. Cloudesley Brereton and Fred Rothwell. New York: Macmillan, 1928.

Bergson, Henri. *Matter and Memory.* 1896. Trans. Nancy Margaret Paul and W. Scott Palmer. London: George, Allen and Unwin, 1911.

Blanchard, I. G. "Eight Hours." 1878. *American Labor Songs of the Nineteenth Century.* Ed. Philip S. Foner. Urbana: U of Illinois P, 1975. 224.

Bolden, Tony. *Afro Blue: Improvisations in African American Poetry and Culture.* Urbana: U of Illinois P, 2004.

Boris, Eileen. *Art and Labor: Ruskin, Morris, and the Craftsman Ideal in America.* Philadelphia: Temple UP, 1986.

Borshuk, Michael. *Swinging the Vernacular: Jazz and African-American Modernist Literature.* New York: Routledge, 2006.

Bourne, Randolph. "Trans-national America." 1916. *The American Studies Anthology.* Ed. Richard P. Horwitz. Oxford: SR Books, 2004. 146–63.

Bowlby, Rachel. "Sad Hearts and Supermarkets." *Textual Practice* 11.2 (summer 1997): 199–218.

Bradley, William Aspenwall. "Four American Poets." *The Dial* December 14, 1916: 528–30.

Braverman, Harry. *Labor and Monopoly Capital: The Degradation of Work in the Twentieth Century.* New York: Monthly Review P, 1974.

Bremer, Sidney H. *Urban Intersections: Meetings of Life and Literature in United States Cities.* Urbana: U of Illinois P, 1992.

Brooks, Cleanth. *Modern Poetry and the Tradition.* Chapel Hill: U of North Carolina P, 1939.

Buell, Lawrence. "Downwardly Mobile for Conscience's Sake: Voluntary Simplicity from Thoreau to Lily Bart." *American Literary History* 17.4 (winter 2005): 653–65.

Buhle, Paul. "Poetry (English Language), 1870–1930." *Encyclopedia of the American Left.* Ed. Mari Jo Buhle et al. Urbana: U of Illinois P, 1992.

Cappucci, Paul R. *William Carlos Williams' Poetic Response to the 1913 Paterson Strike.* Lewiston, NY: Edwin Mellen P, 2000.

Cawein, Madison. "The Voice of April." *The Lyric Year: One Hundred Poems.* Ed. Ferdinand Earle. New York: Mitchell Kennerley, 1912. 42–44.

Chenery, William L. *Industry and Human Welfare.* 1922. New York: Arno, 1977.

Childs, Donald J. *From Philosophy to Poetry: T. S. Eliot's Study of Knowledge and Experience.* New York: Palgrave, 2001.

Chura, Patrick. *Vital Contact: Downclassing Journeys in American Literature from Herman Melville to Richard Wright.* New York: Routledge, 2005.

Cicero, Marcus Tullius. *De Officiias*. Trans. Walter Miller. London: William Heinemann, 1913.

Clark, Christopher C., and Nancy A. Hewitt. *Who Built America: Working People and the Nation's Economy, Politics, Culture, and Society.* Vol. 1. New York: Worth, 2000.

Cocks, Catherine. *Doing the Town: The Rise of Urban Tourism in United States, 1850–1915.* Berkeley: U of California P, 2001.

Coles, Nicholas, and Janet Zandy, eds. *American Working-Class Literature: An Anthology.* New York: Oxford UP, 2007.

Conn, Peter. *The American 1930s: A Literary History.* New York: Cambridge UP, 2009.

Cooper, Wayne. *Claude McKay: Rebel Sojourner in the Harlem Renaissance.* New York: Schocken, 1940.

Cowley, Malcolm. *Exile's Return: A Literary Odyssey of the 1920s.* 1934. New York: Penguin, 1994.

Cowley, Malcolm. "The Revolt against Gentility." Foreword. *After the Genteel Tradition: American Writers since 1910.* 1937. Ed. Malcolm Cowley. Gloucester, MA: Peter Smith, 1959.

Crain, Caleb. "It Happened One Decade." *New Yorker* September 21, 2009: 90–94.

Crane, Hart. "Episode of Hands." *Complete Poems of Hart Crane.* Ed. Marc Simon. New York: Liveright, 1993. 173.

Crane, Joan St. C., comp. *Carl Sandburg, Philip Green Wright, and the Asgard Press, 1900–1910.* Charlottesville: U of Virginia P, 1975.

Crawford, Matthew B. *Shop Class as Soulcraft: An Inquiry into the Value of Work.* New York: Penguin, 2009.

Crawford, Robert. *The Savage and the City in the Work of T. S. Eliot.* New York: Clarendon, 1987.

Cullen, Countee. "Atlantic City Waiter." *My Soul's High Song: The Collected Writings of Countee Cullen.* 1925. Ed. Gerald Early. New York: Anchor, 1991. 85.

Cvetkovich, Ann. *An Archive of Feelings: Trauma, Sexuality, and Lesbian Popular Cultures.* Durham, NC: Duke UP, 2003.

Danbom, David B. *The Resisted Revolution: Urban America and the Industrialization of Agriculture, 1900–1930.* Ames: Iowa State P, 1979.

Dawahare, Anthony. "Langston Hughes's Radical Poetry and the 'End of Race.'" *MELUS* 23.1 (1998): 21–41.

Dawahare, Anthony. *Nationalism, Marxism, and African American Literature between the Wars.* Jackson: UP of Mississippi, 2007.

de Botton, Alain. *The Pleasures and Sorrows of Work.* New York: Pantheon, 2009.

Dell, Floyd. *Love in Greenwich Village.* New York: George H. Doran, 1926.

Devine, Edward T. *Misery and Its Causes.* New York: Macmillan, 1910.

Dickstein, Morris. *Dancing in the Dark: A Cultural History of the Great Depression.* New York: Norton, 2009.

Dijkstra, Bram. Introduction. *A Recognizable Image: William Carlos Williams on Art and Artists.* New York: New Directions, 1978.

Donohue, Kathleen. "What Gender Is the Consumer?: The Role of Gender Connotations in Defining the Political." *Journal of American Studies* 33.1 (April 1999): 19–44.

Dubofsky, Melvin. *We Shall Be All: A History of the Industrial Workers of the World.* 1969. Urbana: U of Illinois P, 2000.

Dunbar, Paul Laurence. "We Wear the Mask." *Lyrics of Lowly Life.* New York: Dodd, Mead, 1898. 167.

Duncan, James. "Efficiency." *Journal of Accountancy* 12.1 (May 1911): 26–34.

Durant, Will. *The Story of Philosophy.* 1926. New York: Simon and Schuster, 2005.

Ehrenreich, Barbara. *Fear of Falling: The Inner Life of the Middle Class.* New York: Pantheon, 1989.

Eliot, Charlotte C. "Before and After in St. Louis." *The Survey* 11.1 (July 1903): 430–32.

Eliot, Samuel Atkins. *A History of Cambridge, Massachusetts, 1630–1913.* Cambridge: Cambridge Tribune, 1913.

Eliot, T. R. [T. S. Eliot]. "Conversation Galante." *Poetry: A Magazine of Verse* 8 (April–September 1916): 292.

Eliot, T. R. "La Figlia che Piange." *Poetry: A Magazine of Verse* 8 (April–September 1916): 292.

Eliot, T. R. "Mr. Apollinax." *Poetry: A Magazine of Verse* 8 (April–September 1916): 293.

Eliot, T. R. "Morning at the Window." *Poetry: A Magazine of Verse* 8 (April–September 1916): 294.

Eliot, T. S. "American Literature and American Language." 1953. *To Criticize the Critic and Other Writings.* Lincoln: U of Nebraska P, 1992. 43–60.

Eliot, T. S. "First Caprice in North Cambridge." *Inventions of the March Hare: Poems, 1909–1917.* Ed. Christopher Ricks. San Diego: Harcourt Brace, 1996. 13.

Eliot, T. S. "Fourth Caprice in Montparnasse." *Inventions of the March Hare: Poems, 1909–1917.* Ed. Christopher Ricks. San Diego: Harcourt Brace, 1996. 14.

Eliot, T. S. "The Hawthorne Aspect." *Little Review* 5 (August 1918): 47–53.

Eliot, T. S. *Inventions of the March Hare.* Ed. Christopher Ricks. San Diego: Harcourt Brace, 1996.

Eliot, T. S. *The Letters of T. S. Eliot.* Ed. Valerie Eliot. Vol. 1. San Diego: Harcourt Brace Jovanovich, 1988.

Eliot, T. S. Preface. *Bubu of Montparnasse.* By Charles Louise Philippe. 1901. New York: Shakespeare House, 1951. NP.

Eliot, T. S. "Second Caprice in North Cambridge." *Inventions of the March Hare: Poems, 1909–1917.* Ed. Christopher Ricks. San Diego: Harcourt Brace, 1996. 15.

Eliot, T. S. *A Sermon Preached in Magdalene College.* Cambridge: Cambridge UP, 1948.

Eliot, T .S. *The Waste Land: A Facsimile and Transcript of the Original Drafts.* Ed. Valerie Eliot. San Diego: Harcourt Brace, 1971.

Eliot, T. S. "What Dante Means to Me." 1950. *To Criticize the Critic and Other Writings.* Lincoln: U of Nebraska P, 1992. 125–35.

Empson, William. *Some Versions of Pastoral.* 1935. New York: New Directions, 1960.

Erkkila, Betsy. *Whitman: The Political Poet.* New York: Oxford UP, 1989.

Evans, Nicholas M. *Writing Jazz: Race, Nationalism, and Modern Culture in the 1920s.* New York: Taylor and Francis, 2000.

Ferris, Timothy. *The 4-Hour Work Week: Escape 9–5, Live Anywhere, and Join the New Rich.* New York: Vermillion, 2008.

Filreis, Alan. *Modernism from Left to Right: Wallace Stevens, the Thirties, and Literary Radicalism.* Cambridge: Cambridge UP, 1994.

Final Report and Testimony: Submitted to Congress by the Commission on Industrial Relations. Vol. 1. Washington, DC: Government Printing Office, 1916.

Foster, George G. *New York by Gas-Light.* New York: DeWitt and Davenport, 1850.

Frail, David. *The Early Politics and Poetics of William Carlos Williams.* Ann Arbor: UMI Research P, 1987.

Frank, Robert H. *Luxury Fever: Why Money Fails to Satisfy in an Era of Excess.* New York: Free Press, 1999.

Freeman, Joshua, et al. *Who Built America: Working People and the Nation's Economy, Politics, Culture, and Society.* Vol. 2. New York: Pantheon, 1992.

Fried, Debra. "Andromeda Unbound: Gender and Genre in Millay's Sonnets." *Critical Essays on Edna St. Vincent Millay.* Ed. William B. Thesing. New York: G. K. Hall, 1993. 229–47.

Furniss, Edgar S., and Lawrence R. Guild. *Labor Problems: A Book of Materials for Their Study.* New York: Houghton Mifflin, 1925.

Gabbard, Krin. Introduction. *Jazz among the Discourses.* Ed. Krin Gabbard. Durham, NC: Duke UP, 1–28.

Gage, Beverly. *The Day Wall Street Exploded: A Story of America in Its First Age of Terror.* New York: Oxford UP, 2009.

"Gaynor Going Slow on Park Changes." *New York Times* July 8, 1910: 7.

Gerstle, Gary. "The Immigrant as Threat to American Security." *From Arrival to Incorporation: Migrants to the U.S. in a Global Era.* Ed. Elliott Robert Barkan et al. New York: New York UP, 2007. 217–45.

Gilman, Charlotte Perkins. *In This Our World.* Boston: Small, Maynard, 1914.

Gilroy, Paul. *The Black Atlantic: Modernity and Double Consciousness.* Cambridge: Harvard UP, 1993.

Glenn, Evelen Nakano. "From Servitude to Service Work: Historical Continuities in the Racial Division of Paid Reproductive Labor." *Working in the Service Society.* Ed. Cameron Lynne Macdonald and Carmen Sirianni. Philadelphia: Temple UP, 1996. 115–56.

Goddard, Henry Herbert. *The Kallikak Family: A Study in the Heredity of Feeble-Mindedness.* New York: Macmillan, 1912.

Golin, Steve. *The Fragile Bridge: Paterson Silk Strike, 1913.* Philadelphia: Temple UP, 1988.

Gompers, Samuel. "The Miracles of 'Efficiency.'" *American Federationist* 18.4 (April 1911): 273–79.

Gordon, Lyndall. *Eliot's Early Years.* Oxford: Oxford UP, 1977.

Graham, Marcus, ed. *An Anthology of Revolutionary Poetry.* New York: Active Press, 1929.

Grandgent, Charles. "The Dark Ages." *Old and New: Sundry Papers.* Cambridge: Harvard UP, 1920. 92–120.

Grandt, Jürgen E. *Kinds of Blue: The Jazz Aesthetic in African-American Fiction.* Columbus: Ohio State UP, 2005.

"The Great Strike." *Harper's Weekly* August 11, 1877: 626–27.

Griffin, Larry J., and Maria Tempenis. "Class, Multiculturalism, and the American Quarterly." *American Quarterly* 54.1 (2002): 67–99.

Gross, Daniel M. *The Secret History of Emotions: From Aristotle's Rhetoric to Modern Brain Science.* Chicago: U of Chicago P, 2006.

Guimond, James. *The Art of William Carlos Williams: A Discovery and Possession of America.* Urbana: U of Illinois P, 1968.

Gussow, Adam. *Seems Like Murder Here: Southern Violence and the Blues Tradition.* Chicago: U of Chicago P, 2002.

Hall, Stuart. "Race, Articulation, and Societies: Structured in Dominance." *Sociological Theories: Race and Colonialism.* London: UNESCO, 1980.

Harrington, Joseph. "Why American Poetry Is Not American Literature." *American Literary History* 8.3 (1996): 496–515.

Harrison, Frederic. "The Cult of the Foul." *Living Age* 54 (1912): 707–13.

Hegel, G. W. F. *Phenomenology of Spirit.* Trans. A.V. Miller. 1807. New York: Oxford UP, 1977.

Henson, Kristen K. *Beyond the Sound Barrier: The Jazz Controversy in Twentieth Century American Literature.* New York: Routledge, 2003.

Herotodus. *The Histories of Herodotus of Halicarnassus.* Trans. Harry Carter. Oxford: Oxford UP, 1962.

Hirsch, E. D. *The New Dictionary of Cultural Literacy.* Boston: Houghton Mifflin, 2002.

Hirsch, Edward. *How to Read a Poem.* San Diego: Harvest, 1999.

Hochschild, Arlie. *The Managed Heart: Commercialization of Human Feeling.* Berkeley: U of California P, 1983.

Hodgkinson, Tom. *How to Be Idle.* New York: Penguin, 2005.

Hoxie, Robert Franklin. *Scientific Management and Labor.* New York: D. Appleton, 1916.

Hueffer [Ford], Ford Madox. "Impressionism—Some Speculations." *Poetry* 1.2 (1913): 177–287.

Huggins, Nathan. *Harlem Renaissance.* New York: Oxford UP, 1971.

Hughes, Langston. *The Big Sea: An Autobiography.* 1940. New York: Hill and Wang, 1993.

Hughes, Langston. "The Negro Artist and the Racial Mountain." *The Portable Harlem Renaissance.* Ed. David Levering Lewis. New York: Penguin, 1994. 91–95.

Hunter, Robert. *Poverty.* New York: Macmillan, 1907.

Hunter, Tera W. "Work That Body: African-American Women, Work, and Leisure in Atlanta and the New South." *Labor Histories: Class, Politics, and Working-Class Experience.* Ed. Eric Arnesen et al. Urbana: U of Illinois P, 1998. 153–74.

Jackson, Kenneth T. *Crabgrass Frontier: The Suburbanization of the United States.* New York: Oxford UP, 1985.

Jain, Manju. *A Critical Reading of the Selected Poems of T. S. Eliot.* New York: Oxford, 1991.

Jemie, Onwuchekwa. "Hughes's Black Esthetic." *Critical Essays on Langston Hughes.* Ed. Edward J. Mullen. Boston: Hall, 1986. 95–120.

Jerving, Ryan. "Early Jazz Literature (And Why You Didn't Know)." *American Literary History* 16.4 (winter 2004): 648–74.

Jimoh, A. Yemisi. *Spiritual, Blue, and Jazz People in African-American Literature: Living in Paradox.* Knoxville: U of Tennessee P, 2002.

Johns, Orrick. "Second Avenue." *The Lyric Year: One Hundred Poems.* Ed. Ferdinand Earle. New York: Mitchell Kennerley, 1912. 132–37.

Johnson, Bob. "'A Whole Synthesis of His Time': Political Ideology and Cultural Politics in the Writings of William Carlos Williams, 1929–1939." *American Quarterly* 54.2 (2002): 179–215.

Jones, Gavin. *American Hungers: The Problem of Poverty in U.S. Literature.* Princeton, NJ: Princeton UP, 2007.

Kaiser, Jo Ellen Green. "Displaced Modernism: Millay and the Triumph of Sentimentality." *Millay at 100: A Critical Reappraisal.* Ed. Diane P. Freedman. Carbondale: Southern Illinois UP, 1995. 27–42.

Kanigel, Robert. *The One Best Way: Frederick Winslow Taylor and the Enigma of Efficiency.* New York: Viking, 1997.

Kilmer, Joyce. "Says 'Vers Libre' Is Prose, Not Poetry." *New York Times* March 19, 1916: SM10.

Kornbluh, Joyce, ed. *Rebel Voices: An IWW Anthology.* Chicago: Charles H. Kerr, 1988.

Kornweibel, Theodor, Jr. *Seeing Red: Federal Campaigns against Black Militancy, 1919–1925.* Bloomington: Indiana UP, 1999.

Kumar, Shiv V. *Bergson and the Stream of Consciousness Novel.* New York: New York UP, 1963.

Lafargue, Paul. *The Right to Be Lazy and Other Studies.* 1883. Trans. Charles H. Kerr. Chicago: Charles H. Kerr, 1907.

"Langston Hughes, 'Busboy Poet' and Writer of 'Weary Blues,' Tells How a Long Shot First Gave Him Chance to Scale Height." *Pittsburgh Courier* January 30, 1926: 2.

Larkin, Margaret. "A Poet for the People—A Review." *Opportunity* March 1927: 84–85.

Larkin, Philip. "Toads." *Collected Poems.* New York: Farrar, Straus and Giroux, 2004. 62–63.

Lawson, Andrew. *Walt Whitman and the Class Struggle.* Iowa City: U of Iowa P, 2006.

Lears, T. J. Jackson. "Beyond Veblen: Rethinking Consumer Culture in America." *Consuming Visions: Accumulation and Display of Goods in America, 1880–1920.* Ed. Simon J. Bronner. New York: Norton, 1989. 73–98.

Lears, T. J. Jackson. *No Place of Grace: Antimodernism and the Transformation of American Culture, 1880–1920.* 1981. Chicago: U of Chicago P, 1994.

Leidner, Robin. *Fast Food, Fast Talk: Service Work and the Routinization of Everyday Life.* Berkeley: U of California P, 1993.

Lentricchia, Frank. *Modernist Quartet.* Cambridge: Cambridge UP, 1994.

Lewis, David Levering. *When Harlem Was in Vogue.* 1981. New York: Penguin, 1997.

Lichtenstein, Nelson, and Howell John Harris, eds. *Industrial Democracy in America: The Ambiguous Promise.* Cambridge: Cambridge UP, 1996.

Lindsay, Vachel. *The Congo and Other Poems.* New York: Macmillan, 1915. 1–11.

Lippmann, Walter. *A Preface to Politics.* New York: Mitchell Kennerley, 1914.

"Living beyond Our Means." *New York Times* November 26, 1905: 8.

Lock, Graham, and David Murray, eds. *Thriving on a Rift: Jazz and Blues Influences in African American Literature and Film.* New York: Oxford UP, 2009.

Lowell, Amy. *Tendencies in Modern American Poetry.* New York: Houghton Mifflin, 1917.

Lowney, John. *The American Avant-Garde Tradition: William Carlos Williams, Postmodern Poetry, and the Politics of Cultural Memory.* Lewisburg, PA: Bucknell UP, 1997.

Lowney, John. *History, Memory, and the Literary Left: Modern American Poetry, 1935–1968.* Iowa City: U of Iowa P, 2006.

Lowry, Helen Bullitt. "Life in Our Village." *New York Times*. June 13, 1920: 66.

Löwy, Michael, and Robert Sayre. *Romanticism against the Tide of Modernity*. Trans. Catherine Porter. Durham, NC: Duke UP, 2001.

MacDonald, Cameron Lynne, and Carmen Sirianni, eds. *Working in the Service Society*. Philadelphia: Temple UP, 1996.

Mao, Douglas, and Rebecca L. Walkowitz, eds. *Bad Modernisms*. Durham, NC: Duke UP, 2006.

Mariani, Paul. *William Carlos Williams: A New World Naked*. New York: Norton, 1990.

Markham, Edwin. *The Man with the Hoe and Other Poems*. New York: Doubleday and McClure, 1900.

Marx, Karl. *Capital: A Critique of Political Economy*. Vol. 1. Trans. Ben Fawkes. 1867. New York: Vintage, 1976.

Marx, Karl. *The Eighteenth Brumaire of Louis Bonaparte*. 1852. New York: International, 1963.

Marx, Karl. *Manifesto of the Communist Party*. 1848. *The Marx-Engels Reader*. Ed. Robert C. Tucker. New York: Norton, 1978. 469–500.

Massachusetts: A Guide to Its People and Places. Boston: Houghton Mifflin, 1937.

Maxwell, William J. *New Negro, Old Left: African-American Writing and Communism between the Wars*. New York: Columbia UP, 1999.

Mayer, John T. *T. S. Eliot's Silent Voices*. New York: Oxford UP, 1989.

McCann, Paul. *Race, Music, and National Identity: Images of Jazz in American Fiction, 1920–1960*. Madison, NJ: Farleigh Dickinson P, 2009.

McCartin, Joseph. *Labor's Great War: The Struggle for Democracy and the Origins of Modern American Labor Relations, 1912–1921*. Chapel Hill: U of North Carolina P, 1997.

McKay, Claude. *Banjo: A Novel*. 1928. New York: Harvest Books, 1970.

McKay, Claude. *Home to Harlem*. 1928. Boston: Northeastern UP, 1987.

McKay, Claude. *A Long Way from Home*. 1937. New Brunswick, NJ: Rutgers UP, 2007.

Millay, Edna St. Vincent. *Conversation at Midnight*. New York: Harper and Brothers, 1937.

Millay, Edna St. Vincent. *Letters of Edna St. Vincent Millay*. Ed. Alan R. MacDougall. Westport, CT: Greenwood, 1972.

Miller, Nina. *Making Love Modern: The Intimate Public Worlds of New York's Literary Women*. New York: Oxford UP, 1999.

Mitford, Nancy. *Savage Beauty: The Life of Edna St. Vincent Millay*. New York: Random House, 2001.

"Mitchell against Brandeis Economy." *New York Times* December 11, 1910: 6.

Moglen, Seth. *Literary Modernism and the Injuries of American Capitalism*. Stanford, CA: Stanford UP, 2007.

Montgomery, David. *Workers' Control in America*. Cambridge: Cambridge UP, 1979.

Morris, William. "Art under Plutocracy." 1884. *Political Writings of William Morris*. Ed. A. L. Morton. New York: International, 1973. 57–85.

Morris, William. *Chants for Socialists*. London: Reeves, 1884.

Morris, William. "Gothic Architecture." 1893. *News from Nowhere and Other Writings*. New York: Penguin, 1993. 329–48.

Morris, William. "The Lesser Arts." *Political Writings of William Morris.* Ed. A. L. Morton. New York: International, 1973. 31–56.

Morris, William. "Useful Work, Useless Toil." *Political Writings of William Morris.* Ed. Arthur Leslie Morton. New York: International, 1973. 86–108.

Muirhead, Russel. *Just Work.* Cambridge: Harvard UP, 2004.

Murger, Henri. *Latin Quarter: Scènes de la Vie de Bohème.* 1851. Trans. Elizabeth Ward Hughes. New York: Dodd, Mead, 1930.

Nelson, Cary. *Repression and Recovery: Modern American Poetry and the Politics of Cultural Memory, 1910–1945.* Madison: U of Wisconsin P, 1992.

Nelson, Cary. *Revolutionary Memory: Recovering the Poetry of the American Left.* New York: Routledge, 2002.

Nelson, Daniel. *Managers and Workers: Origins of the Twentieth-Century Factory System in the United States, 1800–1920.* Madison: U of Wisconsin P, 1995.

"New Lamps for Old." *The Dial* March 16, 1914: 231–33.

The New Oxford Annotated Bible. Ed. Bruce M. Metzger and Roland E. Murphy. New York: Oxford UP, 1991.

Newcomb, John Timberman. "The Footprint of the Twentieth Century: American Skyscrapers and Modernist Poems." *Modernism/Modernity* 10.1 (January 2003): 97–125.

Newman, Charles Henry [Sol Funaroff]. "How Objective Is Objectivism?" *Dynamo* 1.3 (1934): 26–29.

Niven, Penelope. *Carl Sandburg: A Biography.* New York: Scribner, 1991.

Orvell, Miles. *Real Thing: Imitation and Authenticity in American Culture, 1880–1940.* Chapel Hill: U of North Carolina P, 1989.

Perkins, David. *A History of Modern Poetry: From the 1890s to the High Modernist Mode.* Cambridge: Harvard UP, 1976.

Philippe, Charles-Louise. *Bubu of Montparnasse.* 1901. New York: Shakespeare House, 1951.

Pound, Ezra. "Patria Mia." 1913. *Selected Prose, 1909–1965.* Ed. William Cookson. New York: New Directions, 1975. 99–141.

Pound, Ezra. "A Retrospect." 1918. *The Norton Anthology of Modern American Poetry.* Ed. Jahan Ramazani et al. New York: Norton, 2003. 929–38.

"Protecting the Park." *New York Times* July 9, 1910: 6.

Puccini, Giocomo. *La Bohème.* 1896.

Rampersad, Arnold. *The Life of Langston Hughes.* Vol. 1. 1986. New York: Oxford UP, 2002.

Reed, John. *The Day in Bohemia, or Life among the Artists.* New York: N.p., 1913.

Reed, John. "War in Paterson." 1913. *American Working-Class Literature: An Anthology.* Ed. Nicholas Coles and Janet Zandy. New York: Oxford UP, 2007. 271–77.

"Report on the Taylor and Other Systems of Shop Management." *Machinists' Monthly Journal* 24.6 (June 1912): 539–43.

"Review of *Fine Clothes to the Jew,* by Langston Hughes." *Chicago Whip* February 26, 1927: N.p.

Reynolds, David. *Beneath the American Renaissance: The Subversive Imagination in the Age of Emerson and Melville.* Cambridge: Harvard UP, 1988.

Reynolds, George W. M. *The Mysteries of London.* 4 vols. London: G. Vickers, 1845–48.

Rice, Wallace, and Francis Rice, eds. *The Humbler Poets: A Collection of Newspaper and Periodical Verse, 1885 to 1910*. Chicago: A. C. McClurg, 1911.

Rizzo, Sergio. "Remembering Race: Extra-poetical Contexts and the Racial Other in 'The Red Wheelbarrow.'" *Journal of Modern Literature* 29.1 (2005): 34–54.

Rollins, Judith. "Invisibility, Consciousness of the Other, and *Ressentiment* among Black Domestic Workers." *Working in the Service Society*. Ed. Cameron Lynne Macdonald and Carmen Sirianni. Philadelphia: Temple UP, 1996. 223–43.

Rosenstone, Robert A. *Romantic Revolutionary: A Biography of John Reed*. New York: Vintage, 1981.

Ruskin, John. *The Stones of Venice*. Vol. 2. 1853. London: Smith, Elder, 1873.

Russell, Bertrand. *The History of Western Philosophy*. New York: Simon and Schuster, 1945.

Russell, Bertrand. "In Praise of Idleness." 1932. *In Praise of Idleness and Other Essays*. New York: Routledge, 2004. 1–15.

Sandburg, Carl. *Ever the Winds of Chance*. Urbana: U of Illinois P, 1983.

Sandburg, Carl. "John Ruskin: A Man of Ideals." *Lombard Review* 13 (March 1901): 110–11.

Sandburg, Carl. *Letters of Carl Sandburg*. Ed. Herbert Mitgang. San Diego: Harcourt Brace Jovanovich, 1988.

Sandburg, Carl. "Looking 'Em Over." *International Socialist Review* September 1915: 132–37.

Sandburg, Carl. *The People, Yes*. 1936. New York: Harcourt, Brace, 1964.

Sandburg, Margaret, ed. *Poet and the Dream Girl: The Love Letters of Lillian Steichen and Carl Sandburg*. Urbana: U of Illinois P, 1987.

Sandoval-Strausz, A. K. *Hotel: An American History*. New Haven, CT: Yale UP, 2007.

Sappho. *Greek Lyric I: Sappho and Alcaeus*. Trans. David A. Campbell. Cambridge: Harvard UP, 1990.

Schmidt, Regin. *Red Scare: FBI and the Origins of Anticommunism in the United States*. Copenhagen: Museum Tusculanum P, 2000.

Schocket, Eric. *Vanishing Moments: Class and American Literature*. Ann Arbor: U of Michigan P, 2006.

Schulman, Robert. *The Power of Political Art: The 1930s Literary Left Reconsidered*. Chapel Hill: U of North Carolina P, 2000.

Scott, Jonathan. *Socialist Joy in the Writing of Langston Hughes*. Columbia: U of Missouri P, 2006.

Sennett, Richard. *The Craftsman*. New Haven, CT: Yale UP, 2008.

Sheffield, Ada Eliot. *The Charity Director: A Brief Study of His Responsibilities*. New York: Russell Sage Foundation, 1913.

Sheffield, Ada Eliot. *The Social Case History: Its Construction and Content*. New York: Russell Sage Foundation, 1920.

Sigg, Eric. *The American T. S. Eliot: A Study of the Early Writings*. Cambridge: Cambridge UP, 1989.

Simons, A. M. "The Economic Foundations of Art." *The Craftsman* 1.6 (March 1902): 33–42.

Smethurst, James. Review of *History, Memory, and the Literary Left: Modern American Poetry, 1935–1968*, by John Lowney. *Modernism/Modernity* 14.4 (2007): 787–88.

Smith, Grover. *T. S. Eliot's Poetry and Plays: A Study in Sources and Meanings.* Chicago: U of Chicago P, 1956.

Stacy, Jason. *Walt Whitman's Multitudes: Labor Reform and Persona in Whitman's Journalism and the First* Leaves of Grass, *1840–1855*. New York: Peter Lang, 2008.

Stanbrough, Jane. "Edna St. Vincent Millay and the Language of Vulnerability." *Critical Essays on Edna St. Vincent Millay.* Ed. William B. Thesing. New York: G. K. Hall, 1993. 213–28.

Stansell, Christine. *American Moderns: Bohemian New York and the Creation of a New Century.* New York: Metropolitan, 2000.

Starr, Ellen Gates. "Art and Labor." *Hull House Maps and Papers.* New York: Crowell, 1895.

"Staten Island Ferry." *New York Times* April 26, 1917: 12.

Stetson, Charlotte Perkins. *In This Our World.* Oakland, CA: McCombs and Vaughn, 1893.

Stevens, Wallace. "A Window in the Slums." *Collected Poetry and Prose.* New York: Library of America, 1997. 497.

Stickley, Gustav. "The Truth about Work." *The Craftsman* 27.2 (November 1909): 184–90.

Stickley, Gustav. "Waste: Our Heaviest National Liability." *The Craftsman* 20.4 (July 1911): 343–48.

Stromquist, Shelton. *Reinventing "The People": The Progressive Labor Movement, the Class Problem, and the Origins of Modern Liberalism.* Urbana: U of Illinois P, 2006.

Sue, Eugène. *The Mysteries of Paris.* London: Chapman and Hall, 1845.

Sullivan, Louis H. "The Architectural Discussion: Form and Function Artistically Considered." *The Craftsman* 8.4 (July 1905): 453–58.

Taylor, Frederick Winslow. *The Principles of Scientific Management.* 1911. New York: Harper and Row, 1947.

Taylor, Frederick Winslow. *Shop Management.* 1903. New York: Harper and Row, 1947.

Taylor, Frederick Winslow. *Testimony before the Special House Committee.* 1912. New York: Harper and Row, 1947.

Terkel, Studs. *Working: People Talk about What They Do All Day and How It Makes Them Feel.* New York: Avon, 1974.

Thomas, M. Wynn. *The Lunar Light of Whitman's Poetry.* Cambridge: Harvard UP, 1987.

Thompson, E. P. *The Making of the English Working Class.* 1963. New York: Vintage, 1966.

Thoreau, Henry David. *Walden.* 1854. *Walden and Other Writings.* Ed. Brooks Atkinson. New York: Modern Library, 1992.

Tice, Karen Whitney. *Tales of Wayward Girls and Immoral Women: Case Records and the Professionalization of Social Work.* Urbana: U of Illinois P, 1998.

Tillery, Tyrone. *Claude McKay: A Black Poet's Struggle for Identity.* Amherst: U of Massachusetts P, 1992.

Torgovnick, Marianna. *Gone Primitive: Savage Intellectuals, Modern Lives.* Chicago: U of Chicago P, 1991.

Tracy, Steven C. *Langston Hughes and the Blues.* Urbana: U of Illinois P, 1988.

Triggs, Oscar Lovell. *Chapters in the History of the Arts and Crafts Movement.* Chicago: Bohemia Guild of the Industrial Art League, 1902.

T. S. Eliot: A Symposium from Conrad Aiken. Comp. Tambimuttu and Richard March. London: Frank and Cass, 1965.

"Two Recent College Graduates." *Not in the Curriculum: A Book of Friendly Counsel to Students.* New York: Fleming H. Revell, 1903.

Unrau, John. "Ruskin, the Workman, and the Savageness of the Gothic." *New Approaches to Ruskin: Thirteen Essays.* Ed. Robert Hewison. London: Routledge and Kegan Paul, 1981. 33–50.

Untermeyer, Louis. "Caliban in the Coal Mines." *The Lyric Year: One Hundred Poems.* Ed. Ferdinand Earle. New York: Mitchell Kennerley, 1912. 266.

Untermeyer, Louis, ed. *Modern American Poetry.* New York: Harcourt, Brace, 1921.

Van Dyke, Robert. *Essays in Application.* New York: Charles Scribner's Sons, 1906.

Van Dyke, Robert. *The Friendly Year.* New York: Charles Scribner's Sons, 1906.

Van Dyke, Robert. Preface. *A Book of Princeton Verse.* Ed. Henry Van Dyke et al. Vol. 2. Princeton, NJ: Princeton UP, 1919. v–ix.

Van Dyke, Robert. "Work." *The Van Dyke Book: Selected from the Writings of Henry Van Dyke.* Ed. Edwin Mims. New York: Charles Scribner's Sons, 1921. 141.

Van Kleeck, Mary. "Women and Machines." *Atlantic Monthly* February 1921: 250–60.

Veblen, Thorstein. *The Instinct of Workmanship and the State of the Industrial Arts.* 1914. New York: Augustus M. Kelley, 1964.

Veblen, Thorstein. *The Theory of the Leisure Class.* 1899. New York: Penguin, 1994.

Vogel, Shane. "Closing Time: Langston Hughes and the Queer Poetics of Harlem Nightlife." *Criticism: A Quarterly Journal for Literature and the Arts* 48.3 (2006): 396–425.

Vogel, Shane. *The Scene of Harlem Cabaret: Race, Sexuality, Performance.* Chicago: U of Chicago P, 2009.

von Hallberg, Robert. "The Politics of Description: William Carlos Williams in the 'Thirties." *English Literary History* 45.1 (1978): 131–51.

Wald, Alan. *Exiles from a Future Time: The Forging of the Mid-Twentieth-Century U.S. Left.* Chapel Hill: U of North Carolina P, 2001.

Wald, Alan. *Trinity of Passion: The Literary Left and the Antifascist Crusade.* Chapel Hill: U of North Carolina P, 2007.

Walkowitz, Rebecca L. "Shakespeare in Harlem: The Norton Anthology, 'Propaganda,' Langston Hughes." *Modern Language Quarterly: A Journal of Literary History* 60.4 (1999): 495–519.

Ware, Caroline. *Greenwich Village, 1920–1930: A Comment on American Civilization in the Post-war Years.* Boston: Houghton Mifflin, 1935.

Waterworth, James A. "The Conflict Historically Considered." *The Labor Problem: Plain Questions and Practical Answers.* Ed. William Eddy Barns. New York: Harper and Brothers, 1886. 17–51.

Watkins, Gordon S. *An Introduction to the Study of Labor Problems.* New York: Thomas Y. Crowell, 1922.

Weaver, Mike. *William Carlos Williams: The American Background.* Cambridge: Cambridge UP, 1971.

Weber, Max. *The Protestant Ethic and the Spirit of Capitalism.* 1904. Trans. Talcott Parsons. London: Routledge, 1992.

Webster's New World College Dictionary. 3rd ed. New York: Macmillan, 1997.

Weigel, John C. "Town Topics." *Galesburg Gazette* September 11, 1934: N.p.

Wetzsteon, Ross. *Republic of Dreams: Greenwich Village, the American Bohemia, 1910–1960*. New York: Simon and Schuster, 2002.
Wharton, Amy S. "Service with a Smile: Understanding the Consequences of Emotional Labor." *Working in the Service Society.* Ed. Cameron Lynne Macdonald and Carmen Sirianni. Philadelphia: Temple UP, 1996. 91–112.
"What the Others Are Saying." *Common Cause* 1.4 (April 1912): 109–13.
Whitman, Walt. "Out of the Cradle Endlessly Rocking." *Leaves of Grass.* Ed. Sculley Bradley and Harold W. Blodgett. New York: Norton, 1973. 246–53.
Whitman, Walt. "The Tramp and the Strike Questions." *Complete Prose Works.* Philadelphia: David McKay, 1891. 329–30.
Whybrow, Peter C. *American Mania: When More Is Not Enough.* New York: Norton, 2006.
Williams, Raymond. *The Country and the City.* Oxford: Oxford UP, 1978.
Williams, Raymond. "The Politics of the Avant-Garde." *The Politics of Modernism: Against the New Confromists.* Ed. Tony Pinkney. New York: Verso, 1989. 49–63.
Williams, William Carlos. *The Autobiography of William Carlos Williams.* New York: Random House, 1951.
Williams, William Carlos. "Ballad of Time and the Peasant." *Poems.* Urbana: U of Illinois P, 2002. 7–8.
Williams, William Carlos. "A Beginning on the Short Story (Notes)." *Selected Essays of William Carlos Williams.* New York: Random House, 1954. 295–310.
Williams, William Carlos. "A Comment on *Contact.*" 1921. *A Recognizable Image: William Carlos Williams on Art and Artists.* Ed. Bram Dijkstra. New York: New Directions, 1978. 64–68.
Williams, William Carlos. "A Letter." *Furioso: A Magazine of Verse* 1.2 (1940): 21–23.
Williams, William Carlos. "Hymn to the Spirit of Fraternal Love." *Poems.* Urbana: U of Illinois P, 2002. 31.
Williams, William Carlos. *I Wanted to Write a Poem: The Autobiography of the Works of a Poet.* Ed. Edith Heal. Boston: Beacon, 1958.
Williams, William Carlos. *In the American Grain.* 1925. New York: New Directions, 1956.
Williams, William Carlos. "Letter to Ezra Pound." March 5, 1935. *Pound/Williams: Selected Letters of Ezra Pound and William Carlos Williams.* Ed. Hugh Witemeyer. New York: New Directions, 1996. 165–67.
Williams, William Carlos. "The Neglected Artist." 1936. *A Recognizable Image: William Carlos Williams on Art and Artists.* Ed. Bram Dijkstra. New York: New Directions, 1978. 82–96.
Williams, William Carlos. *Paterson.* New York: New Directions, 1995.
Williams, William Carlos. "A Point for American Criticism." *Selected Essays of William Carlos Williams.* New York: Random House, 1954. 80–90.
Williams, William Carlos. *The Selected Letters of William Carlos Williams.* Ed. John Thirwell. New York: McDowell, Obolensky, 1957.
Williams, William Carlos. "Walker Evans: American Photographs." 1938. *A Recognizable Image: William Carlos Williams on Art and Artists.* Ed. Bram Dijkstra. New York: New Directions, 1978. 136–39.
Wilson, Elizabeth. *Bohemians: The Glorious Outcasts.* New Brunswick, NJ: Rutgers UP, 2000.

Wiltse, Jeff. *Contested Waters: A Social History of Swimming Pools in America.* Chapel Hill: U of North Carolina P, 2007.

Winthrop, John. "A Model of Christian Charity." 1629. *The Norton Anthology of American Literature.* Vol. 1. Ed. Nina Baym. New York: Norton, 1998. 214–25.

Witkin, Robert W. "Why Did Adorno 'Hate' Jazz?" *Sociological Theory* 18.1 (2002): 145–70.

Woodhull, Victoria. "'And the Truth Shall Make You Free': A Speech on the Principles of Social Freedom, Delivered in Steinway Hall, Monday, Nov. 20, 1871, and Music Hall, Boston, Wednesday, Jan. 3, 1872." New York: Woodhull, Claflin, 1872.

Wright, Frank Lloyd. "The Art and Craft of the Machine." 1901. *Frank Lloyd Wright: Writings and Buildings.* New York, Horizon, 1960. 55–73.

"Writer Sent to Jail." *New York Times* April 29, 1913: 2.

Yaffe, David. *Fascinating Rhythm: Reading Jazz in American Writing.* Princeton, NJ: Princeton UP, 2005.

Yanella, Philip. *The Other Carl Sandburg.* Jackson: UP of Mississippi, 1996.

Young, Neil. "My My, Hey Hey (Out of the Blue)." *Rust Never Sleeps.* Reprise, 1979.

Index